LOVE'S VIRTUES

LOVE'S VIRTUES

Mike W. Martin

UNIVERSITY PRESS OF KANSAS

© 1996 by the University Press of Kansas
All rights reserved

Published by the University Press of Kansas (Lawrence, Kansas 66049), which was organized by the Kansas Board of Regents and is operated and funded by Emporia State University, Fort Hays State University, Kansas State University, Pittsburg State University, the University of Kansas, and Wichita State University

Library of Congress Cataloging-in-Publication Data

Martin, Mike W., 1946–
    Love's virtues / Mike W. Martin.
        p.   cm.
    Includes bibliographical references and index.
    ISBN 0-7006-0766-8 (cloth) — ISBN 0-7006-0767-6 (pbk.)
    1. Love. 2. Marriage. I. Title.
BD436.M334   1996
177′.7–dc20   95-50403

British Library Cataloguing in Publication Data is available.

Printed in the United States of America

10 9 8 7 6 5 4 3 2 1

The paper used in this publication meets the minimum requirements of the American National Standard for Permanence of Paper for Printed Library Materials Z39.48-1984.

For SHANNON, with love

CONTENTS

CONTENTS
viii

ACKNOWLEDGMENTS

I wish to thank Renford Bambrough, Steve Duck, Tom Ford, Robert Ginsberg, Lawrence Houlgate, Otto Neumaier, Joseph Runzo, and Elizabeth Truax for their helpful comments on earlier drafts of various chapters. I also benefited from discussions with Donald R. Booth, Terri Joseph, Otto Neumaier, and Virginia L. Warren. I am especially grateful for comments on the entire draft by Robert C. Solomon and an anonymous reviewer for the University Press of Kansas.

My students provided a valuable stimulus as I explored ideas for this book in various classroom settings. A half-year sabbatical from Chapman University enabled me to complete this book earlier than would otherwise have been possible.

After long neglect, the topic of love is undergoing a renaissance of philosophical interest. As indicated in the text and footnotes, I have benefited from the recent writings of a number of distinguished philosophers, including Annette Baier, Lawrence A. Blum, Robert Brown, J. F. M. Hunter, Robert Nozick, Martha C. Nussbaum, Gerasimos Santas, Roger Scruton, Irving Singer, Alan Soble, and Robert C. Solomon. I have also drawn widely from literature and literary criticism, psychology, sociology, feminism, and philosophical works on the virtues.

Several chapters were published earlier as the following articles, and I thank the editors of these journals for permission to reprint the essays with minor changes.

Chapter 3: "Love's Constancy," *Philosophy* 68 (1993): 63–77.
Chapter 4: "Adultery and Fidelity," *Journal of Social Philosophy* 25, no. 3 (1994): 76–91.

Chapter 6: "What's Fair in Love?" *The Southern Journal of Philosophy* 31 (1993): 393–407.
Chapter 7: "Honesty in Love," *The Journal of Value Inquiry* 27 (1993): 497–507.

Most of all, I am grateful to my mother, Ruth Lochhead Martin, and to my wife, Shannon Snow Martin, for their inspiration and for their love.

INTRODUCTION:
EROTIC FAITH

In everything concerning love there is a need
for far more clarity, honesty, idealism. . . .
—*Isak Dinesen*[1]

Moral ideals focus, guide, and structure love. Like lenses, they determine how and what we perceive. Like landmarks, they give us our bearings in uncertain terrain and also enter into what is there to be appreciated. Like ligaments, they structure the emotions, desires, attitudes, commitments, and relationships of love. Like leitmotivs, they provide coherence and meaning to lives. In large measure, ideals define what love is.

Love is a way to value persons morally, and to be valued in return. More accurately, love encompasses a wide variety of virtue-structured ways in which persons value each other as having irreplaceable worth. The valuing is *moral* because it involves affirming the moral worth of persons, but primarily because it must be understood in terms of moral virtues and their corresponding ideals. Caring is love's central virtue. It is manifested in and interwoven with additional virtues, which I discuss in separate chapters: faithfulness, sexual fidelity, respect (including self-respect), fairness, honesty, wisdom, courage, and gratitude. Other virtues deserve chapters of their own—for example, self-control, perseverance, responsibility, humility, and hope. I have not attempted to make an exhaustive study of love's virtues, but I do hope I have explored enough of them to unfold a conception of love as virtue-structured ways to value persons.

1

Values structure all types of love, including parental, filial, sibling, friendship, humanitarian, and religious. Here my interest is erotic love, that is, love involving sexual desires and, in particular, monogamous marital love. Marriages, as I understand them, are moral relationships that involve sexual desires (at some time during the relationship) and which are based on long-term commitments to love one's partner (whether or not the commitments are formally sanctioned by legal or religious authorities). In this sense, marriages are not restricted by the gender or sexual orientation of partners; spouses may be lesbian, gay, bisexual, or heterosexual.

This moral definition of marriage differs from but overlaps the ordinary legal definition. Most states recognize "common law marriages" between partners who live together in a sexual relationship for a certain number of years without participating in legal or religious ceremonies. Prior to reaching a largely arbitrary number of years, couples who are committed to staying together are married in all but (legal) name only. Indeed, today many couples consider themselves married despite forgoing public ceremonies. To be sure, ceremonies have important social, economic, and legal implications, but for many couples ceremonies have become matters of personal symbolism, much like decisions about whether to wear wedding rings, change last names, and share bank accounts. The symbols are morally significant insofar as they express moral ideals, but they should not be confused with the ideals themselves.

As this definition of marriage suggests, my approach to marital love is both traditional and modern. It is traditional in that I seek to understand the moral significance of relationships based on long-term commitments to love, especially commitments that are intended to be lifelong. It is modern because I proceed within a pluralistic framework that affirms many kinds of erotic love, depending on the ideals a couple embraces, their particular commitments, and their interpretations (within limits) of what love's virtues imply. As a result, love is morally complex and ambiguous but also morally rich and creative. Love encompasses a multitude of possibilities for valuing persons morally, consistent with such fundamental values as caring, respect for autonomy, and self-fulfillment.

Different kinds of values enter into marital love: sexual values that celebrate human embodiment, aesthetic values of appreciating beauty, prudential values of self-interest, legal values of socially mandated conduct, and religious values that define the sacred. Nevertheless, the moral virtues are central. Virtues are desirable ways of relating to other persons, as well as to communities, social practices, animals, the environment, and ourselves.[2] They are patterns of character that correspond to ideals about the kinds of persons we aspire to be and the kinds of relationships we find desirable. In this way, virtues are essentially moral ideals as embedded in character and relationships, in many different ways and degrees.

Is this virtue-oriented approach to love excessively "idealistic" in a pejorative sense, that is, unrealistic and naive? On the contrary. The virtues I discuss are eminently practical, even pragmatic.[3] As will become clear, they provide a basis for renouncing the dangerous illusions and excesses of Romantic conceptions of love, including the fanciful myths that there can be perfect oneness between couples, that love conquers all, and that love is all we need. At the same time, love's virtues combine aspiration with earthiness in ways beautifully expressed by Elizabeth Barrett Browning.

> I love thee to the depth and breadth and height
> My soul can reach, when feeling out of sight
> For the ends of Being and ideal Grace.
> I love thee to the level of every day's
> Most quiet need, by sun and candlelight.[4]

The poet wrote these lines when she and Robert Browning were courting.[5] At the time she had achieved international renown as a poet, but she lived under the tyranny of a father who forbade marriage for his children, perhaps because of his racist fear that his lineage contained the blood of black slaves. She was also a London recluse, an invalid, and a morphine addict who, at age thirty-nine, had few hopes for romance. Still, love took root, providing the couple with the courage to escape to Italy where they raised a child and pursued a creative literary partnership for two decades. Everyday kindness, fairness, and mutual honesty made their marriage one of the most fulfilling in the nineteenth century.

That century also produced cynics about marriage. Witness Leo Tolstoy, who began *Anna Karenina* with the famous pronouncement, "All happy families are like one another; each unhappy family is unhappy in its own way."[6] Tolstoy then confronts the reader with a marital upheaval caused by Prince Oblonsky's sexual liaison with the family's French governess. Apparently, Prince Oblonsky has fallen out of love with his wife, the mother of their five children. Their quarrels, suffering, and rationalizations immediately engage us and prepare us for an engrossing love affair between Count Vronsky and Anna Karenina, who is trapped in a frustrating marriage. Tolstoy is at his best in portraying characters who learn that marriage is hell and extramarital romance heavenly, at least until that romance ends in death. It is not long before we grasp the meaning he intends in his opening sentence: Unhappy marriages are distinctive and interesting whereas happy marriages are all alike — bland, boring, and probably nonexistent.

In fact, the unhappy families Tolstoy describes are not as dissimilar as he suggests. Essentially they are variations on an archetypal marriage that begins with love and moves through stages of "disillusionment, rage, disgust, acquiescence."[7] Repeatedly he draws on the artistic resources from his own marriage — "one of the most miserable marriages in history."[8] To be sure, Tolstoy was not a cynic about love, which he portrays with great beauty and power, sensitive (like Anna Karenina) to its many forms: "What I think is . . . that as there are as many minds as there are heads, so there are as many kinds of love as there are hearts."[9] Tolstoy's cynicism is limited to the prospects for joining marriage with love in ways that are fulfilling and enduring.

Needless to say, Tolstoy is not alone in his marital cynicism and skepticism. Disillusionment with marriage is a recurring theme in the twentieth century; most of us experience it on some occasion. Affirming marital love has become an act of faith, for me a living faith grounded in personal experience. This marital faith blends with a wider *erotic faith*, in Robert M. Polhemus's sense: "an emotional conviction . . . that meaning, value, hope, and even transcendence can be found through love — erotically focused love, the kind of love we mean when we say that people are in love. . . . Men and women in the hold of erotic faith feel that love can redeem personal life and offer a reason for being."[10] They are confident that love transforms lives by redirecting desires, reordering priorities, and renewing hopes so as to deepen life's meaning and joy.[11]

As a general trust in the possibilities of erotic love, marital faith is distinct from the specific faith placed in one's marriage and one's partner, yet the two faiths are connected. As reasonable persons, we avoid ways of life that seem futile. If we lack any confidence in the general prospects for marriages, we will experience considerable difficulty in sustaining specific faith about our own marriage.

Turning to specific faith, why is a couple's shared faith in each other and in their relationship so important? Faith is not a mere causal prerequisite to love. Like love's other virtues, faith partly constitutes love. Indeed, faith is interwoven with most of love's other defining virtues, each of which must be exercised on a foundation of trust. Mutual caring, faithfulness, sexual fidelity, and courage all imply a shared willingness to trust, which in turn implies faith in each other. Honesty entails trustworthiness, which makes one worthy of a partner's faith. Similarly, mutual respect is strengthened by faith in each other. And no aspect of wisdom is more important than knowing when, how much, and in what ways to trust in one's partner and marriage.

Of course, saying that marital faith is essential to a successful marriage does not justify that faith, even given the tendency of faith to be self-fulfilling by providing motives for greater effort. It is marriage itself that cynics renounce. Is marital faith reasonable? Specific faith in one's spouse may or may not be justified, depending on the circumstances, but what about general faith in marriage? Can it be anything but foolish, given our current confusion about marriage?

We need to understand the origin of that confusion, which conservative, radical, and liberal social critics diagnose in very different ways. Conservatives decry the culture of permissiveness and promiscuity that threatens marriages grounded in commitments to love. They affirm, as a canonical view, that marriage is the only permissible sexual relationship and that marital obligations are virtually absolute. Marriage is a divinely ordained sacrament that, once entered into, creates unconditional obligations. Divorce is always a moral failure.

Radicals, by contrast, see the lingering influence of conservative perspectives as the major source of confusion. Sex and love are matters of personal happiness, not obligations. Marriage has no special moral importance. If anything, it is morally suspect because of its tendency to inflict violence on the spirit and often on the body. Not only does marriage tend to be unfair to women, but it harms women and men alike through sexual and psychological confinement. If we choose to marry, we should do so with great caution and feel free to leave whenever greater happiness can be found elsewhere.

Liberals approach love and marriage in terms of rights. Marriages are essentially highly flexible agreements that create limited obligations which can be broken for many legitimate reasons. Liberals diagnose our confusion about marriage as the result of unprecedented economic pressures on individuals and relationships, together with an exciting array of career opportunities that threaten long-term relationships. Happy marriages have a limited moral dimension (centered on rights and respect for rights), but they are primarily a matter of good fortune in finding a partner who proves to be compatible under a range of largely unforeseeable circumstances. Accordingly, rather than criticizing other persons' marriages and divorces, we should seek greater tolerance of diversity and freedom to make decisions about personal relationships.

All these critics have insights, but all neglect love's virtues. Responsibilities are important in marriage, as conservatives urge, but love is primarily a set of virtue-structured ways to value persons. Violence and misery characterize many marriages, as radicals emphasize, but that does not warrant neglecting the moral possibilities of virtue-guided marriages. And although love should be understood within a pluralistic society that respects rights, as liberals insist, virtue-focused love makes possible special ways of valuing persons. Caring and its related virtues enable us to create and sustain processes of mutual support, intimacy, tenderness, and joy that are sometimes not as readily achievable in other types of relationships.

The differences among conservative, radical, and liberal diagnoses of marital confusion reflect substantial differences among value perspectives. Is general confusion about moral values another source of confusion about marriage? Surely it is. My purpose in writing this book is to clarify the role of moral values in understanding love at a time when that role has become obscure. Nevertheless, I am convinced that social critics have exaggerated our moral confusion.

Consider *Habits of the Heart,* a best-seller written by sociologist

Robert N. Bellah and his colleagues, which portrays Americans as utterly confused about moral concepts and, in particular, about the moral significance of marriage. Their research is guided by a largely conservative perspective that contrasts canonical (especially biblical) and egoistic ("individualistic") paradigms of love and marriage. Americans are confused, they charge, about which of these paradigms to embrace. In particular, Americans are "torn between love as an expression of spontaneous inner freedom, a deeply personal, but necessarily somewhat arbitrary, choice, and the image of love as a firmly planted, permanent commitment, embodying obligations that transcend the immediate feelings or wishes of the partners in a love relationship."[12] Couples were usually most comfortable with a self-centered vocabulary: "Even the most secure, happily married of our respondents had difficulty when they sought a language in which to articulate their reasons for commitments that went beyond the self."[13]

Now, undoubtedly the people interviewed by Bellah's group were somewhat unclear about moral concepts. We all are. However, the study itself suffers from moral blinders and conceptual constrictions that lead the authors to exaggerate the problem. In conducting and interpreting interviews, they rely on simplistic dichotomies: obligation versus egoism, commitment versus self-seeking, community versus individualism.[14] As a result, they often fail to hear the language of love's virtues, which bridges these dichotomies, and they fail to appreciate how many of the couples they interviewed understand love as virtue-structured ways to value one another.

For example, in characterizing his ten-year marrriage to a "special person," one man remarked, "I think there is an element, a small element of obligation. But I think mostly it's just, you know, this person is really good. It's worked so well up to now, and it continues to do that because you expect it to, and it does, by and large."[15] The man's remarks about the relationship working, based on an expectation that it will, at least hint at the virtue of marital faith. More to the point, the man's affirmation of the goodness of his wife might be understood in terms of my thesis: Love is a way to value persons morally, as singularly important — "really good," "special." Instead, Bellah's group disparages the man for using a self-centered vocabulary to express "the romantic idea that his wife Debby is 'special,'" as if romance in this sense is somehow selfish.[16]

To cite a more striking example, another man remarks, "My viewpoint of a true love, husband-and-wife type of relationship is one that is founded on mutual respect, admiration, affection, the ability to give and receive freely."[17] Directly and indirectly, this man is appealing to love's virtues—respect, caring, fairness, and reciprocity. Rather than highlighting this virtue language, however, Bellah's group faults the man for appealing to personal happiness in justifying why he finds this conception of love appealing. Apparently they want him to appeal to religious faith or civic responsibilities or at least to some systematic moral perspective about the purposes of human life. By contrast, I am struck by the man's simplicity, directness, and ease in speaking of love as a virtue-structured relationship that he apparently values for itself and for its contribution to personal happiness.

Our moral ideals guide what we see and hear concerning love. Bellah is preoccupied with community ideals and hence he listens for the language of duty and social responsibility, neatly separated from appeals to personal happiness. As a consequence, he fails to attend to love's virtues in characterizing how couples value each other. Sometimes virtue language is prominent in the interviews, and other times it lies just below the surface when couples talk about their relationships. Perhaps because some virtue terms can sound a bit stuffy in everyday speech, couples tend to use colloquial variations: "expect" for "have faith," "not cheat" for "sexual fidelity," "stick together" for "be faithful," "balance" for "fairness," "guts" for "courage," "level with" for "be honest with," and "savvy and sensitivity" for "wisdom." Adjusting for these variations, Bellah's interviews reveal that love's virtues play a vital role in everyday discourse about love.

To return to our question, is marital faith justified? Obviously not a blanket faith. A reasonable faith will be selectively focused on marriages that substantially embody love's virtues. It will be nuanced according to our understanding of those virtues, as well as our grasp of how good luck also plays an essential role in the best of marriages. And it will be balanced by faith in other desirable ways to value persons, including friendship, civic participation, voluntary community service, service through the professions, and artistic expression.

Understanding love as virtue-structured ways to value persons is itself a step toward renewing marital faith. Thus, in its entirety this book is my attempt to offer a justification of marital faith. I provide an internal justification which proceeds by making salient the moral dimensions of love that make it desirable insofar as its virtues are embedded in marriages. External justifications are also possible, such as empirical studies highlighting the contributions of marriage to parenting and social stability. I suspect, however, that external justifications are incapable of creating a personal faith where none exists. Morally, love speaks from within.

1

LOVE AND MORALITY

"Do you love Clara?" he asks, as if love were something
well defined, something you either have or don't have,
something you give or withhold, like money in your
purse; as if the word "love" (like the word "orchid")
did not cover an almost infinite number of varieties.
                                        —*Esther Tusquets*[1]

How is love related to morality? Are the two external to each other,
so that love can be defined independently of moral values? If so, are
they antagonists, with morality functioning as a censor to restrain
and impede love? Or are they allies, with morality serving as a care-
taker who fences and prunes a garden that gives pleasure in return?[2]
I will explore yet another possibility: Love is internally related to
morality. Moral values partly constitute love from within, rather
than merely constraining it from without. Moral values define love
as ways to value persons.

Where to begin? No aspect of life is more complex than love, with
its bewildering mixtures of promise and peril, delight and destruction, coherence and confusion. In exploring this complexity I focus
first on language, specifically on the expression "true love." This
ubiquitous expression reminds us that genuine love can be elusive
and easily confused with a variety of superficial attractions. It also
provides a first clue about how moral values enter into love, along
with personal preferences. These linguistic observations are quickly
augmented by references to philosophy, literature, and social science, a pattern repeated in subsequent chapters.

10

How love and morality are related depends, of course, on what morality is. In the second half of this chapter I place my conception of love's virtues within a pluralistic framework. Without attempting to offer a comprehensive ethical theory, I reject any narrow or univocal understanding of the values defining love. Insofar as our moral ideals of goodness differ we will have different conceptions of what love is. Some conceptions, such as those that systematically oppress women, violate minimum moral decency and hence should be rejected, but a great variety of other conceptions embody alternative forms of goodness that are desirable without being obligatory. Within wide limits, diversity of moral conceptions of love should be celebrated for creating new ways to value persons morally.

"TRUE LOVE"

The word "love" has a tangled web of meanings, mirroring the complexity of love itself. "Love" may refer to more or less brief *feelings* of strong attraction, *emotions* of tenderness and affection, *desires* to make love, and *commitments* to share a life together. It might also refer to complex *sentiments* and *attitudes* expressed in a wide range of emotions — affection, caring, and joy, but also pride, anger, jealousy, hatred, disappointment, fear, and grief.[3] When reciprocated, love becomes a *relationship* involving the full spectrum of human emotions, shared activities and commitments, mutual support and economic interdependency, fighting and reconciliation, compromise and forgiveness, and indeed every other aspect of human life.[4] Most intriguing, when we speak of "true love" we refer to *values,* including moral values. The reference may be direct, by thinking of love per se as a moral value, or indirect, by alluding to desirable experiences, attitudes, and relationships that define what it means to value persons morally.

Or is this reference to moral values clear? Perhaps we should first consider other possible meanings. Occasionally "true love" is used in a purely value-neutral way to describe or classify types of love. Alternatively, it may refer to personal tastes rather than to moral ideals. Most often, "true love" refers simultaneously to moral values and personal preferences, mixed together in various combinations. Let us consider each of these meanings.

Classifying Sense

We contrast "true" Arabian horses with thoroughbred horses without implying that thoroughbreds have less value. Similarly, the expression "true love" can be applied in a value-neutral way to classify emotional states and to distinguish love from related attitudes with which it might be confused. In this descriptive or classifying sense, "true love" refers to any strong positive attraction, in contrast with less potent attractions.[5] Hence, to identify what we truly love is simply to discover what most strongly attracts us.

Using this meaning, we can love all kinds of things: painting, parties, peace, peaches, penguins, people, perfumes, piccolos, places, poetry, and power—to sample only one letter of the alphabet. The type of attraction depends in part on the object that attracts us. To love parties is to enjoy attending or hosting them, whereas to love peace is to actively promote it. The type of attraction also depends on which features in the object attract us: Musicians love playing piccolos, musicologists love studying them, and merchants love marketing them.

Similarly, love for persons varies according to our connection with them or the reasons for our attraction. For example, parental love is love for one's children (in part because they are one's children). By contrast, erotic love, in a purely descriptive sense, is any strong attraction involving sexual desire and at least some affection. The presence of sexual desire distinguishes erotic love from parental—as well as from filial, sibling, humanitarian, friendship, and Platonic—love.

The classifying sense can also be used to specify different kinds of erotic love. Suppose we want to pinpoint "true" (genuine) infatuation for someone who has never experienced it. Dorothy Tennov's list of typical features might suffice: preoccupation with someone such that thoughts and feelings involuntarily intrude on consciousness; "a general intensity of feeling that leaves other concerns in the background"; dependency on the moods of the beloved; intense longing for the beloved to reciprocate with similar reactions; fear of rejection; "an aching of the 'heart' (a region in the center front of the chest) when uncertainty [about reciprocity] is strong"; "acute sensitivity to any act or thought or condition that can be interpreted favorably" as a sign of reciprocated passion; "buoyancy (a feeling of walking on air) when reciprocation seems evident"; marked emphasis on the admirable traits of the beloved and avoidance of the negative; and within wide limits, the tendency for passion to increase through adversity.[6] Upon reading this list of features we might agree: Yes, that's genuine infatuation, the real McCoy. Or we might disagree and modify the list. Either way, we would be describing and classifying, not evaluating.

At the same time, Tennov's list of features explains why infatuation is usually not counted as true love. We say, "It was *only* an infatuation, not the real thing." What exactly does that mean?

There are various possibilities, depending on our preferences and values. Perhaps the infatuation was intense but fleeting, whereas we wanted a long-lasting relationship based on commitment. Perhaps the attraction centered too exclusively on sex and inspired too little caring and respect, or it was pervaded with illusion rather than honest attempts at mutual understanding. Maybe the relationship was one-sided rather than reciprocal and fair, or it became stagnant instead of fostering growth. These contrasts combine preferences with morality, what we desire with what is desirable.

I believe that most everyday talk about true love combines, and sometimes oscillates between, expressions of personal preferences and references to moral values. Proceeding cautiously, however, I will attempt to pry apart a sense of "true love" that could be used simply to express personal preferences without implying moral judgments.

Preference Sense

In a preference sense, "true love" is used to express subjective tastes. We might lack reasons for those tastes, just as we might prefer the taste of chocolate over strawberry yogurt without having a justification to offer. Erotic preferences are as richly varied as food preferences. For example, we respond differently to the following sexual stimuli: personality features (intelligence, sense of humor, character traits); styles of dress, movement, and speech; facial features; hair color (blond, brunette, red); parts of bodies (face, chest, buttocks); patterns of sexual intercourse (frequency, vigor, positions); and sexual identity of partners (male, female, both). No doubt there are *causes* that shape our erotic preferences, but there need not be *reasons* that justify them, beyond the pleasures they happen to bring, and when we cite those pleasures we may be explaining our behavior rather than justifying it with intersubjective reasons.

To be sure, sometimes we do have reasons for our preferences, although reasons that fall well short of objectively justifiable claims applicable to others. Thus, I might prefer Victorian architecture because of its visual richness, warmth, and imaginative charm. These aesthetic reasons are subjective in that they provide no basis for criticizing people who prefer instead the simplicity and austerity of Bauhaus architecture, but they also play an intersubjective role in clarifying and supporting judgments of aesthetic value. Similarly, persons who prefer to date athletic and sports-oriented "types" have no basis for criticizing people who prefer to date intellectuals.

What about love? Critics who reject my conception of love as virtue-structured might reduce all talk about true love to the preference sense, insisting that moral values have little to do with love. *De gustibus non est disputandum:* There is no disputing tastes.

The sociologist John Alan Lee adopts such an approach to love, partly in the name of morally neutral social science and partly as a moral objection to the excessive moralization of love. Lee believes there are as many legitimate love preferences or "love-styles" as there are colors.[7] The colors of love include three primary colors — eros, storge, and ludus — together with six secondary hues that are variations on the primary colors. One, *eros* is a strong physical attraction to people having a particular body type we prefer; typically it is experienced as love at first sight. Two, *storge* (friendly love) is affection and caring that develops gradually. Three, *ludus* (playful love) refers to noncommittal flirtatious involvements. Four, *mania* is the obsessive and possessive preoccupation with the beloved. Five, *pragma* is the pragmatic choice of lovers who use the criteria of compatability and likelihood of long-term relationships. Six, *agape* is selfless altruism, often based on beliefs about a duty to love. Seven, *storgic eros* combines caring with a wider standard for beauty. Eight, *ludic eros* is the playful enjoyment of a range of partners with different body types. Nine, *storgic ludus* combines affection with the desire for playful and temporary involvements with many partners. All these love-styles, Lee concludes, are "valid according to each person's taste."[8] None is more justified than any other. He allows that there are reasons or "ideologies" for each style, but the reasons are entirely subjective and do not establish any style as objectively better or worse.

Should we follow Lee in reducing love to mere preferences? Can we? His distinctions are interesting, but his wholesale attempt to demoralize love is simplistic. In fact, he has difficulty maintaining his view consistently, hinting in several places that objective values do play a role in love. Thus, in one passage he insists that mania should not be dismissed as mere infatuation because doing so "denies some of the valuable aspects of manic experience. For example, it can be beneficial to realize how deeply, how intensely you are capable of loving another person. Later, in some other choice of love-style, this realization can add considerably to your self-esteem and to your ability to love a worthy partner."[9] These allusions to self-esteem, worthy partners, and loving deeply imply values beyond mere preferences, if only the value of self-fulfillment. Even so, by declaring the independence of love and morality, Lee's approach impoverishes our understanding of love.

Moral Sense

"True love" usually refers to attitudes and relationships that are desirable in moral terms, in addition to expressing personal preferences. For most people, genuine love refers to caring, honesty, and fairness; it is incompatible with systematic cruelty, untruthfulness, and exploitation. The reference to values is not incidental. Moral values enter into the very meaning of genuine love by structuring relationships and shaping experiences.

Consider falling in love. Depending on individual ideals of love, the experience may differ considerably. One person experiences overwhelming sexual desire tinged with affection; another feels deep caring accompanied by a desire to express that caring sexually; yet another has a sense of complete ease and peace with a partner and a readiness to make a lasting commitment. Even more dramatically, moral values structure subsequent stages and relationships of love. Love that emphasizes caring and commitment differs in kind from love centered on convenient pleasures. And love grounded in honesty, fairness, self-respect, and mutual respect is fundamentally different from love that lacks these virtues.

The moral sense of "true love" is ubiquitous in popular stories, songs, soap operas, and everyday struggles to give life meaning. It also has a long history in philosophy. All the characters in the *Symposium,* the first philosophical masterpiece on love, distinguish between higher and lower forms of love, each in his own way, although within the general value perspective of fourth-century B.C. Greek culture. Remarkably, many of their distinctions sound quite contemporary.

> It is the common, vulgar lover, who loves the body rather than the soul, the man whose love is bound to be inconstant, since what he loves is itself mutable and unstable. The moment the body is no longer in bloom, "he flies off and away," his promises and vows in tatters behind him. How different from this is a man who loves the right sort of character, and who remains its lover for life, attached as he is to something that is permanent.[10]

This passage is echoed in contemporary ideals that define genuine love as more than short-lived and skin-deep.

Even some psychological theories allude to moral values in understanding love. To cite one interesting example, psychologist Robert Sternberg develops a "triangular" theory of love that yokes together three ideas: intimacy, passion, and decision/commitment.[11] Intimacy is caring, manifested in sharing, promoting the good of the beloved, mutual enjoyment, common understanding, and personal communication. Passion combines sexual desires with desires for increased self-esteem gained through mutual attachments. And decision/commitment combines the decision that one loves a particular individual and the commitment to sustain the love. Configurations of these three (compound) elements yield types of love. Passion by itself is "infatuation"; commitment by itself is "empty love"; commitment on the basis of passion without intimacy is "fatuous love." By contrast, ideal, "consummate, or complete love" unites substantial degrees of intimacy, passion, and decision/commitment.

Clearly, these are not the labels of a neutral observer. Because of Sternberg's nonneutrality, Lee charges him with bias and lack of scientific rigor, but that is a mistake.[12] Psychologists are not prejudiced simply because they relate scientific fact to human aspiration. In particular, Sternberg is not prejudiced when he stresses the element of caring in love. A complete absence of caring would lead most of us to deny the presence of love, and hence a psychological theory that ignored caring would be of little use in understanding love. Of course, it is important to identify the points at which science merges with value judgments, lest the mantle of scientific authority is abused by confusing science with moral inquiry.

Henceforth, I will use "love" in its moral sense, aware that the moral sense blends with the preference sense in colloquial usage. Before proceeding, however, consider an objection. I began with the thesis that love is a way to value persons morally. Then I explored the morally loaded sense of "true love" in which love implies moral values. But surely this linguistic analysis cannot establish that moral values are essential in understanding what love is. For all that has been said so far, perhaps we should simply refrain from using the moral sense, replacing it with Lee's terminology of love-styles and colors of love.

In reply, notice that something has been achieved. We have identified a perfectly familiar way of talking about love that directly links love to such virtues as caring and constancy, fairness and fidelity. That manner of discourse leads naturally into philosophical and psychological theories about worthwhile forms of love, theories that articulate the value standards implicitly used as criteria in applying the expression "true love." To be sure, identifying a moral *concept* (sense) of "love" is only a preliminary step to exploring moral *conceptions* (perspectives) of love rooted in moral ideals. Nevertheless we have made progress, and we can now use an example to introduce the virtues discussed in subsequent chapters.

In the first scene of Ingmar Bergman's *Scenes from a Marriage*,

Marianne and Johan appear contented in a ten-year marriage centered around material comforts and everyday pleasantries. The couple meet Marianne's initial definition of happiness: "Happiness is being content. I don't long for anything. Except for the summer, of course. I wish it could always be like this. That nothing ever changed" (25).[13] Their complacency is punctured when they are forced to make an abortion decision; later it collapses when Johan announces he loves another woman. As their marriage unravels, removing their patina of politeness, they are forced to admit how stagnant their marriage had become. They "killed off love" with a rigid formality, an unwillingness to quarrel, and a fear of asserting their individual needs and frustrations, even when asserting them could have produced greater happiness (148). They became blind to warning signals of boredom and sexual difficulty. In retrospect, they begin to appreciate the ideal of love to which they were tacitly committed all along, even when they failed to live up to it. A fuller realization of that ideal, as embodied in love's virtues, might have preserved their marriage. Conceivably it might yet open a path of reconciliation.

Marianne's initial characterization of a good marriage captures many aspects of *caring:* daily kindness, affection, and comradeship, in addition to politeness and tolerance (16). But as she and Johan eventually discover, caring requires a fuller responsiveness to each other's needs. More than comfort, those needs include a deeper sharing of emotions, a willingness to explore ideas together, including ideas about which they differ, and wider areas of shared involvement. In particular, they had lost their ability to make shared decisions about major plans for their life together.

Johan comes to appreciate his capacity for *faithfulness,* that is, for constancy in sustaining a commitment to love. Earlier his view was that even spouses are emotionally isolated from each other. "Loneliness is absolute," and to believe in fellowship, whether through love, religion, or art, is to believe in an illusion (115–116). He finds he cannot live with this cynicism and that he needs "something to long for . . . something to believe in" (196). He also learns he is capable of an enduring love, and that he continues to love Marianne — "In an earthly and imperfect way" (200).

What about the narrower sense of faithfulness as *sexual fidelity?*

Both of them have extramarital affairs, and each is hurt by them, especially by Johan's recent affair that precipitates their divorce. Extramarital affairs are warnings that something is amiss in their relationship, warnings that they failed to recognize (149, 187). At the same time, they do not explicitly commit themselves to sexual exclusivity, and it is an open question whether they could have reached a more honest mutual understanding about outside affairs.

Gradually and painfully, they attain greater *self-respect* than they had during their marriage, and with it greater *respect* for each other. Marianne is able to affirm her individuality and the legitimacy of asserting her needs. Johan abandons his cynical tendency to devalue human life, including his own, and to respond more sensitively to Marianne's feelings, especially when they do not coincide with his own. Both achieve greater integrity in respecting their own and each other's needs for change and growth.

Honesty makes possible their process of self-discovery, including honesty about their earlier lack of truthfulness with each other and with themselves. Despite their superficial candor, they had "made do with convenient half-truths" and buried many of their emotional needs and fears (189). In doing so they disregarded possibilities for deeper levels of trust in each other. At the same time, they wisely avoided making honesty an absolute that would "pulverize" a marriage by destroying all personal privacy.

Both become aware that their marriage fell short of complete *fairness*. Their dual careers provided economic balance, but an emotional power imbalance existed. Johan's outlook dominated their discussions. Once, while discussing an Ibsen play they had attended together, Johan erupted in sexist bombast that for the first time explicitly conveyed his attitudes about women. Marianne was disturbed but unwilling to criticize his superficial stereotypes of women and the women's movement. As a result, they failed to discuss how Johan's attitudes may have affected the balance of benefits and burdens in their relationship.

Johan achieves greater *courage* in confronting his previous cowardice, manifested in his unwillingness to acknowledge his vulnerability and emotional dependence within the marriage. Marianne discovers the element of cowardice in her attempts to please everyone rather than to assert her own needs and her occasional anger.

Gradually she learns to express herself and yet, in loving, to "forget about myself, even though I don't efface myself" (200). She learns that personal courage is not only compatible with caring but sometimes an important manifestation of caring.

During their marriage, neither of them fully appreciated the life they shared. They lacked *gratitude* for each other's love and the joy it made possible. Marianne concludes, "Sometimes I feel that you and I were both born with silver spoons in our mouths, but we've squandered our resources and find ourselves poor and bitter and angry" (145). In acknowledging his ingratitude, Johan concludes, "I was bound to you in a different and deeper way than I realized. I was dependent on all those things that are called home and family and regular life and quiet everyday routine" (153).

Finally, they lacked *wisdom*, both the understanding required for achieving the other virtues and the good judgment to know how to keep their relationship alive and creative, instead of becoming sterile. Part of their difficulty was in becoming complacent and passive in conforming to the expectations of their family circle. Instead they should have tried to "escape far away and create something worthwhile on our own terms" (123). But the primary difficulty was in failing to try hard enough to understand and to have their marriage serve each other's needs beyond a life of material security and comfort.

It might be objected that this example does not establish my thesis — that virtues and ideals enter into defining what love is. Granted, love's virtues play an enabling role in contributing to the success or failure of the love and the marriage. They guide and partly motivate good conduct that enables the marriage and the love to prosper in ways that bring mutual fulfillment. But these virtues play no constitutive role. They are not part of the love itself; they do not define love as a virtue-guided way to value persons.

Look more closely. Love's virtues are essential in defining the love between Marianne and Johan. To the extent these virtues are present, their love is present, vibrantly alive; as these virtues recede, their love shrivels. The love shrivels not as a causal aftermath of the virtues' absence, but as part of the meaning of the relationship defined by those virtues. That is obvious with regard to caring. Without deep caring the relationship might involve pleasant coexistence but not love. But in addition, the caring is embedded in many of the other virtues, including faithfulness, courage, and gratitude. Again, try abstracting from the virtues of respect, honesty, and fairness and see if the marriage would amount to the same thing. These virtues structure and define what their love is, how they value each other, and how they value their relationship.

TRADITION AND PLURALISM

In urging greater attention to love's virtues, Iris Murdoch once called for "a moral philosophy in which the concept of love, so rarely mentioned now by philosophers, can once again be made central."[14] My aim, conversely, is to make moral philosophy central to understanding love. Yet the tasks overlap. To explore love's virtues is to elucidate the significance of love for morality and for moral philosophy. Part of that significance lies in overthrowing a powerful paradigm that has dominated moral philosophy for nearly three centuries.

According to this *impartiality paradigm,* morality consists of a set of universal rules for right conduct. This paradigm has three prominent features. First, it makes obligations primary: Morality is essentially a matter of required conduct. Second, the obligations are universal, both in application and justification: Valid moral principles apply to everyone and would be recognized by all rational persons as binding on them in the same way. Third, the obligations demand impartiality: Moral principles set forth requirements to treat everyone alike (in certain ways), without giving preference to particular individuals.

Ethical theorists have developed the impartiality paradigm in many directions. Rights ethicists (John Locke, Thomas Jefferson) formulate it in terms of respect for universal human rights, the rights that people have simply because they are human. Duty ethicists (Immanuel Kant, David Ross) formulate it in terms of categorical imperatives, the unconditional duties incumbent on all rational beings to obey universal duties motivated by a concern for duty. Act utilitarians (Jeremy Bentham, John Stuart Mill) say there is one universal rule to produce the greatest good for the greatest number of people, weighing the good of each person impartially. Rule utilitarians (Richard Brandt) instead develop a set of more specific rules that, when adopted as a code within a particular society, produce the most good for the most people. And contract theorists (John Rawls) seek a set of principles that rational persons would endorse in a hypothetical situation of impartiality where they lacked detailed knowledge about themselves and their relationships.

All of these versions of the impartiality paradigm give minimal attention to love's virtues and, simultaneously, little attention to love. The simultaneity is no surprise, given my conception of love as virtue-structured ways to value persons. After all, how could the moral significance of love be appreciated in terms of abstract principles of mandatory conduct? Erotic love is characterized by extraordinary partiality in the singling out of one individual (or at most a few) to be cherished as unique and irreplaceable within a shared life of intimacy and caring. To be sure, general rules such as keep promises, avoid deception, and refrain from harm do play a role in love. But the impartiality paradigm regards these rules as external constraints on love rather than inherent in the virtues that structure love. If anything, it would seem that the impartiality paradigm creates a presumption against giving preferential treatment to a spouse or lover at the expense of helping many others. That explains why so many thinkers contrast morality and love rather than understanding love as structured by moral values.

The impartiality paradigm led moral philosophers to neglect love, but it also distorted the work of those few philosophers who did write about love. Irving Singer is a striking example. His masterful trilogy, *The Nature of Love,* begins with a suggestion that influenced me: love is a way to value persons. Immediately, however, he insists that the valuing is *non*moral: "In loving another person . . . we enact a nonmoral *loyalty.*"[15] To explain, Singer describes a mother whose love for her criminal son leads her to stand by him, refusing to turn him in to the police and blinding her to the seriousness of the harm he causes. Her devotion "will not be a moral love." In general, "love is not *inherently* moral. There is no guarantee that it will bestow value properly, at the right time, in the right way."

The last claim is undeniable. Whether overall or in limited respects, instances of love can be morally flawed. It does not follow, however, that love is a nonmoral loyalty. Moral imperfection does not imply moral insignificance, and love that is primarily bad can still embody elements of goodness. If the mother's love is flawed, it is also admirable in some ways. It embodies the moral virtues of caring, faithfulness, and loyalty, even though these virtues have mostly bad consequences in her situation—primarily because they are not balanced and guided by good judgment and wisdom.

Why does Singer overlook these seemingly obvious points? It is because he is in the grip of the impartiality paradigm, specifically the Kantian version that construes partiality as the violation of universal principles about acting for the sake of duty. Consider this passage: "It is almost impossible to imagine someone bestowing value without caring about the other person's welfare. To that extent, love implies benevolence. And yet the lover does not act benevolently for the sake of doing the right thing."[16]

To begin with, why "almost" impossible? Surely we cannot conceive of love without caring, at least in some minimal degree. Moreover, apparently benevolence is a moral virtue, which blocks Singer's conclusion (in the same paragraph) that love is nonmoral loyalty. As the passage reveals, Singer thinks of morality in Kantian terms, as acting "for the sake of doing the right thing," as obeying duty for duty's sake. Kant's influence is unmistakable when he adds that "ethical attitudes," unlike love's "nonmoral loyalty must consider the individual in his relations to other people, as one among many who have equal claims." Of course, if morality required us to treat everyone's claims as equal, then love would have little to do with morality; indeed they would be in opposition. By jettisoning this paradigm, we can begin to appreciate love as virtue-structured and highly particularized ways to value persons morally.

To his credit, Singer is a pluralist who celebrates many alternative forms of love. In a similar spirit, but discarding the impartiality paradigm of morality, I will next place my conception of love within a pluralistic perspective of moral values.

According to the impartiality model, all ideally rational and morally sensitive persons would agree on fundamental moral principles. This view is sometimes called *ethical monism* because it asserts there is only one justified moral perspective. Applied to erotic love, this view implies there is one canonical view of sex, love, and monogamy: Always sex should express love and always it should do so within marriage. The canonical ideology begins and ends with obligations, leaving little room for alternative forms of good to be achieved through different kinds of relationships.

Much of the history of erotic love is a tale of bigotry, of fierce wars waged among ethical monists who insist on their canonical truths. Sex without love, erotic love outside marriage, homoerotic love, and divorces have all been condemned as deadly sins. Today, clashing attitudes about sexual love underlie disagreements in American politics over homosexuality, abortion, teenage sex, pornography, feminism, AIDS, and government control over marriage.[17] Perhaps we should not be surprised at the prominence of erotic love within the culture wars. Even apart from the impartiality paradigm, deep psychological forces render it difficult for us to accept alternative forms of love. Our ideals of love dramatically shape our sense of identity and self-worth because they concern some of life's most important goods. As a result, most of us feel some anxiety in confronting opposing ideals of love. In affirming the moral goods embedded in our relationships, we feel the need to legislate that everyone else should pursue those goods.

Ethical pluralism acknowledges a plurality of justified moral perspectives. It affirms reasonable variations in how moral values are understood and applied. Of course, not all moral perspectives are equally justified. Moral perspectives may be more or less clear, comprehensive, consistent, rich and enriching, and compatible with the most carefully considered convictions of morally sensitive and reasonable persons. Nevertheless, there are probably many perspectives that satisfy these criteria in equal degrees, and there is no one canonical view of the morally good life.

Pluralism itself takes various forms, and here I endorse a version developed by John Kekes as six theses. I should emphasize that Kekes does not accept the implications for love that I draw from his theses. Like Singer, Kekes believes that love is a nonmoral value and that "erotic love . . . [is] only incidentally concerned with moral values."[18] He seems to be led to this view for reasons other than the impartiality model, but his reasons are obscure. Thus, he says love is nonmoral because moral values "depend on producing deserved benefits and not producing undeserved harms," implying that love generates undeserved benefits, perhaps because it is a gift. Yet surely gifts have moral implications, and in any case love is far more complex morally than simple gifts.

In any case, Kekes's six theses are both plausible and provide a helpful framework within which to explore the moral significance of love. Here I offer only a few illustrations about how the theses apply to love, leaving fuller development to later chapters.

Thesis 1. There are many moral values, none of which is so fundamental that it overrides all the others in all circumstances. With regard to marital love, these values include autonomy, mutual fulfillment, mutual caring, fairness and justice, and all the other major virtues that add value to relationships. Couples will assign different weights to these values. For example, some will see complete honesty as essential, whereas others will give greater weight to fairness. Because there is no impartial universal schema that dictates a mandatory way of ranking these virtues, virtue-structured love encompasses a wide variety of ways to value persons and a wide diversity of morally valuable relationships.

Thesis 2. Given the importance of moral values and the complexity of life, disturbing conflicts among values are inevitable, and there is no single reasonable way to resolve many of those conflicts. With regard to marriage, the conflicts will be worked out together by spouses in ways that are not mandatory or canonical for other couples. For example, one partner might give high priority to sexual fidelity and interpret it as forbidding any form of extramarital sex, while the other partner might interpret the virtue less strictly and give lower priority to it compared to sexual freedom. The agreement a couple reaches may be essential to the success of their love, but their agreement cannot be a universal requirement for others.

Thesis 3. Many moral conflicts, including some very fundamental ones, can only be (rationally) resolved by compromises and mutual adjustments through democratic processes, rather than through a substantive consensus. This thesis may seem more applicable to communities than to couples, because successful marriages typically require large areas of shared values. In fact, couples may well differ over some fundamental issues, while maintaining a wide area of shared moral convictions and commitments. They work out mutually satisfactory, or at least workable, adjustments in how to raise children, how to balance work hours and time spent together, and about which social causes to contribute to.

Thesis 4. Moral disagreements often play a positive role in drawing attention to alternative possibilities for morally significant lives. This thesis applies especially to differing views about sex and erotic love. Pluralists reject the ideas that marriage (or else chastity) is the best choice for everyone, sex ought to be limited to marriage, divorce should be difficult to obtain, and marriage should be restricted to heterosexual couples. Nevertheless, ethical pluralism does leave room for obligations to sustain love, after autonomous individuals make commitments to each other.

In this connection, recall John Stuart Mill's defense of diversity in *On Liberty*. Mill urged that "there should be different experiments of living; . . . free scope should be given to varieties of character."[19] These experiments call for "spontaneity" and "originality," rather than "ape-like imitation" and blind obeisance to custom, but they do not mean ignoring the "higher [more valuable] pleasures" of love, friendship, and art. Nowhere are experiments more important than with regard to erotic love, as Mill's personal life testifies. He and Harriet Taylor had to confront considerable bigotry. When they first met, Taylor was married and had two children. She and Mill agreed to keep their relationship platonic, responding to what they saw as justifiable moral claims on them, including the concern for the children and Taylor's continuing affection for her husband, not to mention social decorum. They waited two decades, until after the death of Taylor's husband, before they married. Thus, in affirming a variety of experiments in loving, Mill also affirmed the value of traditional ideals of marriage.

Thesis 5. There are limits to what counts as reasonable moral views; some conventions, social practices, and personal conduct are immoral. In particular, pluralism allows us to make firm moral judgments criticizing betrayal, exploitation, cruelty, and violence in marriages. There are minimal standards of decency that are not merely relative, whether we understand those standards in terms of human rights (rights ethics), respect for autonomy (Kant's duty ethics), or the promotion of human welfare (utilitarianism). Moreover, some relationships are better than others in the degree they instantiate important virtues. That is, they are better with regard to the presence of those virtues, although not necessarily overall.

Thesis 6. There is such a thing as moral progress in moving toward morally better practices and communities. Measures of progress include fundamental ideals like justice and compassion. Another measure is the moral richness of the society in respecting diversity of forms of moral goodness, in particular those manifested in friendship and love, as ways to value persons morally. Perhaps the most striking example of moral progress in marriages during the twentieth century has been in rethinking the meaning of fairness in personal relationships. As I see it, another form of progress that has yet to be socially achieved lies in social acceptance of nonheterosexual marriages.

Defending these six theses would take us too far afield, for they are general claims about moral values that require a book-length defense of the sort Kekes provides. I want to highlight, however, three considerations that make ethical pluralism plausible and inviting: Pluralism affirms objective values, liberty and tolerance of diversity, and the moral significance of personal caring relationships.

First, ethical pluralism retains a belief in objective values, including some values that have widespread and even universal application, together with other values that have more limited but still reason-backed intersubjective significance. Many values should find wide intersubjective agreement and recognition among morally concerned persons, even though their precise applications are open to disagreement. Hence, pluralism is not to be confused with ethical relativism, the view that moral values are entirely reducible to the social conventions of particular times and places, a view that reduces morality to the vagaries of custom. With regard to sex and erotic love, relativists claim that no form of sexual expression is any better or worse than others; there are only various erotic preferences that societies and groups selectively endorse. Ethical relativism permits any form of cruelty, for example the systematic suppression of women, if a given society or group accepts it. As such, ethical relativism is a form of skepticism about the possibility of objective moral reasoning. By contrast, ethical pluralism leaves considerable room for objective moral reasoning while leaving equal latitude for personal moral choices — especially about ideals of goodness such as those defining love.

Second, ethical pluralism affirms human freedom and diversity. It does so in part by way of celebration: Liberty is valuable both inherently and for its good consequences. It does so in part by way of resignation: There are problems that arise from liberty, but the alternatives of political tyranny and psychological repression are far worse. Tolerance is a fundamental virtue. Just as we value our own capacity to make choices, we should respect the autonomy and dignity of other persons as free and rational beings. Tolerance is consistent with praising some love-styles and relationships as better, because they embody important virtues, without condemning the alternatives as immoral. It is also consistent with praising several love-styles as equally good, albeit in different ways and for different reasons.

Third, ethical pluralism affirms the moral importance of caring relationships, especially in family, friendship, and love. It denies the impartiality paradigm, rejecting the attempt to formulate all moral values as universal principles to treat people impartially. One reason for this denial is a stubborn fact: Millenia of responsible discourse among rational and morally concerned persons have failed to yield a univocal view of moral goodness. Instead, that history of reasoned discourse has yielded increasing moral diversity on many issues. A more positive reason for rejecting the impartiality paradigm is to open our moral vision to how personal relationships of love, friendship, and family create morally desirable ways to value persons.

In the chapters that follow, my aim is to explore traditional marital ideals within a pluralist framework. I approach traditional ideals as virtue-structured ways to value persons and thereby to create morally good relationships, rather than as stipulating obligatory ways of life. This combination of pluralism and tradition opens me to criticism from all sides. Ethical monists will be upset by my acceptance of many forms of erotic love, especially homoerotic love and marriage. Some pluralists will suspect that concentrating on traditional values surrounding erotic love conceals an unjustifiable bias in favor of one way of life. And relativists will find the attempt to seriously reason about values otiose. Without hoping to convert critics to my viewpoint, I offer the following invitations.

To ethical monists, I invite ecumenical dialogue, confident of the goodwill to be found among them. Almost invariably, canonical views are grounded in religious convictions concerning *the* good life for humans based on particular religious beliefs.[20] Yet, canonists disagree among themselves as much as they disagree with pluralists, often with greater acrimony as religious absolutes clash with opposing absolutes. Again, some canonists are committed to narrow and intolerant dogma, but others are known for their tolerance and ecumenical commitments. Now, just as pluralists regard some sexual relationships as morally richer than others, canonists might admit that alternative moral ideals are valuable, even if less than those guided by their own ideals. Hence there is a large middle ground where canonical and pluralistic outlooks converge. Exploring traditional marital virtues within a pluralistic framework will help identify this common ground.

Dialogue will be minimal if religious doctrines about love are embraced uncritically, as the directives from a deity who commands whimsically, without reasons.[21] We can assume, however, that a morally perfect God would have good moral reasons for endorsing particular values, thereby inviting dialogue about what those reasons are. In particular, it is fruitful to discuss the possibility that a loving God who is concerned for human well-being, and who is cognizant of alternative ways that erotic love promotes well-being, would endorse the values of autonomy and tolerance (within limits) in matters of erotic love. Hence, even though humanistic pluralism does not share religious views about the supernatural, there is much room for mutually enriching dialogue.

To ethical pluralists who suspect that my sympathy for traditional forms of erotic love conceals a bias, I emphasize how my approach to traditional marital virtues is nontraditional. One way is already indicated in my definition of marriage as including gay, lesbian, and bisexual relationships. Another way is my emphatic denial that marriage is the most desirable erotic relationship for everyone. Other ways will emerge later, for example in my definition of sexual fidelity in terms of a couple's mutual understanding rather than an absolute "Thou shalt not commit adultery." And my approach to many of the other virtues, such as honesty and fairness, allows considerable flexibility in how they are interpreted and applied in relationships.

In the eyes of some pluralists, marriage is an archaic, foolishly romantic, and "bourgeois" mainstay of an establishment that needs to be dismantled in order to achieve social freedom and justice. Now, clearly the practice of marriage has a mixed history, as feminists especially have shown. For one thing, marriages have been governed by harmful laws, such as those making divorce difficult and those giving males property ownership and unilateral authority.[22] For another thing, until recently marriages provided an area of privacy protected from social scrutiny. As such, they have been sites of "privatized power imbalances" in which "men have been able to assault, batter, and rape the women to whom they were married, and parents can assault, batter, and impound their children."[23]

But are these abuses due to marriage per se or instead to grafted-on cultural traditions of male domination that have permeated all social practices and institutions? Marriage is a flexible practice that can be modified to avoid the abuses. The flexibility is implied by my moral definition of marriage, but it is even true in the legal definition. During a relatively short historical period, laws changed so as to permit relatively easy divorce, and the trend in the law is to demand minimally decent conduct between spouses. For example, the concepts of marital abuse and marital rape are entering into the law as legitimate grounds for prosecution, however difficult they may be to prove.

Finally, to ethical relativists I grant that moral judgments need to be made in relation to specific situations and contexts, as I will emphasize in thinking about love. Those contexts include variable social allegiances, ethnic identities, and customs that are morally relevant in making cogent moral judgments concerning love. But relevance is one thing; reduction of morality to *mores* is something else. The easy slide into relativism that pervades our society is a combination of confusion and loss of moral faith. There are few relativists who consistently believe that all forms of human cruelty and degradation are morally permissible when backed by group approval (and there is always some group prepared to endorse a given form of cruelty). Can customs justify violence, whether in the form of spouse abuse, acquaintance and marital rape, or mutilation of female genitals? Can we seriously believe that racism, sexism, and exploitation are merely matters of convention and cannot be criticized morally?

To conclude, love encompasses a variety of virtue-guided and virtue-structured ways to value persons. Understood within a pluralistic perspective, love makes possible morally creative forms of shared caring, a theme to which I return in the next chapter.

2

CARING

> For what is love itself, for the one we love
> best? — an enfolding of immeasurable cares
> which yet are better than any joys outside
> our love.
> —*George Eliot*[1]

Caring is the central virtue defining love, and as such it is a topic throughout this book. In this chapter, I discuss two related questions. First, when and why is caring a virtue? Is it a virtue only when it has good consequences, or are good motives and intentions most important? I will argue for a complex view: Within erotic love relationships, caring is a virtue partly when it has good motives and intended objects, partly because (as such) it tends to produce good consequences, and partly because of its connections with other virtues. Caring is directed toward persons in their full individuality, motivated in part by a concern for their well-being and tending with any luck to produce good consequences. In love, as elsewhere, caring must be understood within a tapestry of additional virtues that limit, condition, augment, and express it.

Second, what is distinctive about the caring involved in marriages? Perhaps more than any other type of relationship, marriage is defined by mutual caring within a shared life. That life includes shared commitments, interests, agency, identity, happiness, fulfillment, meaning, and moral creativity within relationships based on intimacy and trust.

A third theme emerges in discussing both of these questions: Love

32

is morally creative, in addition to being a primary source of inspiration in the arts and sciences. This theme is familiar in world religions and is celebrated in popular talk about the "power of love" to transform lives. It is also central to Plato's *Symposium,* which I discuss in the first section. In the second section I explore moral creativity as producing valuable new results within marriages based on shared caring.

CARING AS A VIRTUE

The word "caring" has many meanings.[2] To *care for* is to desire and to promote the well-being of others, at least in part for their sake rather than solely for oneself. To *care about positively* is to want someone (or something) to prosper, whereas to *care about negatively* is to want them not to prosper. *Having cares* is having concerns that may be burdensome; *having care of* is being responsible for; *taking care of* is looking after; and *taking care* is being suitably cautious (careful). When I say that marital love makes possible special ways to care for persons, I intend yet another meaning—caring as a virtue. This is the honorific sense in which we speak of *being a caring person,* either in general or with regard to a person one loves. As a virtue, caring can be defined using the other senses: Caring persons care for and (positively) care about other people in desirable ways; typically they have cares and responsibilities, take care to meet them, and take care of others when appropriate.

Yet, not all caring for and caring about (positively) is virtuous, at least not overall and in every respect, and the same is true of love.[3] Is caring a virtue only when it has good consequences?

Good Consequences

Certainly, good consequences are relevant in evaluating caring. At the very least, there is a presumption that caring is undesirable when it produces horrendous results, even though that presumption may be overridden by other considerations in particular situations.

Consider a case of pathological caring in which an individual's conduct becomes largely impermeable to reason. Psychotherapist Irvin Yalom describes a seventy-year-old married woman who came to him as a patient. Thelma, as he calls her to conceal her identity, was for eight years obsessed with a previous therapist with whom she made love once, before he broke off their month-long romance.[4] The obsession disrupted her marriage and made her life a nightmare of unrelenting depression and torment. No amount of reasoning or therapy could ease her obsession until the previous therapist agreed to meet with her. He confessed that at the time of their romance he was recovering from a psychotic episode in which he believed he could achieve a perfect oneness with her, and with everything else in the universe. Since then, he abandoned his career as a therapist and became an administrator in a health maintenance organization. The woman's condition began to improve slightly when he agreed to meet with her socially. Yalom acknowledges that the woman's infatuation helped her endure a rather dreary existence, and it also revealed an endearing side of her personality. He leaves no doubt, however, that her caring and love were undesirable overall, both in deepening her unhappiness and in wreaking havoc on her family.

Love and caring can manifest more vice than virtue even in the absence of full-blown mental illness. In Émile Zola's novel *Thérèse Raquin*, Laurent begins an intense affair with Thérèse Raquin, "a relationship in blood and sensuality."[5] When her husband becomes a threat to the affair, Thérèse hints at the possibility of killing him. Knowing her husband cannot swim, Laurent arranges a boat ride and during a gruesome struggle throws him overboard, making his death look like an accident. After waiting long enough to avoid any appearance of wrongdoing, Laurent and Thérèse marry. Although their passion revives intermittently, gradually it turns to hatred as they torture each other with accusations about the murder.

We need not turn to fiction for such examples. About half of all murders are committed within families and among lovers. Consider Thomas Bird, a minister in the Flint Hills of Kansas, and his secretary Lorna Anderson.[6] Both were married, although not happily, and each had children. They fell in love and began having a affair. Ruling out divorce and remarriage on the grounds that it would hurt his career, Reverend Bird argued—in the name of love!—that the lesser evil in their situation was to kill their spouses. He drove his wife to a bridge, hit her with a car jack, and, as she desperately clung to the railing, kicked her off the bridge to her death. Then he pushed the car over the bridge to create the appearance of a car crash. Four months later, Lorna Anderson drove with her husband to a prearranged location where, after she feigned illness, Reverend Bird shot him. The pair were arrested before Lorna could collect her husband's $300,000 life insurance.

We are unlikely to see much virtue in whatever caring Anderson and Bird, and Thérèse and Laurent, felt for each other. True, we might attempt to trace the bad consequences to their hatred for their spouses rather than their caring for each other. Yet, the hate and caring cannot be neatly separated, and it seems clear that the caring entered substantially into the motives for murder. Alternatively, we might suspect there was more lust than (virtue-structured) love involved. Either way, we will hesitate to invoke the language of virtues lest we seem to praise affections that are so dramatically overshadowed by evil.

Nevertheless, we cannot in general infer that caring is not virtuous simply because it has bad consequences in a particular situation. Bad luck, unfortunate circumstances, and harm caused by third parties can frustrate the most genuine and admirable caring. We celebrate the love of Romeo and Juliet, Tristan and Isolde, and Heloise and Abelard, despite its tragedy—or rather because of it.

Moreover, the caring involved in the earlier examples failed to be virtuous for reasons beyond bad consequences. The caring itself was corrupt or unhealthy. In the cases of Thérèse-Laurent and Anderson-Bird, the caring was mixed with selfishness, lust, ambition, greed, and cruelty. In the case of Thelma, the caring was pathologically motivated. These features of the caring generate the bad consequences, thereby suggesting that caring is a virtue, at least in part, because of good motives and intentions.

Good Intentions and Moral Creativity

According to Plato, love and caring are desirable because of their constitution rather than primarily because of their consequences.

Love is desirable only when it is directed toward good objects, in particular toward ideals of beauty and goodness, and only when accompanied by intentions to pursue those ideals. Nevertheless, good objects tend to inspire moral creativity and thereby to produce good results. These views, that love is valuable because of its intended objects and also because it tends to be morally creative, are genuine insights even if we reject, as I think we should, Plato's characterization of the specific objects and intentions in love.

Each of the speakers in the *Symposium* portrays love as morally creative in some way. Phaedrus, the first speaker, praises love for inspiring virtues in lovers, especially honor, courage, and self-sacrifice. The greatest army would be one composed of lovers who, "in battle side by side, would conquer all the world. . . . For a man in love would never allow his loved one, of all people, to see him leaving ranks or dropping weapons."[7] Pausanius, the next speaker, distinguishes between higher and lower forms of love depending on how strongly the love inspires virtue. Higher love is more constant and increases wisdom because it is aimed at the soul (rather than the body) of a wise person. Both Phaedrus and Pausanius focus on love between persons, as does Alcibiades, who concludes the dialogue by making a passionate overture to the virtuous Socrates. By contrast, Eryximachus portrays love as a cosmic force that creates harmony and reconciles opposites in all areas of life, and Agathon praises love as a deity who inspires virtue in humans.

Framed between the speeches of Eryximachus and Agathon, Aristophanes sets forth the most famous of the person-focused theories of love in the *Symposium*. According to his wonderfully humane myth, which affirms homosexual and heterosexual love alike, human ancestors were round creatures with double sets of heads, limbs, and genitals. Rebellious and powerful, the creatures affronted the gods, who then retaliated by dividing them in half, leaving them wounded and lonely for their other half. Originally there were three types of round creatures—female-female, male-male, and female-male—which explains why the divisions created three sexual orientations: lesbian, gay, and heterosexual. Whatever one's sexual orientation, "love is born into every human being; it calls back the halves of our original nature together; it tries to make one out of two and heal the wound of human nature."[8] Here the theme

of moral creativity is expressed as re-creating ourselves in our original wholeness so as to restore health and produce happiness.

As a character in the dialogue, Socrates most fully expresses Plato's own views.[9] Socrates challenges Aristophanes' person-centered
theory of love. He portrays the highest forms of love as aimed at
ideals of beauty and goodness, rather than at people. In doing so, he
explicitly links moral creativity to the objects of love: Love is morally
creative when it is directed toward beauty and goodness.

More fully, Socrates connects good objects with moral creativity in
three ways. First, he sets forth a myth about the origins of Love, that
is, the god of love. Love's mother is the god of poverty and need,
which explains lovers' desperate neediness for each other. Love's father is the god of resourcefulness, making Love "a schemer after the
beautiful and the good; he is brave, impetuous, and intense, an awe-
some hunter, always weaving snares, resourceful in his pursuit of intelligence, a lover of wisdom through all his life, a genius with en-
chantments, potions, and clever pleadings."[10] Inspired with at least
partial wisdom, lovers become creative in expressing and securing
their love (an idea I develop in the chapter on wisdom).

Second, moving beyond metaphor, Socrates says that love is directed toward the good: "Love is wanting to possess the good for-
ever," both one's own good and an objective moral good.[11] Because of
this focus on the good, love's function is to be morally creative in
"giving birth in beauty," enabling lovers to achieve a kind of personal immortality through creating a lasting good.[12] The lower form
of creativity, which centers on sexual beauty, leads to giving birth to
children (a view that reflects Greek misogyny). The higher form
consists of creating works of art, philosophy, and science, and especially moral virtue.

Third, Socrates ranks types of love according to the moral value of
their objects and, correspondingly, according to the creative products those objects inspire. Love is better depending on whether a
lover is attracted by the beauty found in objects whose value is
ranked on an ascending scale: one body, all bodies, souls (the inner
beauty of character), social practices and laws, knowledge, or
Beauty itself (the Form, or metaphysical exemplar, of Beauty). Correspondingly, there are varying levels of creativity in the ideas and
virtues these objects inspire. The highest love, which is aimed at im-

personal abstractions of beauty and goodness, inspires philosophical creativity.

What are we to make of this theory? Plato deserves credit for moving beyond an exclusive focus on good consequences. He links the value of love to its objects and intentions, and he uses them to explain why genuine love is morally creative. Unfortunately, Plato gives a perplexing account of the objects of interpersonal love. He construes the objects as ideals (of beauty, goodness, wisdom) that are manifested in the beloved. But our topic is interpersonal love, and surely interpersonal love is the love of persons. I agree with Plato that ideals play an essential role in loving persons, but rather than invoking ideals to understand love for persons he seems to reduce that love to the love of ideals.

Admittedly, there are difficulties in interpreting Plato, especially his Socratic ascent toward increasingly valuable objects. Does communion with the Form of Beauty imply abandoning love of persons, thereby sublimating sexual love in order to love ideals (as the expression "platonic love" suggests)? Or can love for (virtuous) persons be one way to love ideals? (Similar questions of interpretation surround religious doctrines about loving God in and by loving persons.) The latter reading is supported by Plato's decision to end the *Symposium* by presenting Alcibiades' love for Socrates. It is also supported by the *Phaedrus,* Plato's other important dialogue on love, in which love for persons is celebrated rather than sublimated.[13]

Ultimately, however, little turns on whether Plato replaces love for persons with love of ideals or instead allows that love for persons can be one way to love ideals. Either way, his theory draws us away from valuing persons for their own sake, in their full particularity, individuality, uniqueness, and irreplaceability. As Gregory Vlastos stated, Plato's theory bids us to "love persons so far, and only insofar, as they are good and beautiful. . . . It does not provide for love of whole persons, but only for love of that abstract version of persons which consist of the complex of their best qualities."[14] In my terms, Plato describes the love of ideals through persons, or at most the love of persons as instantiating ideals. By contrast, I think we love persons "through" moral ideals and within virtue-structured relationships.

Plato's theory of love has another problematic feature. He describes love as self-seeking. Its guiding intention is the pursuit of enlightened self-interest. What about altruism? As I understand caring and love, the lover's intention is (in part) to promote the good of the beloved, for the sake of the beloved. At least to some degree, love is a *particularized altruism* — caring focused on the good of the beloved, by contrast with general benevolence toward humanity. It is also an active altruism, by contrast with mere wishing and fantasizing. More fully, the object of genuine love is the well-being of the beloved together with the shared well-being of the two lovers. By focusing on ideals rather than personal relationships, Plato overlooks the sharing, mutuality, and reciprocity in love, a topic to which I turn in a moment.

Good Motives

Caring embodies particularized altruism, but it is not entirely selfless. Having rejected Plato's wholly self-seeking *eros,* we should avoid the opposite extreme of wholly selfless *agape.* Within personal relationships, the agape ideal would encourage masochism and frustration, just as Plato's eros ideal would encourage narcissistic struggles. To be sure, the predominant human motive (or reason for action) is self-seeking, and hence it should come as no surprise to discover that self-seeking is the primary motive in love.[15] But we also have altruistic capacities to care for others for their sake. Love not only interweaves altruism and self-interest; it fuses them. Love transcends the dichotomy between eros and agape by creating motives to promote the shared good of two (or more) people.

Irving Singer describes this fusion of self-interest and altruism as a mixture of individual appraisal with bestowal. "Individual appraisal" means valuing persons because of how they satisfy our needs and desires. (By contrast, "objective appraisals" evaluate persons in terms of how well they meet wider community standards).[16] "Bestowal," however, "goes beyond all appraisive categories" in that it is caring for others beyond how they answer to our desires. As such, bestowal creates new value: "In relation to ourselves it gives another being a special goodness, a personal worth, that emanates from our own capacity to love. . . . Love is a bestowal of value which supplements, and sometimes overrides, our attitudes of appraisal. As bestowal, love accords a person preferential status that is unearned in any appraisive sense."[17]

Whereas Plato thought love was morally creative because of its focus on good objects, Singer says love, as bestowal, is a creative process of giving new value to the beloved. This is an intriguing suggestion, but in making it Singer conflates two senses of "creating value." In the first sense, which I endorse, bestowal is an appreciative recognition. It is a response to the beloved as being singularly important—in his or her own right, and not just because of how that person answers to another's needs. As a result, mutual acts of bestowal elevate lovers' self-esteem and enrich the meaning in their lives. That explains why we want to be loved: Love convinces us that we matter to people who matter to us.

In the second sense, which I reject, bestowal is the origin of human worth: "In themselves, in their individual human souls (whatever that may be), people have neither 'infinite worth' nor infinite worthlessness. They acquire value and the lack of it only as they are valued or value themselves in their relations with one another."[18] Here Singer reduces the worth of persons to how they are actually valued. That reduction is unwarranted, both in psychological and moral terms. On the one hand, it does not ring true in terms of the psychology of love. Granted, we experience our beloved's love as a gift that affirms and expands our sense of self-worth. But the converse is not true. As lovers we do not experience ourselves as creating value where none exists. Instead, we experience ourselves as appreciating the inherent worth of the beloved, a worth we recognize rather than create. As one of Singer's critics remarks, "If I thought your love was added from nowhere, and if I seriously believed that my love for you was entirely a matter of my giving you a gift you didn't deserve, decent relationships would be more fragile than they are. What is pure gift, answering to no value in the beloved, can be withdrawn as spontaneously as it was given—without explanation, without justification. Intimacy does not work on such principles."[19]

On the other hand, these psychological observations reflect a moral truth. Love *reveals* value. In love we discover and appreciate the value of the beloved, as someone unique and irreplaceably dear.

Other people might fail to appreciate the people we love, and perhaps sometimes the people we love undervalue themselves.[20] We do
not fill the gap by creating a new value, ex nihilo, where none existed before. Instead we respond to the value that a person already
has. Of course, the person we love takes on special importance to us,
but that is because we recognize a value he or she already possesses.

Having said this, I agree with Singer that motives and reasons for
love are focused simultaneously on the beloved (through bestowal in
the first sense) and on oneself (through appraisal). Love is reason-
based in ways that evoke self-interest, and yet it interweaves self-interest with an appreciation of the inherent value of the beloved.[21]
Using Singer's distinctions, we can understand shallow caring as primarily self-interested appraisal with little other-focused bestowal.
By contrast, the deep caring defining genuine love implies high degrees of bestowal mixed with appraisal. We can also understand
deep caring in terms of the particular types of appraisal-reasons for
love. In deep caring, the reasons for love center on the entire person;
they target central aspects of his or her identity and character. By
contrast, shallow caring centers exclusively on such things as a person's body or money.

It is now clear that our discussion of love's reasons and motives is
connected with the earlier discussion of love's objects. Deep caring
implies love for persons, not just for some of their qualities. As Jeffrey Blustein writes, "One's attractive or valuable qualities (or combination of such qualities) are what one is loved for, or why one is
loved, not all that is loved. We might put it this way: particular persons are invaluable to us not because they exhibit certain *qualities,*
but because *they* exhibit certain qualities."[22] If I love someone just
for her money, beauty, or kindness to me, then she becomes replace-
able by other partners who provide these things, perhaps in even
greater quantity. Of course, we love the person who has particular
features, and the person is not separable from all those features. But
the features are not abstract properties, such as intelligence, beauty,
good character, that are repeatable in innumerable other individuals. Instead the features are *particularized:* They are embedded in
the highly individual *style* of the beloved.[23] Rather than loving a
package of general properties, we love a person with that style.

Tapestry of Virtues

The caring involved in genuine love is directed toward persons in their full individuality, motivated in part by a concern for their well-being and tending with any luck to produce good consequences. Caring, in this sense, is the central virtue defining love, yet it cannot be understood alone, in abstraction from other virtues. It is expressed in, conditioned on, enhanced or limited by, and in general interwoven with other virtues within a complex moral tapestry (explored throughout this book). This view of caring should not be confused with Aristotle's doctrine of the unity of the virtues, which says that possessing one cardinal virtue implies possessing them all. The virtues are not as tightly linked as that, but nor are they entirely isolated. As the metaphor of a tapestry suggests, they are interconnected in many complicated patterns.

Virtues are not monolithic structures. They enter into character in different ways and degrees. They may be manifested in some contexts but not others, contrary to Aristotle who portrayed the virtuous person as having fixed and invariable dispositions. (Think of the politician who is genuinely honest within his private circle of friends, mostly honest with his spouse, and often dishonest toward the public.)

Again, it is tempting to link each virtue to specific aspects of marriage: caring to helping, honesty to intimacy and trustworthiness, fairness to balanced sharing of goods, faithfulness to preserving constancy in love, sexual fidelity to maintaining sexual commitments, and so on. I will develop some of these linkages. Nevertheless, a given virtue often influences additional aspects of a marriage, and caring interacts with nearly all aspects of a marriage and hence with all the other virtues.

To develop the idea of a tapestry of virtues, with caring made central, it is helpful to discuss Carol Gilligan's *In a Different Voice*. Gilligan distinguishes a "morality of caring" from a "morality of justice," which focuses on rights and fairness. I want to show that caring and justice are too tightly interwoven within the tapestry of virtues to allow any such neat separation. In doing so, however, I want to draw on Gilligan's insights in identifying four features of caring that are important in thinking about love: sensitivity to context, balancing needs, acceptance of personal responsibility, and understanding self-identity in terms of relationships.

First, caring is context-sensitive: It is a response to particular situations and to the specific needs of individuals we care for. In this connection Gilligan quotes George Eliot, "Moral judgments must remain false and hollow unless they are checked and enlightened by a perpetual reference to the special circumstances that mark the individual lot."[24] As Eliot also points out, morality requires "growing insight and sympathy," not abstract rules applied "without the trouble of exerting patience, discrimination . . . [and] a wide, fellow feeling with all that is human."

Gilligan fails to ask, however, which features of context the caring person attends and responds to.[25] The tapestry of virtues provides the answer. Choices about where to focus, when, and with what salience and weight presuppose other values such as justice, fairness, self-respect, and honesty (with oneself and with others). To use an extreme example, racists and sexists attend to different features in their patterns of caring than egalitarians do. Again, insensitive people attend to some features while either omitting finer-grained detail or wider-grained features that provide perspective. Gilligan herself emphasizes the idea of needs, which is a normative concept that singles out some desires and human functions as more important than others.[26] In any case, caring is not the foundation for a separate ethics that can be understood independently of other virtues.

Second, Gilligan emphasizes that caring persons must reasonably balance their needs with the needs of others. This balancing is essential to love, for otherwise relationships become distorted by subservience and dominance. Yet how is this balancing achieved? Once again other moral values are relevant—especially self-respect and fairness. Gilligan wisely suggests that a morality of caring should be complemented by a morality of justice, but she does not fully appreciate how the very concept of caring implies sensitivity to justice and rights. Justice concepts are essential in understanding the kind of balancing of concerns that are vital in avoiding harm to oneself and others.[27]

Third, Gilligan says that caring is responsible concern for the needs and desires of others, but what does that mean? One alternative is to define caring in terms of ideally responsible conduct, thereby establishing caring as an umbrella virtue that encompasses all the others. Another alternative, which I prefer, is to understand caring as a dependent virtue, that is, a virtue only when it is combined with at least a minimum of other goods and virtues.[28] Thus, caring is not virtuous when it motivates murder, as in the earlier examples. Genuine caring need not be accompanied by completely responsible conduct, but it implies a minimum degree of decency and integrity. Once again, caring is linked to many other virtues, rather than being the basis for a separate ethics.

Fourth, Gilligan says a morality of caring understands personal identity in terms of relationships with other people. By identifying with them, we understand our own well-being as tied to their well-being. Both my identity and my well-being are found in the relationships I participate in rather than the rights I exercise. This aspect of Gilligan's work brings to mind the paradox of caring: We find our good by caring for the good of others. The paradox is expressed in various ways: Self-sacrifice promotes self-fulfillment; self-surrender wins personal freedom; promoting others' happiness for their sake contributes to one's own happiness; in giving we receive. Nowhere is this paradox more applicable than with regard to spouses who share a life in which caring and self-interest are inextricably interwoven.

As Gilligan is aware, this paradox is dangerous, especially if caring is misconstrued as self-abnegation.[29] The call for selflessness has often been used to exploit women who are urged to serve husbands by following their "natural" tendency to be more caring than men. Selflessness in love needs to be understood as concern for others' good while giving due attention to one's own needs. This implies, however, that caring requires the virtues of wisdom, prudence, and self-respect in discerning how to balance the needs of the self with those of others. Once again, caring emerges as part of a tapestry of moral virtues, a tapestry that in marriage unfolds within a shared life.

SHARED LIVES

Reciprocal caring is manifested in all dimensions of marital sharing, including shared commitments, interests, agency, identity, happiness, fulfillment, meaning, and moral creativity. Each of these dimensions contributes to love as virtue-structured ways to value persons.

Shared Commitments

Traditional marital love is grounded in lifelong commitments to love actively and supportively "til death us do part." These commitments affirm the unique importance of the beloved by being exclusive (to one person only) and lifelong (intended to last as long as the partner is alive). As Robert R. Ehman writes, "The assertion of love implies that the beloved has a value for the lover above that of others and that the lover regards his relation to his beloved as more important than his other relationships."[30]

Lifelong commitments affirm the beloved's entire life, as opposed to a time-slice of it. In this way, they are unlike temporary liaisons of convenience that recognize the value of the person at present and in limited respects. Lifelong commitments are also unlike fixed-time commitments, such as to pursue a relationship during college until career plans necessitate separation. Time-limited commitments automatically make lovers secondary, whether to education, work, or other relationships. By contrast, commitments intended to be lifelong place the relationship first, with the understanding that all other goals will be pursued within the framework of the relationship. The strength of commitment to the beloved diminishes as the relationship is made secondary to other concerns.[31]

Lifelong commitments are far more than vows made in wedding ceremonies. They are affirmed each day in acts of concern and support, "to the level of everyday's / Most quiet need, by sun and candlelight."[32] The commitments establish a framework in which all aspects of two lives intermingle, thereby multiplying opportunities for mutual expressions of caring and affection.

Sex is only one way to express affection, but typically it is an especially important way. Marriage increases occasions and transforms contexts for expressing caring in and through sex. We do not make love to a body. We make love to a person, to an embodied consciousness. Insofar as consciousness is always undergoing change, sex provides a kaleidoscope of ways to express caring—with tenderness, re-assurance, passion, release from anger or depression, joy in bodily expression.

Shared Interests

The common interests of spouses are varied: shared activities, social involvements, intellectual enthusiasms, moral and religious goals, economic needs, and especially emotional interdependence. Caring means that partners desire each other's good and are willing on oc-casion to make sacrifices to promote it. Caring also means delight-ing in a partner's good fortune, taking pride in his or her accom-plishments, sharing the sadness over disappointments, and feeling anger at wrongs done to the other. In innumerable ways, things that happen to one partner happen to both partners.

Does it follow that spouses want all the preferences of their part-ners satisfied? Roger Scruton thinks so: "All distinction between my interests and your interests is overcome. Your desires are then rea-sons for me, in exactly the same way, and to the same extent, that my desires are reasons for me. . . . The mere fact that you want something enters the forum of my practical reasoning with all the imperative character of a desire that is already mine. If I cannot dis-suade you, I must accept your desire, and decree in my heart 'let it be done.' "[33] Scruton is exaggerating. Caring establishes a strong pre-sumption against supporting a partner's self-destructive desires.[34] Moreover, love is compatible with merely tolerating minor, irritating aspects of a partner rather than affirming each of them as a basis for supportive action. Scruton is right, however, that "the tendency of love is towards the identity of interests." Love tends to be troubled insofar as partners cannot support each another's major interests.

Shared Agency

Caring couples make many decisions about their relationship to-gether. Some decisions are minor: how to arrange furniture, where to have lunch, what to watch on television. Others are fundamental:

career changes, major allocations of money, whether to have and how to raise children. Spouses voluntarily restrict some of their independent decision-making rights. As Robert Nozick writes, "Each [lover] transfers some previous rights to make certain decisions unilaterally into a joint pool; somehow, decisions will be made together about how to be together."[35] Invoking rights in connection with love may sound too formal. Certainly the habitual appeal to rights signals trouble for a relationship. Nevertheless, Nozick's idea of pooling agency rights captures an authentic element of love, namely, limiting individual freedom in order to make shared agency possible.

Even when partners make separate decisions they try to act on behalf of each other and the relationship. In this way, the separate actions of partners express their joint will. This is true of the most mundane activities, such as buying groceries, doing yardwork, and caring for children. There is an analogy here with how the actions of managers, acting within their job descriptions, count as actions of the corporation that employs them.[36] In certain areas even the law recognizes that one partner can act for both. When a spouse draws money from a joint bank account, the act counts as the couple's action in that both are legally responsible for it. In moral terms, something analogous to this, but much more extensively, occurs when couples pursue endeavors on the basis of common purpose and shared responsibility.

Shared Identity

Spouses who care deeply for each other live with a sense of belonging together. As Gilligan says of all caring, but far more here than elsewhere, marital caring defines spouses' identity. To apply the metaphor from Aristophanes' myth, lovers experience themselves as halves of a whole.

Inspired by Aristophanes' myth, Robert C. Solomon makes shared identity central to understanding love: "Love is fundamentally the experience of redefining one's self in terms of the other."[37] Lovers form their self-images in terms of how their partners view them, and in turn those self-images form the primary basis for their sense of self-worth. Solomon suggests that the search for stable self-worth is the primary motive for love. In modern societies, self-worth is continually threatened by social fragmentation, competition, and conflicting value perspectives. Erotic love responds to those threats by providing a clear focus for defining our identity and worth in the eyes of the beloved.[38] As Solomon points out, this risky dependence on one's partner makes us vulnerable, as is especially visible in the explosive emotions generated when marriages unravel.

I take issue with Solomon on one point. Solomon (like Singer) lapses into an overly subjective account of the valuing that occurs in love. He says that love fosters self-esteem by creating "private virtues," that is, one's desirable traits as seen by one's lover: "In love, accordingly, we pick a single, supreme judge who alone has the power to acknowledge and encourage what we ourselves see as our most noble attributes, our most important virtues, even if the whole of the rest of the world fails to appreciate them."[39] This casts love as a kind of mutual vanity, an egoism a deux with all its attendant dangers. Of course, mutual vanity and accenting each other's attributes play a role in love, but mutual vanity is not the primary way in which love elevates self-esteem. Nor is it the heart of lovers' shared identity. Spouses and lovers want to be valued as important, as persons who matter greatly to each other. This affirmation comes through caring, which affirms our unique value as individuals rather than our particular features or "private virtues."

Shared Happiness

Deep caring provides a framework for the shared pursuit of happiness. What is happiness? It is not merely satisfying our desires. Satisfied desires need not be satisfying; they can leave us bored, humiliated, and full of regrets. Is happiness, then, taking pleasure in what we get—wanting what we get, rather than getting what we want? But a life rich in pleasures can still be unhappy unless the desires satisfied are important ones and also add up to something that is valued by us (where the "adding up" is not purely quantitative). A happy life implies an overall satisfaction with life, and that implies an affirmation of the entire pattern of desires, activities, and relationships that generate pleasures (as well as pains).[40] Similarly, relationships are happy insofar as we are satisfied with them overall.

Love contributes to happiness in many ways, often bringing excitement, comfort, emotional stability, financial security, self-esteem, and joy. Often a couple finds these goods together or not at all. At the same time, happiness and love are related in complex ways, and a relationship (like an entire life) can be happy in varying degrees and limited respects.

Mutual Fulfillment

Lifetime commitments create a framework for individuals to pursue self-fulfillment together. Self-fulfillment implies happiness, but in addition it implies developing our individual talents and interests, as well as our more generic human capacities to think, feel, be independent, and relate socially.[41] As Jungian therapist Adolf Guggenbuhl-Craig suggests, marriage is a way for two people to jointly work out their fulfillment or "secular salvation": "The life-long dialectical encounter between two partners . . . can be understood as a special path for discovering the soul, as a special form of individuation," that is, a way to pursue self-fulfillment.[42] There are many other paths to self-fulfillment, but marriage provides distinctive ways for two people to interact continuously in seeking self-fulfillment within a give-and-take relationship over most of a lifetime.

Shared Meaning

Caring-based marriages create much of the meaning spouses find in life. In part, that meaning is subjective: a stable feeling of worthwhileness. In part, it is objective: the objectively justified values that structure the marriage. Meaningful lives are coherent and worthwhile. They are coherent in that they hang together intelligibly rather than being a mere hodgepodge of experiences. They are worthwhile in terms of moral values as well as the values of religion, the arts, science, sports, friendship—and love. These features are connected: Meaningful lives are coherent (intelligible) in terms of values that make life worth living.

Caring, grounded in long-term commitment, unifies lives so as to contribute to a sense of meaning. As Søren Kierkegaard points out in *Either/Or*, without enduring commitments our lives are fragmented, chaotic, and ultimately in despair because our multifarious desires pull us apart in many conflicting directions. Commitments enable us to unify our personalities, thereby serving our highest task "to order, cultivate, temper, enkindle, repress, in short, to bring about a proportionality in the soul, a harmony."[43] In particular, marital commitments decisively structure and harmonize the personality throughout a lifetime. In this way, moral duty is a supportive companion and friend of "true love": "For duty loves only true love and has a mortal hatred of false love."[44]

The deepened sense of value that love brings is transforming. Rather than just being an added-on area of value, it permeates every aspect of life, making all endeavors feel more worthwhile precisely because the endeavors serve a shared rather than a separate purpose. Successful marital love is fulfilling not only because of the external benefits it yields, but because of what it is in itself—a virtue-structured relationship of intimacy, trust, and caring.

Shared Creativity

Both internally and externally, love is often morally creative, as Plato knew and personal experience confirms. Happy, fulfilling, and meaningful love relationships are morally creative in this sense: They tend to generate new and valuable products.[45] Newness can be judged from different vantage points; for example, individuals, groups, traditions. Values may also be assessed on different scales. Here I am interested in couple-relative creativity, that is, creating products that are new with regard to a couple's past achievements. What are *morally* creative products?[46] They include fresh ideas about morality—solutions to moral problems, innovative moral perspectives, and insights into which ideals and virtues are most important in a particular context. They are also the achievements in implementing morally valuable ideas in conduct, organizations, and relationships.

How much room is there for morally valuable newness within love relationships and elsewhere? Not much, if we reduce morality to a set of fixed, universal, and clear-cut rules to which individuals passively conformed. But moral rules are vague, indeterminate, and open-ended in their requirements and hence call for interpretation and even creative application. They also come into conflict with each other, as well as with nonmoral values, in ways that call for creative insight as well as good common sense about situational priorities (that cannot be captured in abstract rules). Most important, in addition to moral rules about obligations, there are also moral ideals of goodness that can be pursued creatively, in many ways and degrees.

Talk of "creativity" conjures up fears of subjectivity of a sort incompatible with moral values. Thus, at the opposite extreme of a fixed-rule conception of morality is the extreme view that moral ideals are radically subjective. In this view, moral creativity, like painting pictures, is largely a matter of personal taste. Jean-Paul Sartre set forth this view in his early existentialist writings: "Does one ever ask what is the picture that he ought to paint? As everyone knows, there is no pre-defined picture for him to make"; hence, "there is this in common between art and morality, that in both we have to do with creation and invention."[47] Sartre's art analogy reminds us that morality has a personal dimension in which we have discretion to pursue optional ideals of goodness, including ideals of love. But Sartre's radical subjectivity amounts to skepticism about moral values, not to mention skepticism about aesthetic standards.[48]

A more fruitful analogy compares moral creativity with creativity in the "scientific arts," such as engineering or medicine. Here there are certainly objectively justifiable values, but they leave considerable room for reasonable differences in interpreting and balancing them within ever-changing situations. Like engineers confronting design problems, we are confronted with new situations that impose constraints but also leave room for innovation in applying values.[49]

"Creative intelligence," to use John Dewey's expression, consists of making a decision that preserves all important values relevant in a given context, "which coordinates, organizes and functions [in] each [moral] factor of the situation which gave rise to conflict, suspense and deliberation."[50] As James D. Wallace elaborates, moral decision-making calls for "intelligent, calculated improvisation and the virtue of resourceful inventiveness in adapting our practical knowledge to unprecedented difficulties."[51] Nowhere is this more true than in putting our ideals of love into practice and in resolving practical problems within relationships. Valuable forms of love typically embody some degree of moral creativity in how relationships are pursued, how difficulties are confronted, and how virtues structure relationships. Properly conceived, marriages are flexible rather than rigid structures. As such, they permit selective emphases within the tapestry of virtues so as to achieve mutually fulfilling relationships.

Here are three examples. First, moral creativity in marriage might be shown in creating nontraditional marriages by negotiating new roles for partners—new because they transcend the models for marriages with which individuals were raised. Think of the open marriage between Jean-Paul Sartre and Simone de Beauvoir. Their love began with a decade-long sexual relationship involving several short-term commitments to remain together, living in separate apartments, tolerating outside affairs, and demanding exceptional candor. For over fifty years the relationship continued, grounded in solidarity with each other as caring intellectual companions. As Beauvoir said, they "had become necessary to each other" in a way that critics did not understand because their only referent was traditional marriages. "It's true, we knew each other so well, no one ever understood us as we understood each other. But rather than to see us as senile old people, too lazy or too tired to change, which is how most old married couples become, they should have said that all our shared experiences made us supremely at ease and comfortable with each other."[52] Their relationship generated problems, especially the inevitable jealousies and hurt caused by their extramarital affairs. There are also questions about whether Beauvoir tended to give Sartre more credit for ideas they generated together. Still, it remained a relationship based on exceptional degrees of honesty, as well as caring and respect.

Second, some couples creatively adapt more traditional patterns of marriage. An example is the monogamous lesbian marriage between Gertrude Stein and Alice B. Toklas. For thirty-nine years, until Stein died, they maintained a morally and artistically creative partnership that embodied an array of virtues. Their caring, mutual respect, and faithfulness were grounded in a detailed understanding of each other's needs. Toklas, who was well attuned to Stein's idiosyncratic working schedule and considerably exalted ego, "knew when to be self-effacing and when to call the tune" in order to protect Stein's time.[53] Stein, in turn, knew Toklas sufficiently well to capture her voice and vision of life in *The Autobiography of Alice B. Toklas*. They established a shared understanding about sexual fidelity that was thoroughly traditional. Stein could probably have tolerated a more sexually experimental arrangement, but Toklas was "fiercely possessive and jealous and wanted absolute fidelity."[54] They also revealed a shared wisdom and courage in maintaining the arrangements needed to protect their love: "They were so emphatically and uncompromisingly themselves, that the world could do nothing less than accept them as they were."[55]

What about fairness? Some observers see their marriage as lacking equality, indeed, as amounting to a same-sex variation on conventional domination by one partner. The relationship was focused around Stein's literary career, and Toklas sacrificed much in her role as helpmate, secretary, editor, housekeeper, and promoter of Stein. Nevertheless, Toklas exercised substantial power within the relationship, as an organizer, manager, and literary agent. Moreover, she and Stein autonomously agreed to the arrangement and found in it shared happiness and fulfillment.

Third, moral creativity in love can be shown in bridging differences. Think of marriages involving multicultural and multiracial differences, such as the marriage between Simone and André Schwarz-Bart. At one level, it would be difficult to think of two more dissimilar persons: Simone is a black woman, born in Guadeloupe, with an African-Caribbean heritage; André is a white man, born in France, with a Jewish heritage. At a deeper level their lives share a common identification with communities of suffering: She is a descendent of black slaves relocated during colonial years, and he is a survivor of the Holocaust in which both his parents were killed. That identification led to a shared commitment to artistic and moral expressions of the dignity of oppressed people, he most famously in *The Last of the Just* and she in *Hommage à la femme noire*. Their writings seek to appreciate the distinctiveness of their cultural traditions, but both their work and their relationship "testify to the strength of the human spirit and love's capacity to build bridges."[56] Simone once expressed that capacity when, after the New York opening of one of her plays in 1988, she was challenged by an audience member for being insufficiently political by failing to portray black and white personal relationships. Her reply was that this particular play was about love and that, "As for my husband, when I look at him I just see someone I love. For me, he isn't any color at all."[57]

To conclude, whatever combination of traditional and nontraditional elements, caring-structured marriages provide a framework for integrating all aspects of lives, including careers, avocations, community involvements, children, and innumerable challenges. Achieving this integration requires both good judgment and shared creativity. Caring is central in love, but it must be understood within a tapestry of virtues that define, delimit, and embody it. That complex moral tapestry is studied throughout this book, beginning next with faithfulness, the virtue most definitive of the long-term caring essential to marriages.

3

FAITHFULNESS

"Promise you'll never really be unfaithful to me."
Silence.
Emmy raised her head. "You won't promise?" she
said incredulously.
"I can't, Emily. . . . You could change, I could
change, I could meet somebody—."
—Alison Lurie[1]

"Faithfulness" refers to faithful love for a spouse or lover to whom
one is committed, rather than the narrower idea of sexual fidelity.
The distinction is clearly marked in traditional wedding vows. A
commitment to love faithfully is central: "to have and to hold from
this day forward, for better for worse, for richer for poorer, in sickness and in health, to love and to cherish, til death us do part . . .
and thereto I plight [pledge] thee my troth [faithfulness]."[2] Sexual
fidelity is promised in a subordinate clause, symbolizing its supportive role in promoting love's constancy: "and, forsaking all other[s],
keep thee only unto her/him.[3]
Marital commitments to love have been subjected to a barrage of
objections. They have been criticized as unintelligible, unreasonable, inhumane, unnecessary, nonbinding, and incompatible with
love. I respond to these objections in the first section, seeking to uncover the partial truths as well as the confusions they embody. Then,
in the following section, I explore why marital faithfulness is a virtue, that is, a morally desirable feature of spouses who make lifelong
commitments, rather than simply a matter of individual prefer-

ences. Throughout, I continue to develop a conception of love as virtue-structured attitudes and relationships that constitute special ways to value persons.

COMMITMENTS TO LOVE

Consider the following conversation from Tolstoy's *Kreutzer Sonata:*

> "Yes, but how is one to understand what is meant by 'true love'?" said the gentleman. . . .
>
> "Why? It's very simple," she said, but stopped to consider. "Love? Love is an exclusive preference for one above everybody else," said the lady.
>
> "Preference for how long? A month, two days, or half an hour?" said the grey-haired man and began to laugh.
>
> "Excuse me, we are evidently not speaking of the same thing."[4]

The cynical gentleman, who we learn later has killed his wife, thinks of erotic love as a feeling based on sexual desire, a feeling that comes and goes with sexual interest. The lady portrays love as a paramount preference, hinting that love is a way of valuing persons, an attitude that involves but is not reducible to feelings. In her subsequent remarks, however, she follows the gentleman in speaking of love as a feeling, and the disagreement then shifts to how long the feeling can last. This brings us to the first objection to marital commitments.

Objection 1: Love and Will

Commitments to love are unintelligible given the nature of love. A commitment implies a resolve or pledge to engage in actions that are under our voluntary control. But love is an emotion, not an action. As such it happens to us; we do not choose it. The idea of committing ourselves to love is as incoherent as committing ourselves to grief.

This objection assumes that commitments to love refer to love as a feeling or emotion. I suggest instead that the love referred to is primarily an attitude and a relationship. A commitment to love is a commitment to sustain an attitude of valuing the beloved as singularly important in one's life. Spouses who say to each other "I love you" are typically expressing a complex and durable attitude that is revealed in patterns of conduct rather than a momentary feeling.

In addition, a commitment to love implies taking on responsibility for a relationship. It is a commitment to activities that sustain the relationship — activities of caring and support, of sharing resources, of living together harmoniously. It is also a commitment to avoid and to give up things that hurt the relationship. As George Eliot wrote, "Faithfulness and constancy mean something else besides doing what is easiest and pleasantest to ourselves. They mean renouncing whatever is opposed to the reliance others have in us, whatever would cause misery to those whom the course of our lives has made dependent on us."[5]

In general, talk about "true love" alludes to desirable attitudes and value-guided relationships. Ideals enter into their very meaning. One traditional ideal is to value another person above others based on a lifelong commitment. This ideal is hardly reducible to sexual desire and feelings, although it involves sexual attraction as an important aspect of valuing the beloved (at least throughout much of the relationship). The ideal, as well as the attitude and relationship grounded in it, are in part constituted by the virtues of caring, fidelity, honesty, fairness — and faithfulness. These "constitutive virtues" contrast with enabling virtues, such as prudence and perseverance, which help love to flourish.

Of course, emotions are centrally involved in loving attitudes and relationships. They include strong affection but also delight, joy, concern, hope, gratitude, jealousy, anger, pride, guilt, shame, and grief. Hence the objection can be rephrased: Commitments to love imply commitments to have emotions; those commitments are unintelligible because we cannot choose to feel emotions; therefore, commitments to love are unintelligible.

In reply, note first that the issue is not whether love can be created from scratch by a spasm of will. A strong predisposition to love's emotions is already present when the commitment to love is made, especially if we are dealing with freely chosen rather than arranged marriages. In the early stages of love we are largely passive, as ordinary language testifies: we fall in love, get struck by lightning, and are swept away by passion. We cannot voluntarily generate the deeply felt rush of emotions that signal love. We can, however, willingly open or close ourselves to experiences of love and choose whether to pursue those experiences. Most important, commitments to love are not aimed at creating emotions from scratch; they are aimed at sustaining an already present disposition to have them, and to enable feelings of mutual caring and delight to grow deeper.

These commitments make sense because emotions are somewhat under our control. To be sure, the idea of committing ourselves to feel exactly this or that emotion at a particular time is problematic, at least for complex emotions. We can promise to try to enjoy a party, when that means setting aside worries for awhile, but complex genuine emotions are heartfelt, not mentally manufactured. Nevertheless, commitments to love are consistent with these facts. They do not imply manipulating our emotions or turning emotions on and off like a faucet. Instead, they imply assuming responsibility for sustaining patterns of acts and thoughts that foster emotions conducive to love.[6]

Conduct influences emotions. A commitment to love implies a strong willingness to choose activities that promote love-enhancing emotions and to avoid love-threatening emotions. Couples can avoid situations that they know cause anger, jealousy, or anxiety, and they can choose activities that bring mutual pleasure and evoke mutual affection and intimacy. They can set aside time together and prevent work from encroaching on their privacy. And they can learn coping skills, such as the ability and willingness to compromise, to communicate clearly, and to fight fair (in ways that minimize long-term tension and hostility).

In addition, reflection influences emotions. At the core of most emotions are beliefs, attitudes, and patterns of attention that may be more or less reasonable.[7] The activity of assessing reasons can alter this core and thereby shape emotions. For example, couples can choose to dwell on the bright side of situations so as to encourage positive emotions, or allow themselves to dwell on the negative so as to evoke fear, anxiety, and doubt.[8] They can bring to mind a shared history of good times and look forward to positive change in order to encourage hope, or wallow in frustrations so as to nurse despair. They can think through mitigating circumstances in order to become more forgiving of each other and of themselves. In short, conduct and reflection can promote an already present disposition to love's emotions within virtue-structured relationships.

Objection 2: Ought Implies Can

Lifetime commitments to love are not morally binding, given the nature of morality. Commitments imply obligations and hence "oughts." As Kant said, "ought implies can": We are obligated to do only what we can do, or at least what we can reasonably be expected to do. Yet, many individuals cannot sustain lifetime commitments since they involve far too many unforeseeable events (not just emotions) beyond their control. In J. F. M. Hunter's words, "a promise is binding only to the extent that its performance is reasonably within the power of the person promising. If I promise to return your book by Thursday . . . you have some right to complain of bad faith if I fail; but if I promise to enjoy a certain film, to become a millionaire, or to be your friend for twenty years, then no matter how serious you take me to be, you would not have a clear right to complain if I failed to deliver. Now, a marriage vow can be seen as a promise of the latter kind."[9]

To begin with, we should be careful in interpreting the slogan "ought implies can." Although the word "ought" is most often used to prescribe conduct, and although there is no point in prescribing the impossible, "ought" has other uses as well.[10] It is used to ascribe obligations that persons may have even after rendering themselves unable to meet them. Thus, all drivers ought to drive safely; that is their obligation, an obligation which does not disappear when they become too drunk to meet it. At the time they are intoxicated it may be pointless to tell them they ought not to be driving, but it is true nonetheless and later (retrospectively) there may be a point in reminding them of how they rendered themselves unable to do what they ought to have done.

Most obligations do imply the general capacity to meet them. Morality is realistic in this sense: We are obligated to avoid stealing, to show gratitude, and to help others only insofar as we have the general capacity to do so without unreasonable sacrifice. These examples, however, concern duties we all have, independently of our commitments, whereas the objection concerns commitments to do what turns out not to be possible. Do such commitments ever create obligations?

Consider those overly ambitious and naive businesspersons who enter into contracts that they cannot meet, given their talents, other resources, and the limitations imposed by the world. Their commitments are unrealistic, but nevertheless they generate legal and moral obligations. Declaring bankruptcy may cancel the legal obligation, but an apology or more substantive expression of guilt and compensation may be appropriate where great harm is done. What about those lovers who commit themselves to what turns out to be impossible, a lifetime together? Is that what they promise? Normally they promise to do everything in their power to make a marriage work, not to do the impossible. Hence, in each case we need to look at why the relationship did not work out. If the cause is general irresponsibility or lack of effort, then keeping their commitments may not have been impossible at all. If instead the cause was that one partner abandoned the other for no good reason, or that poverty or tragedy drove the couple apart, we readily excuse or forgive.

In short, lifetime promises may prove impossible to keep because of unforeseeable difficulties that were beyond the ability of a couple to handle or beyond what is reasonable to expect them to do. It is often difficult to tell when that is, as I will emphasize later. But until those difficulties become clear, couples can intelligibly make morally binding lifetime commitments.

I should add that marital faithfulness involves a commitment *to a person* — to love, honor, and cherish one's spouse. It is faithfulness *to a promise* in a secondary, symbolic way. Why should the wedding promise be kept? The secondary answer is that the promise was made; the primary answer is to preserve, further, or restore the love that led a couple to make the promise in the first place and which leads them to keep their commitments alive. In this way, faithfulness is aimed primarily at the substance of the wedding vow — the loving relationship itself — rather than at the one-time marital promise.[11]

The longer the love continues, the wider the scope of faithfulness: Faithfulness is to the love in its full historical development, in its actual past, present achievements, and projected future.

Objection 3: Changing Identities

Lifelong commitments to love are not morally binding. They lack moral import because they are unconditional and falsely presume that spouses will retain their present identities. Each of us will change dramatically over a lifetime, so much so that we can think of a person as a series of different selves rather than one unified self. How can my present self morally bind a substantially different later self to do anything several decades from now? That is like trying to make a promise for another person, whereas promises are only binding on the person who makes them. Again, how can I (with moral cogency) commit myself to a partner who will be remarkably different several decades later? That is like making a blanket promise to someone I do not even know.

Are marriage vows unconditional? Surely wedding vows implicitly contain some conditions. As Hunter argues, in the course of a marriage

> a couple may become entirely different persons, with ambitions, tastes, idiosyncrasies or emotional attachments or aversions that could not initially be foreseen, and given which it would be utterly absurd for them to marry. That being the case, it seems reasonable to treat such vows at a minimum as implicitly containing some such clause as "assuming you are substantially the person I believe you to be, and that neither of us changes, as the years go by, in ways more extreme than are common to human beings as they grow older."[12]

Susan Mendus rejects this view and insists that marital vows are unconditional. She draws a "distinction between . . . the person who promises to love and to honour but who finds that, after a time, she has lost her commitment (perhaps on account of change in her husband's character), and . . . the person who promises to love and to honour only on condition that there be no such change in character."[13] The latter person is not committed unconditionally, in the spirit of traditional marriage vows. The former person makes the appropriate commitment and revokes it later, something that is perfectly intelligible as a morally binding promise which, perhaps for good reason, must be broken. There is a genuine obligation, but it is prima facie rather than absolute; there are conditions under which it is justifiably broken. She adds that vows are unconditional when "I cannot now envisage anything happening such as would make me give up that commitment."[14]

Mendus's distinction is important, but her account of unconditional vows is implausible. Surely most spouses can envisage circumstances that would lead them to abandon their commitments to love each other, at least if "envisage" means imagine. For one thing, they can imagine their spouse being transformed into a spouse-beating, child-abusing monster.[15] In making their lifelong commitments, they presuppose that will not occur, and in that sense their commitments are conditional.

For another thing, they can imagine their spouse leaving them; indeed, most spouses fear such abandonment at one time or another, whether as a general possibility (given today's 50 percent divorce rate) or for reasons directly related to their partner. They would not feel obligated to stay married if their spouse abandoned them, and hence this is a second way their marital vows are conditional. In short, no matter how vaguely restricted to extreme situations, wedding vows have "escape clauses." They are implicit in the wedding ceremony in which vows are made together, conditional on their partner's reciprocal vows.

If there are always conditions, why do marriage vows fail to mention them and even seem to rule them out—"for better for worse, for richer for poorer, in sickness and in health?" And why don't enlightened couples mutter under their breath, "unless one of us changes radically?" The answer is obvious but important. Couples have faith that their marriage will endure, that they will keep their commitments, and at the very least that neither will turn into a monster. That faith can waver periodically, and it is compatible with realism about the risk that things will not work out. But marriage is an act of faith, of placing trust in, rather than merely hoping or expecting.

That faith is exactly what the unconditional tone of lifetime vows conveys. And the faith is essential, not only as an expression of love but because it tends to be self-fulfilling by providing the security and trust in which relationships prosper.

Reasonable faith is not blind. With time and effort, partners often can get to know each other well enough to form valid judgments about each other's character as well as reasonable judgments about their own character, judgments that serve as a basis for lifelong commitments. In addition, those commitments themselves dramatically shape the personal identity that will endure through innumerable changes in circumstances and character. When taken seriously, lifelong marital commitments are among the most stable foundations for an enduring core of self-identity. In short, rather than ongoing commitments being wholly contingent on continuity of identity, continuity of identity is in large measure created by lasting commitments to one's partner.

Objection 4: Motives for Loving

Ironically, lifelong commitments to love are incompatible with love. Commitments create obligations that threaten love by generating an onerous sense of duty to abide by a contract. As Robert Solomon once wrote, "Love is not . . . a commitment. It is the very antithesis of a commitment. The legal tit-for-tat quasi-'social contract' thinking of commitment talk fatally confuses doing something because one *wants* to do it and doing something because one *has* to do it, whether or not one wants to at the time."[16] He continues, "The essence of romantic love is a decision, open-ended but by the same token perpetually insecure, open to reconsideration at every moment and, of course, open to rejection by one's lover at every moment too."[17]

Not so! Lifetime commitments do close options — decisively. Only in that way can they open better options within sustained, stable, trusting relationships. There are, of course, alternative ideals of love that keep all options open. Those Romantics and existentialists, not to mention Don Juans and libertines, who treasure the right to change their mind at any moment (without culpability), do well to avoid lifelong commitments. These alternate ideals, but not commitments and responsibilities, are incompatible with traditional marital love.

Solomon is right about this much: Relationships are in trouble once they degenerate into a quasi-legal, tit-for-tat struggle, with each partner preoccupied with asserting the rights generated by promises. But moral commitments are not reducible to contracts in the way he implies. Commitments generate responsibilities that support rather than threaten love's constancy. They do so largely by remaining in the background, perhaps surfacing in times of conflict and temptation as reminders that help stabilize relationships. They are reinforcements of, not replacements for, caring.

It is important to distinguish between having a commitment to love and the motives for keeping that commitment.[18] The motives are primarily love, caring, and joy, as well as self-interest, and only secondarily (and supportively) a sense of responsibility. The same is true of parents, for example, who have responsibilities to care for their children, but who are primarily motivated by love mixed with elements of self-interest.

Objection 5: The Power of Love

Lifelong commitments are unnecessary, given the power of love to conquer obstacles. Commitments and the obligations they imply are inessential: "The devotion and particularity of love are such that commitment is quite unnecessary, although it may well present itself as an expression of love."[19] Lasting devotion does not require commitments, which generate obligations, but only a "decision to stick with it and see it through."[20]

So it seems, at least in the early stage of romance when love promises to make everything possible, certainly its own continuance. But honeymoons end, and the world intrudes with problems — about money, jobs, health, religion, in-laws, child care, schedules, tastes in furniture, and a thousand other things. Active love, understood as an ideal-guided and virtue-structured relationship, typically requires commitments if it is to remain constant (and growing) throughout a lifetime.

Not just the world but lovers themselves change, as an earlier objection emphasized. They grow and regress and undergo a variety of experiences that can mute romance. Commitment generates a sense of responsibility that provides stable trust through fluctuations in temperament. As Mary Midgley said in a related context, "Campaigners against [marriage] . . . have been remarkably crass in posing the simple dilemma, 'either you want to stay together or you don't—if you do, you need not promise; if you don't, you ought to part.' This ignores the chances of inner conflict, and the deep human need for a continuous central life that lasts through genuine, but passing, changes of mood."[21] Commitment is not sufficient to maintain love, but it adds an additional motive for not succumbing to, much less seeking out, temptations that threaten love.

Objection 6: Creative Divorce

Lifetime commitments are inhumane. They are essentially commitments never to divorce, and that amounts to cruelty and torture when one or both partners find a marriage unbearable. Divorce can be creative as well as a painful necessity. Lifetime commitments are immoral because they preclude divorce.

This objection applies within societies that forbid divorce but not to contemporary societies governed by liberal and even "no-fault divorce" laws. Suppose that in good faith, with trust and faith that divorce will not occur, partners make lifetime commitments and then do everything they can to make things work out. They do not succeed, and the marriage disintegrates to the point where it is no longer worthwhile. After every effort is made to repair damage, one or both partners may be fully justified in abandoning their commitment.

Objection 7: Prudence

Lifetime commitments are unreasonable, irrational, imprudent. They fail to show proper regard for one's long-term good. A prudent person forms a plan of life that takes into account how changing circumstances or new knowledge can radically alter one's present conception of good as well as the means to it. Right now love brings happiness, but who knows what it will bring decades later? Lifetime commitments sacrifice far too many options, and hence it is prudent to make only short-term commitments.

Of course, lifetime commitments are unreasonable for some individuals. What is in one's interests and what serves the mutual good of couples vary too widely to generalize about. The same reason, however, should lead us to reject a universal objection to lifetime commitments. That objection omits the good-promoting features of lifetime commitments, in particular the framework they provide for ongoing mutual caring, support, joy, and fulfillment. Marriage closes some options but opens others that may be far preferable, depending on our ideals of love.

Lifetime commitments to love are not prisons; they are vehicles for helping partners deal together with changing situations, interests, and needs. Partners do commit themselves to put the relationship first, to accommodate other things to it, including careers. Other than that, however, relationships are as accommodating and flexible as partners choose to make them.

FAITHFULNESS AS A VIRTUE

Is marital faithfulness a virtue, that is, a character trait which is morally desirable and admirable? Presumably virtues are intrinsically good. Marital constancy, however, is desirable in some cases but undesirable in others, depending on how well a marriage promotes the good of spouses and others (especially children). Faithfulness seems more a matter of self-interest, luck, and simple compatibility than of morality. Perhaps commitments to love should be understood in terms of intentions but not obligations. That would also free us to approach divorce without being preoccupied with betrayal and accusation. In short, shouldn't the entire topic of marital duration be de-moralized?

No, *if* we value the good made possible in long-term marriages. Here I will make six comments by way of clarifying faithfulness as a virtue.

First, we can acknowledge that when a marriage is disastrous and hopeless, constancy can be bad rather than virtuous in that it prolongs a bad thing. But it doesn't follow that faithfulness is not a virtue. Virtues are context-dependent. Michael Slote pointed out that "many virtues only count as such when they are attended by certain other virtues."[22] For example, conscientiousness is a virtue, or at least a highly admirable virtue, only when it involves attention to duties that promote human good, as opposed for example to the conscientiousness of a Nazi. Similarly, Eva Braun's faithfulness in loving Hitler is not a virtue, nor is faithful love for a wife-beating, child-abusing, sadistic husband. In general, faithfulness is desirable and admirable only insofar as there is something good about the love. That good centers on caring—mutual caring, support, kindness, and joy—which is morally desirable in itself and which contributes to the fulfillment of persons.

Second, taking moral commitments seriously does carry with it the possibility of betrayal—of one's spouse, of oneself, and of one's ideals of love. At the same time, given a variety of possible factors beyond our control, not meeting an ideal does not automatically imply moral failure and blameworthiness. Marital betrayal is usually the result of not trying or not trying hard enough. But all the effort in the world cannot by itself achieve marital success without luck.

Some loves are lucky; others are unfortunate, even tragic, due to circumstances that spouses can only partially influence.[23] Luck, as well as good judgment, plays a role in finding a promising partner whom one finds attractive physically, intellectually, morally, socially, and in terms of shared interests and values. Then, if a permanent relationship is to emerge, partners must be able to trust each other's commitments. During their shared history, the basis of love must remain sufficiently constant to overcome inevitable difficulties, such as money problems, major illness, temporary separations, and changing interests. Later, the relationship must survive the ravages of old age, and at any time the threat of death to one of the partners. In addition, there is luck in having the gifts of temperament conducive to monogamy, gifts that are in part genetic and in part the product of our upbringing.[24] All these factors call for great reserve in judging people who are unable to meet their marital commitments. In general, issues of moral criticism and blame should not be conflated with issues about the virtues and moral ideals that make possible special ways to value persons.

Third, it is true that talk about faithfulness and betrayal should be set aside in special contexts. The therapist's office is one such context. In order to help couples or individuals deal with marital or divorce difficulties, counselors do well to keep matters focused on problem-solving skills, not accusation and self-aggrandizement. So do couples themselves as they try to improve their relationship (rather than engage in exercises in self-righteousness). And observers who know little about the obstacles confronting a marriage should be wary of passing judgment. This does not, however, negate the appropriateness of moral language in other contexts, such as marriage ceremonies that publicly express solemn acts of acquiring responsibilities.

Fourth, acknowledging the role of luck does not remove the vital contribution of effort, responsibility, and moral virtue in shaping good relationships. Unless we are fatalists, who view human life as determined in ways that remove moral responsibility, we must recognize that faithfulness plays an important role. Precisely what role in a given case can be difficult to answer.

Thus, in examining individual cases, whether ourselves or others, we confront ambiguities that make it difficult to tell whether inconstancy is the result of temperament, luck, or irresponsibility of the sort that leads us to talk of betrayal and unfaithfulness. Consider Bertrand Russell, who reports that seven years into his marriage he suddenly fell out of love with his wife. "I went out bicycling one afternoon, and suddenly, as I was riding along a country road, I realized that I no longer loved Alys. I had had no idea until this moment that my love for her was even lessening."[25]

What does Russell mean by "love?" He goes on to state that he was no longer sexually attracted to Alys and that he had also become preoccupied with her character faults. In his autobiography, however, he admits the unfairness and self-righteousness in his criticisms of Alys, and in a passage omitted from the final draft of the book he explained the breakup by appealing to his temperament: "I now believe that it is not in my nature to remain physically fond of any woman for more than seven or eight years. As I view it now, this was the basis of the matter, and the rest was humbug."[26]

We need not accept Russell's explanation as authoritative, any more than he had to accept his own earlier interpretation of events. Some might interpret the bicycle experience as a symptom of the "seven-year itch" that other couples deal with through marriage counseling or by taking a long vacation together. Possibly Russell was not only self-righteous but, like the gentleman in *The Kreutzer Sonata,* guilty of bad faith in reducing his love to sexual desire and related feelings.[27] He prides himself on his honesty in promptly telling Alys that his love was gone, but perhaps full honesty would lead to a quite different conversation with Alys in which they explored his troubled feelings together.

As another possibility, perhaps Russell had undergone a fundamental change in his ideals since making his wedding vows. Perhaps he was rebelling against the Victorian ideals he had been raised with. Not temperament but a new ideal of love was the reason he could so quickly conclude that his sexual relationship with Alys was over. In any case, some individuals do change their ideals, rejecting marital faithfulness after having earlier made lifelong commitments in good faith. Anaïs Nin, for example, arrived at this view of faithfulness after entering a fairly traditional marriage: "I really believe that if I were not a writer, not a creator, not an experimenter, I might have been a very faithful wife. I think highly of faithfulness. But my temperament belongs to the writer, not to the woman."[28] A year later, in the midst of her tumultuous affair with Henry Miller, her attitude changed again: "The ideal of faithfulness is a joke" and the essential value in love is "sincerity with one's self."[29]

Fifth, appreciating marital faithfulness as a virtue does not mean making it the supreme value. Marital obligations are not absolute in the sense of always overriding all other considerations. Consider Paul Gauguin, who after a decade into his marriage, and after fathering five children, quit his job as a successful stockbroker to become a full-time artist. For most of the remainder of his life he did not earn enough money to support his family. It is difficult to avoid saying he was unfaithful. It is also difficult to avoid admiring what he did—in one respect—if we value the art he produced and realize that it could not have been produced except at the expense of his family.[30] Perhaps like him, we may regret that the world did not make possible a happier accommodation of art and family, but we may also view aesthetic values and the moral value of self-fulfillment as providing some reasons for his conduct.

Sixth, we tend to think of faithfulness in terms of staying the same in the midst of changing circumstances, especially changes in our spouse. As Shakespeare wrote,

> Love is not love
> Which alters when it alteration
>   finds,
> Or bends with the remover to re-
>   move:
> O, no! it is an ever-fixed mark
> That looks on tempests and is never
>   shaken.[31]

Yet it is more accurate, albeit more prosaic, to say that faithful love constantly modifies and adjusts in response to changes. Rigidity can contribute to unfaithfulness.

Dorothy Day recounts how her common-law marriage with Forster Batterham ended because he could not adjust to her decision to have their child and herself baptized in the Catholic church. Prior to her decision, the marriage had been joyous and deeply rooted in a shared devotion to social justice, a devotion that Day sustained throughout her subsequent leadership in the Catholic worker movement. Yet Batterham was also adamantly anti-religious: "He was averse to any ceremony before officials of either Church or state. He was an anarchist and an atheist, and he did not intend to be a liar or a hypocrite. He was a creature of utter sincerity, and however illogical and bad-tempered about it all, I loved him."[32] In order for Batterham to remain faithful, his love would have had to adjust so as to accept, or at least tolerate, Day's new religious outlook.

The best marriages, like the best persons, are often seriously flawed. Faithfulness is a virtue when it supports good though imperfect relationships. The same is true of tolerance and humility. Nietzsche was no booster of marriages, but what he said of strong characters applies to strong marriages: "'Giving style' to one's character [and marriage]—a great and rare art! It is exercised by those who see all the strengths and weaknesses of their own natures [and marriage] and then comprehend them in an artistic plan until everything appears as art and reason and even weakness delights the eye. . . . Here the ugly which could not be removed is hidden; there it has been reinterpreted and made sublime."[33]

4

SEXUAL FIDELITY

The great problem of the shifting relation between
passion and duty is clear to no man who is capable
of apprehending it. . . . [M]oral judgments must
remain false and hollow unless they are checked and
enlightened by a perpetual reference to the special
circumstances that mark the individual lot.

—George Eliot[1]

Sexual fidelity is a complex virtue. Its dimensions include the most
mundane details about exercising self-control as well as the most
subtle and creatively sensuous ways to sustain sexually fulfilling relationships. No aspect of sexual fidelity, however, is more complicated
than what it implies concerning adultery. Philosophers have devoted
little attention to adultery,[2] generally leaving it as a topic for theology, social science, and literature. Certainly novelists have had much
to say: "To judge by literature, adultery would seem to be one of the
most remarkable of occupations in both Europe and America. Few
are the novels that fail to allude to it."[3]

Both in making our own decisions about adultery and in making
judgments about others, we often find ourselves immersed in confusions and ambiguities that are both personally and philosophically
troublesome. I will seek a middle ground between absolute prohibitions and trendy permissiveness. A humanistic perspective embraces
a pluralistic moral outlook that affirms a variety of forms of sexual
arrangements. At the same time, it can justify a very strong pre-

sumption against adultery for individuals who embrace traditional marital ideals.

The ethics of adultery divides into two parts: making commitments and keeping them. The ethics of making commitments centers primarily on commitments to love, where love is a virtue-guided attitude or relationship, and secondarily on the promise of sexual exclusivity (the promise to have sex only with one's spouse), which some couples make in order to support the commitment to love. The ethics of keeping commitments has to do with balancing initial marital commitments against other moral considerations.

MAKING COMMITMENTS

Adultery has recently entered prominently into evaluations of public figures. Bill Clinton's 1992 presidential campaign was nearly derailed by allegations about a twelve-year extramarital affair. Shortly thereafter England's royal family engaged in extensive damage control as public revelations surfaced about the love trysts of Prince Charles and Lady Diana. Earlier, in 1987, Gary Hart's "womanizing" forced his withdrawal as the leading Democratic presidential candidate. About the same time, charges of adultery contributed to the downfall of television evangelist Jim Bakker.

It is not clear what most upsets (or intrigues) us in such cases. Is it the adultery per se, the deception used to conceal it (from spouses or the public), the hypocrisy in professing contrary religious beliefs, or the poor judgment in failing to keep it discrete (including the bravado of Gary Hart in baiting the press to uncover his affairs)? Nor is it clear how the adultery itself is pertinent to public service, even if we think the adultery is immoral. Character is not a seamless web, and integrity can be present in one context (public service) and absent in another setting (sexual conduct).[4] Many notable leaders had extramarital affairs, including Franklin D. Roosevelt, Dwight Eisenhower, John F. Kennedy, and Martin Luther King, and public scrutiny of marital intimacy might discourage worthy candidates from seeking public office. What is clear, however, is that adultery is morally perplexing.

To begin with, what is adultery? Inspired by the New Testament, some people employ a wide definition that applies to any significant sexual interest in someone besides one's spouse: "You have heard that it was said, 'Do not commit adultery.' But I tell you that anyone who looks at a woman lustfully has already committed adultery with her in his heart."[5] Other people define adultery narrowly to match their particular scruples. For them extramarital genital intercourse may count as adultery, but not oral sex; or falling in love with someone besides one's spouse may count as adultery but not "merely" having sex.[6] Whatever definition we adopt there will always be borderline cases, if only those created by "brinksmanship"—going as far as possible without having intercourse (for instance, lying naked together in bed).[7]

By "adultery" I will mean married persons having sexual intercourse, of any kind, with someone other than their spouse.[8] I am aware that the word "adultery" is not purely descriptive and evokes a range of emotive connotations. Nevertheless, I use the word without implying that adultery is immoral; that is a topic left open for investigation in specific cases. Like "deception," the word "adultery" raises moral questions about possible misconduct, but it does not answer them. By contrast, I will continue to use a wide sense of "marriage" that refers to all monogamous (two-spouse) relationships formally established by legal or religious ceremonies *and* closely analogous moral relationships such as committed relationships between homosexual or heterosexual couples who are not legally married.

A moral understanding of adultery turns on an understanding of morality. If we conceive morality as a set of rules, we will object to adultery insofar as it violates those rules. "Do not commit adultery" is not an irreducible moral principle, but many instances of adultery violate other familiar rules. As Richard Wasserstrom insightfully explained, much adultery violates one or more of these rules: Do not break promises (viz., the wedding vows to abjure outside sex, vows that give one's partner "reasonable expectations" of sexual fidelity); Do not deceive (whether by lying, withholding information, or pretending about the affair); Do not be unfair (by enjoying outside sex forbidden to one's spouse); Do not cause undeserved harm (to one's spouse who suspects or learns of the affair).[9] Wasserstrom points out that all these rules are prima facie: In some situations they are overridden by other moral considerations, thereby justifying some instances of adultery.

Moreover, adultery is not even prima facie wrong when spouses have an "open marriage" in which they give each other permission to have extramarital affairs. In this connection Wasserstrom raises questions about the reasonableness of traditional marital promises of sexual exclusivity. Wouldn't it be wiser to break the conventional ties between sex and love, so that the pleasures of adultery can be enjoyed along with those of marriage? Alternatively, should we maintain the connection between sex and love but break the exclusive tie between sexual love and one's spouse, thus tolerating multiple simultaneous loves for one's spouse and for additional partners? No doubt the linking of love, sex, and exclusivity has an instrumental role in promoting marriages, but so would the patently unreasonable practice of allowing people to eat decent meals (beyond bread and water) only with their spouses.

In my view, a rule-oriented approach to morality lacks the resources needed to answer the important questions Wasserstrom raises. We need an expanded conception of morality as encompassing ideals — in particular the moral ideals of love that provide the point and significance of marital commitments — together with the virtues manifested in pursuing those ideals. The ethics of adultery centers on the moral ideals of and commitments to love. The commitments to love are morally optional in that no one is obligated to make them. Nevertheless, strong obligations to avoid adultery arise for those couples who make traditional marital commitments.

The primary commitment is to love each other, while the commitment of sexual exclusivity is secondary and supportive. This can be seen by focusing on three ideas that Wasserstrom devotes little attention to: love, commitments to love, and trust.

What does Wasserstrom mean by *love?* He seems to use a purely descriptive (value-neutral) sense in which love refers to a strong positive feeling or at most a complex attitude involving many emotions.[10] By contrast, I will continue to use the normative or value-laden sense in which we speak of true love. In this sense, love refers to a set of virtue-structured ways to value persons. As an attitude, love is valuing the beloved, cherishing him or her as unique. Erotic love includes sexual valuing, but the valuing is focused on the person as a unity, not just a body. As a relationship, love is defined by reciprocal attitudes of mutual valuing. The precise nature of this valuing turns on the ideals one accepts, and hence those ideals are part of the very meaning of love. Faithfulness, honesty, trust, and fairness, interwoven with caring and respect, are among the most important virtues in thinking about adultery.

According to the traditional ideal (or set of ideals) of interest here, marriage is based on a *commitment to love:* "to have and to hold from this day forward, for better for worse, for richer for poorer, in sickness and in health, to love and to cherish, till death us do part." As I suggested in Chapter 3, this is not a commitment to have continuous feelings of strong affection, feelings that are beyond our immediate voluntary control. Instead, it is a commitment to create and sustain a relationship conducive to those feelings of strong affection as well as conducive to the happiness and fulfillment of both partners. Spouses assume responsibility for maintaining conditions for mutual caring that in turn foster recurring emotions of deep affection, delight, shared enthusiasm, and joy. The commitment to love is not a promise uttered once during a wedding ceremony; it is an ongoing willingness to assume responsibility for a value-guided relationship.

The commitment to love implies a web of values and virtues. It is a commitment to create a lifelong relationship of deep caring that promises happiness through shared activities (including sexual ones) and through joining interests in mutually supportive ways involving shared decision-making, honesty, trust, emotional intimacy, reciprocity, and (at least in modern versions) fair and equal opportunities for self-expression and personal growth. This traditional ideal shapes how spouses value each other, both symbolically and substantively. Commitments to love throughout a lifetime show that partners value each other as having paramount importance and also value each other as unities, as persons-living-throughout-a-lifetime.

Valuing each other is manifested in a willingness to make accommodations and sacrifices to support the marriage. For most couples, some of those sacrifices are sexual. The promise of sexual exclusivity is a distinct wedding vow whose supportive status is symbolized by being mentioned in a subordinate clause: "and, forsaking all other[s], keep thee only unto her/him." Hopefully, couples who make the vow of sexual exclusivity are not under romantic illusions that their present sexual preoccupation with each other will magically abolish sexual interests in other people and temptations to have extramarital affairs. They commit themselves to sexual exclusivity as an expression of their love and with the aim of protecting that love.

How does sexual exclusivity express and protect love? In two ways. First, many spouses place adultery at the top of the list of actions that threaten their marriage. They are concerned, usually with full justification, that adultery might lead to another love that would damage or destroy their relationship. They fear that the affection, time, attention, and energy (not to mention money) given to an extramarital partner would lessen the resources they devote to sustaining their marriage. They also fear the potential for jealousy to disrupt the relationship.[11] As long as it does not become excessive, jealousy is a healthy reaction of anger, fear, and hurt in response to a perceived loss of an important good.[12] Indeed, if a spouse feels no jealousy whatsoever, the question is raised (although not answered) about the depth of the love.

Second, sexual exclusivity is one way to establish the symbolism that "making love" is a singular affirmation of the partner. The love expressed is not just strong affection, but a deep valuing of each other in the ways defined by the ideals embedded in the marriage. Sex is especially well-suited (far more than eating!) to express love because of its extraordinary physical and emotional intimacy, tenderness, and pleasure. The symbolic meaning involved is not sentimental fluff; it makes possible forms of expression that enter into the substance of love.

In our culture sex has no uniform meaning, but couples are free to give it personal meanings. Janet Z. Giele notes two extremes: "On the one hand, the body may be viewed as the most important thing the person has to give, and sexual intercourse therefore becomes the symbol of the deepest and most far-reaching commitment, which is to be strictly limited to one pair-bond. On the other hand, participants may define sexual activity as merely a physical expression that, since it does not importantly envelop the whole personality nor commit the pair beyond the pleasures of the moment, may be regulated more permissively."[13] Between the two extremes lie many variations in the personal symbolism that couples give to sex, and here we are exploring only those variations found in traditional marital vows.

Trust is present at the time when couples undertake commitments to love, and in turn those commitments provide a framework for sustaining trust. Trust implies but is not reducible to Wasserstrom's "reasonable expectations" about a partner's conduct. Expectations are epistemic attitudes, whereas trust is a moral attitude of relying on others to act responsibly, with goodwill, and (in marriage) with love and support.[14] We have a reasonable expectation that the earth will continue to orbit the sun throughout our lifetime, but no moral relationship of trust is involved. As a way of giving support to others, underwriting their endeavors, and showing the importance of their lives to us, trust and trustworthiness are key ingredients in caring.

To be sure, trust is not always good. It is valuable when it contributes to valuable relationships, in particular to worthwhile marriages.[15] Marital trust is confidence in and dependence upon a spouse's morally responsible love. As such, it provides a basis for ongoing intimacy and mutual support. It helps spouses undertake the risks and undergo the vulnerabilities (emotional, financial, physical) inherent in intimate relationships.

The trust of marital partners is broad in scope. Spouses trust each other to actively support the marriage and to avoid doing things that might threaten it. They trust each other to maintain the conditions for preserving intimacy and mutual happiness. Violating marital trust does more than upset expectations and cause pain. It violates trust, honesty, fairness, caring, and the other moral ideals defining the relationship. It betrays one's spouse. And it betrays one's integrity as someone committed to these ideals.

To sum up, I have avoided Wasserstrom's narrow preoccupation with the promise of sexual exclusivity. Commitments of sexual exclusivity find their rationale in wider commitments to love each other—*if* a couple decides that exclusivity will support their commitments to love *and* where love is understood as a special way to value persons within lasting relationships based on mutual caring, honesty, and trust. Accordingly, marital faithfulness in loving is the primary virtue; sexual fidelity is a supporting virtue. And sexual fidelity must be understood in terms of the particular commitments and understandings that couples establish.

I have also avoided saying that sexual exclusivity is intrinsically valuable or a feature of all genuine love, unlike Bonnie Steinbock: "[Sexual] exclusivity seems to be an intrinsic part of 'true love.' Imagine Romeo pouring out his heart to both Juliet *and* Rosaline! In our ideal of romantic love, one chooses to forgo pleasure with other partners in order to have a unique relationship with one's beloved."[16] In my view, the intrinsic good lies in mutually fulfilling love relationships rather than sexual exclusivity per se, thereby recognizing that some couples sustain genuine love without sexual exclusivity. For some couples sexual exclusivity does contribute to the good found in traditional relationships, but other couples achieve comparable good through nontraditional relationships, for example open marriages that tolerate outside sex without love.[17] We can recognize the value of traditional relationships while also recognizing the value of alternative relationships, as chosen autonomously by couples.[18]

KEEPING COMMITMENTS

I have argued that there is a very strong moral presumption against adultery in traditional relationships, once a commitment to sexual exclusivity is made. Nonetheless, the presumption does not yield an exceptionless, all-things-considered judgment about wrongdoing and blameworthiness in specific cases. I agree with Wasserstrom that even in traditional relationships the prohibition against adultery remains prima facie. I will discuss four of many complicating factors.[19] What if partners wish to revise or change their commitments? What happens when love comes to an end? What if one spouse falls in love with an additional partner? And what about the sometimes extraordinary self-affirmation extramarital affairs may bring?

Changing Commitments

Some spouses who begin with traditional commitments later revise them. Buoyed by the exuberance of romance, most couples feel confident they will not engage in adultery, much less be among the 50 percent of couples who divorce. Later they may decide to renegotiate the guidelines for their marriage in light of changing attitudes and circumstances, although still within the framework of their commitments to love each other.[20] One study suggests that 90 percent of couples believe sexual exclusivity to be essential when they marry, but only 60 percent maintain this belief after several years of marriage (with the changes occurring primarily among those who had at least one affair).[21]

Vita Sackville-West and Harold Nicolson provide an illuminating, if unusual, example. They married with the usual sexual attraction to each other and for several years were sexually compatible. As that changed, they gave each other permission to pursue extramarital affairs, primarily homosexual ones. Yet their original commitment to love each other remained intact. Indeed, for forty-nine years, until Vita died in 1962, their happy marriage was a model of mutual caring, deep affection, and trust: "What mattered most was that each should trust the other absolutely. 'Trust,' in most marriages, means [sexual] fidelity. In theirs it meant that they would always tell each other of their infidelities, give warning of approaching emotional crises, and, whatever happened, return to their common centre in the end."[22] Throughout much of their marriage they lived apart on weekdays, thereby accommodating both their work and their outside sexual liaisons. On weekends they would reunite as devoted companions, "berthed like sister ships."[23]

Just as we respect the mutual autonomy of couples in forming their initial understanding about their relationship, we should also respect their autonomy in renegotiating that understanding — not whimsically, but when circumstances warrant serious reflection. The account I have offered allows us to distinguish between the primary commitment to love and the secondary commitment of sexual exclusivity. The secondary commitment is made in order to support the primary one, and if a couple agrees that it is no longer needed they may revoke it. Renegotiations can also proceed in the reverse direction: Spouses who initially agree on an open marriage may find that allowing extramarital affairs creates unbearable strains on their relationship, thereby leading them to make commitments of exclusivity.

Changing commitments raise two major difficulties. First, couples are sometimes less than explicit about the sexual rules for their relationship. One or both partners may sense that their understandings have changed over the years but fail to engage in discussions that establish explicit new understandings. As a result, one spouse may believe that something is acceptable to the other spouse when in fact it is not. For example, Philip Blumstein and Pepper Schwartz interviewed a couple who, "when it came to a shared understanding about extramarital sex, . . . seemed not to be in the same marriage."[24] The man reported to them, "Sure we have an understanding. It's: 'You do what you want. Never go back to the same one [extramarital partner],'" presumably since that would threaten the relationship. By contrast, the wife reported, "We've never spoken about cheating, but neither of us believe in it. I don't think I'd ever forgive him [if he cheated on me]." Lack of shared understanding generates moral vagueness and ambiguity concerning adultery, whereas periodic forthright communication helps establish clear moral boundaries.[25]

Second, what happens when only one partner wants to renegotiate an original understanding? The mere desire to renegotiate does not constitute a betrayal, nor by itself does it justify adultery if one's spouse refuses to rescind the initial vow of sexual exclusivity. In such cases the original presumption against adultery continues but with an increased risk that the partner wishing to change it may feel adultery is more excusable. Such conflicts may or may not be resolved in a spirit of caring and compromise that enables good relationships to continue. Lacking such resolution, the moral status of adultery may become less clear-cut.

Lost Love

Couples who make traditional commitments sometimes fall out of love, singly or together, or for other reasons find themselves unwilling to continue in a marriage. Sometimes the cause is blameworthy adultery, and sometimes adultery is a symptom of irresponsibility and poor judgment that erodes the relationship in additional ways.[26] Other times there is little or no fault involved. Lasting love is a creation of responsible conduct *and* good luck.[27] No amount of conscientiousness can replace the good fortune of emotional compatibility and conducive circumstances.

Traditional commitments to love are intended to be lifelong, but they are not unconditional. Typically the commitments are based on several tacit conditions, as noted in Chapter 3. One condition is embedded in the wedding ceremony during which mutual vows are exchanged: namely, that one's spouse will make the marital vows and take them seriously. Other conditions are presupposed in the background: the spouse will not turn into a murderer, rapist, spouse beater, child abuser, or psychopathic monster. Usually there are more specific tacit assumptions that evolve before the marriage, for example, that the spouses will support each other's careers. Above all, there is the underlying hope that with sincere effort the relationship will contribute to the overall happiness of both partners. All these conditions remain largely tacit, as a matter of faith. When that faith proves ill-founded or just unlucky, the ethics of adultery becomes complicated.

As relationships deteriorate, adultery may serve as a transition to new and perhaps better relationships. In an ideal world, marriages would be ended cleanly, without moral ambiguity, before new relationships begin. But then, in an ideal world people would be sufficiently prescient not to make traditional commitments that are unlikely to succeed. Contemplating adultery is an occasion for much self-deception, but at least sometimes there may be good reasons for pursuing alternative relationships before officially ending a bad marriage.[28]

New Loves

Some persons claim to (erotically) love both their spouse and an additional lover. They may be mistaken, and later have the honesty to admit as much, but is it impossible to love two (or more) people simultaneously? Impossible in what sense?

Perhaps for some people it is a psychological impossibility, but other individuals do report a capacity to love more than one person at a time. Again, for many persons it is a practical impossibility, given the demands of time, attention, and affection required in genuine loving. But that would seem to allow that resourceful individuals can finesse (psychologically, logistically, financially, and so on) multiple simultaneous relationships. I believe that the impossibility is moral and conceptual — *if* one embraces traditional ideals that define marital love as a singular affirmation of one's spouse and *if* a couple establishes sex as a symbolic and substantive way to convey that exclusive love.[29] Obviously people can experience additional romantic attractions after they make traditional vows, but it is morally impossible for them to actively engage in loving relationships with additional partners without violating the love defined by their initial commitments.

Richard Taylor disagrees with my view. In *Having Love Affairs,* this distinguished philosopher offers a book-length defense of adultery. No doubt his book is helpful for couples planning open marriages, but Taylor concentrates on situations where traditional vows have been made and then searches for ways to minimize the harm to spouses that results from extramarital love affairs.[30] As a result, his book is morally subversive, for he systematically presents only one side of the story in at least five ways.

First, with considerable panache Taylor develops a long list of rules for nonadulterous partners who should be tolerant of their partner's affairs. Here are several examples, followed in each case with the obvious question that he never answers. One, "Do not spy or pry," since that is self-degrading and shows a lack of trust in one's spouse. (But is a commitment-breaking spouse trustworthy?) Two, "Do not confront or entrap," because that would humiliate the spouse. (But what about being humiliated oneself?) Three, "Stay out of it," since good marriages survive adultery. (Is there any empirical support for this sweeping generalization?) Four, "Stop being jealous," since jealousy disrupts marriages. (But what about the case for not provoking jealousy in the first place?)

Taylor also offers rules for the spouse having the affair: Maintain fidelity with one's lover, be honest with one's lover, be discrete rather than boasting about the affair, and do not betray or abandon the lover. In discussing these rules Taylor is oblivious to the infidelity, betrayal of trust, and failure to value one's spouse in the way called for by traditional commitments and the shared understanding between spouses.

Second, Taylor defines infidelity as "a betrayal of the promise to love" and faithfulness as "a state of one's heart and mind" rather than "mere outward conformity to rules."[31] Infidelity, he correctly argues, can be shown in ways unrelated to adultery, such as in neglecting the spouse's sexual needs, selfishly using shared financial resources, and failing to be caring and supportive. The fact that infidelity takes additional forms, however, does nothing to minimize the infidelity in violating marital vows and understandings. Moreover, although faithfulness involves inner states, it also (like other virtues) involves the outward conduct that manifests those inner states. Remarkably, Taylor reminds us that inner states of faithfulness have outward manifestations only in one case: when he condemns infidelity toward an extramarital lover. What about unfaithfulness toward one's spouse?

Third, Taylor tells us that love affairs are natural and avoiding them is unhealthy. "A man, by nature, desires many sexual partners," and "the suppression of the polygamous impulse in a man is . . . bought at a great price" of frustrated and rueful longing for outside love affairs.[32] Granted, most people (male and female) have desires for multiple sexual partners. Yet many people also have monogamous impulses, as shown in their decisions to enter into traditional marriages. The resulting conflicts can make sexual exclusivity notoriously difficult, but they need not result in overall frustration. On the contrary, they often contribute greatly to sexual satisfaction within secure and trusting relationships.

Fourth, "No one can tell another person what is and is not permissible with respect to whom he or she will love. . . . However inadvisable it may be to seek love outside the conventional restraints, the *right* to do so is about as clear as any right can be."[33] Here Taylor equivocates on the word "right," which can mean (1) that others are obligated to leave one alone or (2) that a person's conduct is all right. I agree that people have a right (within limits) not to be interfered with by society as they engage in adultery, but it does not follow that such conduct is all right or morally permissible. Indeed, couples who make traditional commitments waive some rights in relation to each other; in particular they waive the right to engage in adultery that violates their marital agreements.

Fifth, and most important, Taylor praises love affairs as inher-

ently good and even the highest good: "The joys of illicit and passionate love, which include but go far beyond the mere joys of sex,
are incomparably good."[34] On the same page he writes, "This does
not mean that love affairs are better than marriage, for they seldom
are. Love between married persons can, in the long run, be so vastly
more fulfilling" than affairs. I find it difficult to reconcile these
claims: The vastly more fulfilling marriages would seem to provide
the incomparable good, not extramarital affairs that violate the
commitments defining the marriage. Of course many people find
joy in extramarital sex, and for some the joy may be the greatest they
find in life. But Taylor provides no basis for saying that happy traditional marriages never produce comparable joys. Nor does he ever
explain how extramarital joys are morally permissible for individuals who make traditional marriage vows.

Bonnie Steinbock affirms a view that goes too far in the opposite
direction. She suggests that to fall in love with someone other than
one's spouse is already a betrayal: "Sexual infidelity has significance
as a sign of a deeper betrayal — falling in love with someone else. It
may be objected that we cannot control the way we feel, only the
way we behave; that we should not be blamed for falling in love, but
only for acting on the feeling. While we may not have direct control
over our feelings, however, we are responsible for getting ourselves
into situations in which certain feelings naturally arise."[35] I agree
that spouses who make traditional vows are responsible for avoiding
situations that they know (or should know) foster extramarital love.[36]
Nevertheless, deeply committed people occasionally do fall in love
with third parties without being blameworthy for getting into situations that spark that love. Experiencing a strong romantic attraction
is not by itself an infidelity, and questions of betrayal may arise only
when a person moves in the direction of acting on the love in ways
that violate commitments to his or her spouse.

Having said all this, I know of no argument that establishes that
all love-inspired adultery is immoral, all things considered and in all
respects, even within traditional relationships. As I have been concerned to emphasize, there is in fact a serious betrayal of one's
spouse. But to say that ends the matter would make the commitment to love one's spouse a moral absolute, with no exceptions whatsoever. Tragic dilemmas overthrow such absolutes, and we need to

set aside both sweeping condemnations and wholesale defenses of love-inspired adultery.

To mention just one type of case, when marriages are profoundly unfulfilling, and when constricting circumstances prevent other ways of meeting important needs, there is a serious question whether love-inspired adultery is sometimes justifiable or at least excusable — witness *Anna Karenina, Madame Bovary, Lady Chatterley's Lover,* and *The Awakening.* Moreover, our deep ambivalence about some cases of love-inspired adultery reflect how there is some good and some bad involved in conduct that we cannot fully justify nor fully condemn.

Sex and Self-Esteem

Extramarital affairs are often grounded in attractions less grand than love. Affection, friendship, or simple respect may be mixed with a desire for exciting sex and the enhanced self-esteem from being found sexually desirable. The sense of risk may add to the pleasure that one is so desirable that a lover will take added risks. Are sex and self-esteem enough to justify violating marital vows? It would seem not. The obligations created through marital commitments are moral requirements, whereas sex and self-esteem pertain to one's self-interest. Doesn't morality trump self-interest?

But things are not so simple. Morality includes rights and responsibilities to ourselves to pursue our happiness and self-fulfillment. Some marriages are sexually frustrating or damaging to self-respect in other ways. Even when marriages are basically fulfilling, more than a few individuals report that their extramarital affairs were liberating and transforming, whether or not grounded in love. For example, many women make the following statement about their extramarital affair: "It's given me a whole new way of looking at myself. . . . I felt attractive again. I hadn't felt that way in years, really. It made me very, very confident."[37]

In addition, the sense of personal enhancement may have secondary benefits. Occasionally it strengthens marriages, especially after the extramarital affair ends, and some artists report an increase in creative activity. These considerations do not automatically outweigh the dishonesty and betrayal that may be involved in adultery, and full honesty may never be restored when spouses decide against confessing an affair to their partners.[38] But nor are considerations of enhanced self-esteem and its secondary benefits irrelevant.

I have mentioned some possible justifications or excuses for specific instances of adultery after traditional commitments are made. I conclude with a caveat. Specific instances are one thing; general attitudes about adultery are another. Individuals who make traditional commitments and who are fortunate enough to establish fulfilling relationships based on those commitments ought to maintain a general attitude that for them to engage in adultery would be immoral (as well as stupid). The "ought" is stringent, as stringent as the commitment to sexual exclusivity. Rationalizing envisioned adultery with anecdotes about the joys of extramarital sex or statistics about the sometimes beneficial effects of adultery is a form of moral duplicity. It is also inconsistent with the virtues of both sexual fidelity and faithfulness in sustaining commitments to love.

5

RESPECT

Could you really love somebody who was absolutely
nobody without you? You really want somebody like that?
Somebody who falls apart when you walk out the door?
— *Toni Morrison*[1]

Lovers become one, yet remain two. This paradox reflects their deepest dilemma: How can they continually grow closer together while maintaining individuality? This paradox, however, also embodies a creative tension: Lovers must remain two in order to become one, and their unity strengthens their individuality. In Carol Gilligan's words, "We know ourselves as separate only insofar as we live in connection with others, and . . . we experience relationship only insofar as we differentiate other from self."[2] Recast in terms of respect for individuality, self-respect depends on the respect received from the beloved, and yet respect for the beloved presupposes respect for oneself.

I will unravel these paradoxes as two theses. Rather than a mere causal prerequisite for successful love, mutual respect partly constitutes what love is; the same is true for self-respect. The first section explores the *respect thesis:* Respect for the beloved is sufficiently important to enter into the definition of love. The second section discusses the *self-respect thesis:* In order to love others we must respect ourselves.

I begin by noting several connections between caring and respect. Then, using works of literature, I explore three models for thinking about love: the Romantic model of merging, the political model of balanced forces, and the cyclical model of recurring interactions between individuals. Each model expresses some aspects of love, but the cyclical model best conveys the truth contained in the respect thesis.

MUTUAL RESPECT

Respect can mean two things: recognition-respect, or appraisal-respect. *Recognition-respect,* which is owed to all persons equally, is valuing persons as having moral worth.[3] It can also be understood as a virtue, that is, the desirable tendency to show recognition-respect in appropriate ways. *Appraisal-respect* is valuing selected individuals because of their special features — their talents, beauty, virtues, or accomplishments.

It might seem that appraisal-respect is what matters most in love, given love's extraordinary focus on one individual. Certainly it is important. Appraisal-respect is closely related to Irving Singer's idea of "individual appraisal," discussed in Chapter 2, with this difference. Individual appraisal is valuing a person's particular features because of how they answer to our needs and desires, whereas appraisal-respect leaves the question of motives open. Recognition-respect is equally important in love, however. In fact, I will interpret the respect thesis as asserting that recognition-respect, construed as a virtue, is a constituent of love.

At the same time, I will follow Robin S. Dillon in understanding recognition-respect as more personal than is usually thought, and in that regard akin to appraisal-respect. Most modern ethical theories defend an obligation of recognition-respect owed almost impersonally, often as a minimum obligation not to interfere with their conduct. In doing so, those theories conceive of persons in abstract terms, as rational agents (Immanuel Kant), bearers of human rights (John Locke), or loci of happiness (John Stuart Mill). Setting herself against this tradition, Dillon suggests that respect implies sensitivity to the particularities of individuals and at least some concern for their well-being. To emphasize this point, she reinterprets recognition-respect as *care-respect,* caring about persons to the extent of "helping them to pursue their ends and to satisfy their wants and needs."[4] The appropriate degree of help varies according to our relationship with a given individual. Thus, there are wide differences in the appropriate help owed to complete strangers, colleagues, government officials, parents, friends — and spouses.

It may seem that Dillon overextends the idea of recognition-respect. After all, that idea was originally introduced in the philosophical literature to identify the minimum duties owed equally to everyone. Is care-respect perhaps a third kind of respect, distinct from both recognition-and appraisal-respect? Or is Dillon essentially rejecting a libertarian view of recognition-respect, as merely requiring that we leave persons alone to pursue their liberty, and replacing it with stronger requirements to help others? Either way — whether we view care-respect as an interpretation of recognition-respect or as a new concept of respect — Dillon's substantive insights remain. Recognition-respect implies caring for other persons for their sake, and the appropriate expressions of that caring depend on our relationships with them. Even the seemingly impersonal respect for human rights implies caring about persons in some minimal degree.[5] In this way, respect and caring are interwoven within the tapestry of virtues.

To be sure, respect and caring remain distinct virtues, in love as elsewhere. Caring is concern for the good of the beloved, while respect is a more narrowly focused concern for the beloved's individuality and autonomy. Of course, individuality is itself a complex notion, and recognition-respect has corresponding dimensions. Thus, respect for a partner's feelings means acting in appropriate ways so as to avoid hurt. Respect for a partner's views and attitudes implies sensitive listening and sympathetic responses. Respect for a partner's talents and strengths means supporting his or her endeavors, participating in solving problems, and appreciating the other's achievements. Respect for a partner's rights means recognizing areas of personal liberty. And respect for privacy means not being intrusive, something that remains important even in intimate relationships.

Intimate relationships dissolve most impersonal boundaries, replacing complete independence with shared agency, as emphasized in Chapter 2. But not all boundaries disappear. Indeed, new boundaries are negotiated in order both to limit and to sustain intimacy. Couples establish their own rules concerning bathrooms, personal property, time apart, and whether to share sexual fantasies. They continue to respect each other as individuals, rather than extensions of each other, although they are that too. They remain two parts of a couple rather than an undifferentiated unity.

I turn now to three models of love, and their accompanying metaphors and myths, that influence thinking about mutual respect. Most familiar, but also least helpful in appreciating mutual respect, is the "Romantic model" (the capital "R" is used to denote a particular conception of romantic or erotic love). This model sets forth an ideal of complete unity. Lovers do and should aspire to complete oneness — a merging, fusion, and dissolving of two individual identities to form one new identity. Indeed, the nineteenth-century Romantics associated erotic love with aspirations for more thoroughgoing unities with nature, society, and God. "Love's Philosophy," says Shelley in a poem with that title, is to affirm all these unions.

> The fountains mingle with the river
> And the rivers with the Ocean,
> The winds of Heaven melt together
> With a sweet emotion;
> Nothing in the world is single;
> All things by a law divine
> In one spirit meet and mingle.
> Why not I with thine?[6]

The Romantic model carries enormous power. It captures the extraordinary personal transformations as lovers reconceive their entire lives in terms of each other. It highlights the unity of two lives through shared commitments, values, interests, agency, happiness, fulfillment, meaning, and moral creativity. And not to be overlooked, its guiding metaphor of union is rooted in and resonates with the pleasures of sexual intercourse. Nevertheless, the Romantic model obscures the importance of mutual respect. Good marriages do not dissolve individuality; instead, they enable two persons to complement each other so as to expand individuality.

Aristophanes' version of the Romantic myth is at once comical and cautionary. According to the myth, for each of us there is only one perfectly matched "other half" with whom we yearn to fuse. We are asked to imagine two such lovers who have found each other and, while locked in a sexual embrace, are approached by Hephaestus, the god of welding (and other crafts). Hephaestus asks, "Is this your heart's desire, then—for the two of you to become parts of the same whole, as near as can be, and never to separate, day or night? Because if that's your desire, I'd like to weld you together and join you into something that is naturally whole, so that the two of you are made into one. Then the two of you would share one life, as long as you lived, because you would be one being."[7] True soul mates, the story concludes, would welcome the offer as satisfying their deepest desires.

How ludicrous their fusion would be! Restored to their primordial state as one spherical creature, the lovers would awaken, go to the bathroom, work, play, and spend every moment together. Such complete togetherness would destroy joyous interaction. To shift images, their fused bodies might allow them to stare eternally into each other's eyes, like Tristan and Isolde, thereby preventing them from living together creatively, side by side.[8] No wonder the Romantic model ends in promises of "happily ever after," rather than revealing how static, stifling, and boring the "ever after" would become.

Far worse than rigidity, violence is a hidden undercurrent in the Romantic myth. So striking is this undercurrent that it led Denis de Rougement to hypothesize an unconscious death wish embedded in Romantic love.[9] Although de Rougement's critique is one-sided and overlooks healthy minded forms of Romanticism, it contains an important insight.[10] The Romantic passion conceals unacknowledged motives of selfishness that easily turn deadly. The Romantic lover idealizes the beloved, bestowing on the beloved every perfection, but the motive is egotistical.[11] What, after all, could be more self-glorifying than to fuse with a god or goddess? Yet the fusion transfers the power to determine self-worth through the approval or disapproval of a divinity. Then, when the desire for perfect union is frustrated, as inevitably it is, a desperate struggle begins to quickly regain self-esteem. Violence is a familiar recourse, whether aimed at oneself, the lover, or a rival.

Goethe delineates this self-sequence of self-deceiving passions in

The Sorrows of Young Werther. When Werther falls in love with Charlotte he sees her as perfect in every way.[12] She is already engaged to Albert, a fact that is not incidental to Werther's attraction, as Charlotte tries to make him understand: "Do you not sense that you are deceiving yourself and willing your own destruction? Why me of all people, Werther? I belong to another, so why me? I fear, I very much fear that what makes the desire to possess me so attractive is its very impossibility."[13] Werther believes his love is selfless, including his desire to commit suicide in order that Charlotte can be happy with Albert. In fact, he is motivated by repressed hatred, jealousy, humiliation, and vengeance for being rejected as a lover.[14] These motives underlie his request to borrow Albert's pistols, and there is no surprise when Charlotte personally hands them to the servant who delivers them. Unconsciously and symbolically, Werther views Albert and Charlotte as murdering him, just as they murdered his love. Werther's sufferings result from more than unrequited love. They emerge from his Romantic ideal of love.

If the Romantic model obscures and worsens the conflicts inherent in love, perhaps we will do better with a "political model" of love, which is the dominant model of love in the twentieth-century. The political model frankly acknowledges that love can threaten individuality and, as a result, typically generates desires to control and dominate, to place unfair demands on one's partner, to escape responsibility for shared burdens, or to submit masochistically. Mutual respect becomes essential in order to manage conflicts.

In *Women in Love,* D. H. Lawrence uses a political model to illuminate both unhealthy and healthy conflicts. To begin with, Gudrun and Gerald illustrate how the absence of mutual respect produces a deadly struggle for dominance. Gerald's sexual dominance is rooted in his economic power as an industrial magnate who inherited his father's fortune. Just as he reduces his employees to tools defined by the jobs they perform, he reduces women to their roles as sexual objects. Gudrun's dominance derives from participating in Gerald's power and then turning it against him. When she discovers that Gerald will not be exclusively devoted to her, "the deep resolve formed in her, to combat him. One of them must triumph over the other."[15] In the ensuing struggle, each oscillates between sadism and masochism: "Sometimes it was he who seemed strongest, whilst she was almost gone, creeping near the earth like a spent wind; sometimes it was the reverse. But always it was this eternal see-saw, one destroyed that the other might exist, one ratified because the other was nulled."[16] In a final deadly struggle, Gerald strangles Gudrun, releasing her moments before she would have died. He then wanders suicidally in snowbound country until he meets his own death.

Ursula and Birkin, by contrast, illustrate how mutual respect helps manage conflicts. Interestingly, their conflicts are linked to opposing ideals of love. Birkin's ideal is a "mystic conjunction" of two separate beings who exercise "freedom together."[17] Unlike Aristophanes' single sphere that obliterates distinct identities, Birkin pictures two circles — two stars — held in balance by opposing forces of attraction and separation: "What I want is a strange conjunction with you . . . not meeting and mingling . . . but an equilibrium, a pure balance of two single beings; — as the stars balance each other."[18] Ursula also wants to preserve individuality within a balanced relationship, but in addition she seeks "unspeakable intimacies," "complete self-abandon," and "absolute surrender to love."[19] She senses that Birkin's two-star model indicates a refusal of intimacy and a desire to dominate. The novel presents both ideals, of maintaining individuality and surrendering separateness, as valid and in need of reconciliation.[20]

The ideals, however, are never fully reconciled in the novel. Lawrence probably intends a political balance of the ideals themselves, paralleling, at a second order, the balanced stars in Birkin's model. At the levels of both agency and ideals, conflicts would be managed through ongoing conversation and negotiation that identified areas of agreement while leaving areas of disagreement. We might picture this reconciliation as two intersecting circles, with the size of the intersection varying according to the areas of common ground negotiated by the lovers.

The difficulty remains that a political model focuses exclusively on conflicts. Just as the Romantic model with its image of one circle (or one heart[21]) exaggerates unity, the political model with its image of two overlapping circles exaggerates conflict. A better image is the mathematical symbol for infinity: Two circles (personalities) continuously flowing into each other, then temporarily apart. This image pictures a "cyclical model" of love—not complete unity or ongoing conflict, but instead cycles of recurring interaction.

The cyclical model is presented by Milan Kundera in *The Unbearable Lightness of Being*. Kundera's leitmotiv of lightness versus heaviness draws attention to how transitoriness ("lightness") threatens our sense of the meaning and importance ("weight") of our lives. *Einmal ist keinmal*: "What happens but once . . . might as well not have happened at all."[22] Fleeting events feel contingent, pure happenstance. Although love begins with chance events, it does acquire permanence and meaning when two individuals make commitments of ongoing interactions grounded in mutual respect.

Tomas is torn between casual promiscuity, together with a passionate affair with Sabina, and his "com-passionate" love for Tereza. As a libertine, he adopts the rule of threes: Either see a woman three times in a row and then drop her or maintain longer-term relationships in which you see her only once every three weeks. He derives a curious blend of cerebral and sensual power over women by identifying the nuances of their sexual responses. His attempt to separate love and lovemaking, caring and sex, results in a failure to respect Tereza. For her his affairs inflict continual pain and fear and become crass when he comes home with his hair smelling of another woman's vaginal secretions.

Tereza hesitates to make demands. She suffers from the lingering effects of childhood guilt inflicted by a mother who blamed Tereza for making her unhappy, beginning with the childbirth that disfigured her. Like her mother, she is obsessed with her body, and she tries to locate her individuality in the distinctive physical features. Yet she knows her body lacks the power to make Tomas sexually faithful, and as a result she begins to hate her flesh and hence to hate herself. Her suffering includes nightmares in which Tomas gazes on her as one nude body among innumerable others, thus destroying her sense of uniqueness.

Tomas knows he contributes to Tereza's suffering. It takes many years, however, before he grasps how his failures to respect her feelings constitute a failure of love. He learns that respect implies commitments. In turn, commitments generate responsibilities that transform lightness into weight, chance and contingency into a sense of necessity.[23] When Tereza leaves him in Switzerland to return to Czechoslovakia, he feels a temporary sense of freedom (buoyancy, lightness), but he quickly realizes he is bound to her by ties of commitment (weight, responsibility) that demand pursuing her. Later, after they reunite, he realizes that even if he were to find his ideal "other half" described by Aristophanes, he would leave her for Tereza.[24]

Kundera replaces Aristophanes' myth with Nietzsche's myth of eternal recurrence. Nietzsche introduced the myth as a challenge to pursue self-perfection: Am I living in such a way that I would be willing to repeat my life endlessly? Kundera shifts the focus to love: Is my love such that I can will it to continue without limit, as recurring cyles defining a shared life? "Happiness [lightness, joy] is the longing for repetition" (weight, responsibility).[25]

Love can never be wholly selfless, free of demands, accepting, and voluntary. Nevertheless, its repeating cycles blend caring and respect in ways that continuously reaffirm and express love. These cycles include the familiar rituals of making love, sleeping together, talking, acceptance and forgiveness, emotional intimacy, temporary separation, and a thousand other interdependencies that Irving Singer summarizes:

> the casual spending of time with one another, the enjoying of each other's presence, the desire to give and receive pleasure, the exchange of judgments and impressions, the reaching of decisions that affect them both, the cooperative struggle for goals they care about, the rearing of a family as a combined expression of themselves, the participation in a society to which they each contribute, the feeling on various occasions of reciprocal excitement, joy, or sorrow.[26]

The oneness in love is a continuous interaction between two individuals rather than a static unity or a political tension.

The Romantic model expresses the shared identity of lovers, but it omits the importance of mutual respect for individuality. The political model, pictured by twin stars or intersecting circles, expresses the need for maintaining distinct identities, but it downplays the intimacy of love. The cyclical model highlights both intimacy and in-

dividuality. It also prepares us to understand individuality as requiring self-respect.

SELF-RESPECT

In order to love others we must respect ourselves, that is, we must
value ourselves in morally desirable ways. This self-respect thesis was
defended by Erich Fromm in *The Art of Loving,* a book whose influence made the thesis a commonplace in the self-help literature.[27]
Fromm's insights are anything but commonplace, although they
stand in need of interpretation.

According to Fromm, painful isolation is the most striking feature
of the human condition. There are many destructive responses to
this isolation, such as violence and addiction, as well as creative responses, such as community activities and meaningful work. The
most completely satisfying response is "healthy," "mature," "productive" love. These clinical sounding words barely conceal the moral
richness of Fromm's conception of love. Love, he says, is an activity
and an art guided by five values: One, giving, which is productively
expressing oneself in self-affirming ways; two, caring, or the active
concern for the growth of persons we love; three, responsibility, understood as a readiness to respond to their needs; four, respect for
others' individuality, which implies avoiding exploitation and dominance; and five, knowing or understanding the beloved's needs so as
to be able to care responsibly.

Guided by these norms, loving other people implies loving oneself: "If an individual is able to love productively, he loves himself
too."[28] This self-respect thesis applies to all forms of love: "The love
for my own self is inseparably connected with the love for any other
being."[29] What is this "inseparable" connection?

In one interpretation, it is a cause-effect relation: Self-love is a
causal prerequisite for loving others. As such, self-respect is external
to love and separable from it, as a cause is separate from its effect.
Moreover, if causes precede their effects, self-respect would precede
love in time: We must *first* love ourselves in order *then* to love others.
In a second interpretation, self-respect and love are internally related, as a matter of definition and value. In fully desirable relation-

ships, both partners manifest the virtue of self-respect. That is part of what it means for a relationship to be desirable.

The second interpretation best captures Fromm's meaning. Although he does not explicitly list self-love as one of the five features defining love, Fromm tacitly builds self-love into the first feature, productive giving. Productive giving is self-affirming: "This experience of heightened vitality and potency [in giving myself] fills me with joy. I experience myself as overflowing, spending, alive, hence as joyous."[30] These experiences "presuppose" that a person has sufficient self-love to "overcome dependency, narcissistic omnipotence, the wish to exploit others, or to hoard, and has acquired faith in his own human powers."[31]

For similar reasons, self-love also enters into the fourth feature, respect for others. Healthy love between adults means promoting each others' growth, and that requires a secure sense of self-worth. Otherwise partners will bolster their egos through domination (exploitation, sadism) or seek reassurance through subservience (humiliation, masochism). "It is clear that respect is possible only if *I* have achieved independence; if I can stand and walk without needing crutches, without having to dominate and exploit anyone else."[32] Hence, self-love must not be confused with selfishness, which is excessive self-seeking at the expense of others. Selfishness reveals too little self-love. It frustrates our own needs — our needs for self-expression through caring.

Fromm also says that love for oneself and love for others are "inseparably connected," "conjunctive," and "indivisible." In some passages he virtually stipulates that healthy love embodies self-respect: "In contrast to [unhealthy] symbiotic union, mature *love* is *union under the condition of preserving one's integrity,* one's individuality."[33] Integrity and individuality are manifestations of self-love. They are based on a concern that one "should grow and unfold" in accord with one's own nature rather than solely according to others' expectations.[34] Here again Fromm treats self-respect as a defining feature of love, rather than merely as a causal prerequisite for it.

These are insightful ideas, but I should also take note of a flaw in Fromm's defense of the self-respect thesis. He asserts that erotic love for specific individuals is based upon humanitarian love for all persons: "Love is not primarily a relationship to a specific person; it is an attitude, an orientation of character which determines the relatedness of a person to the world as a whole, not toward one 'object' of love. . . . If I truly love one person I love all persons, I love the world, I love life."[35] These claims enter into Fromm's defense of the self-respect thesis. He says we love an individual as "an incarnation of essentially human qualities," that the "love of one person implies love of man as such," and hence that if "an individual is able to love productively, he loves himself too."[36] Thus, loving one person implies loving all persons, and since I am a person, it follows that loving any person implies loving (and respecting) myself.

These claims are inspirational but implausible.[37] Erotic love is characterized by particularity, in a manner that Fromm mentions but cannot make sense of. In addition to unhealthy ("symbiotic") attachments and universal humanitarian love, there is a third possibility: healthy love that is particularized rather than grounded in a love for everyone. Similarly, self-love is a focused response to one particular individual—ourselves—rather than an instantiation of a general love for humanity.

What exactly does self-respect involve? Paralleling the distinction between appraisal-respect and recognition-respect, self-respect takes two forms, according to the reasons for valuing oneself. *Appraisal self-respect* is self-respect based on evaluating ourselves as meeting certain standards. Some evaluations are nonmoral, such as those based on social standing, talents, charm, or physique. Others are moral appraisals of our character. Whether moral or nonmoral, appraisal self-respect is a matter of degree, and it is deserved or undeserved depending on whether the relevant excellences are present.

Appraisal self-respect can be specific or global.[38] When specific, it is targeted narrowly toward our admirable features; we value just those features, and we value ourselves only in those limited respects. When global, it affirms our entire person, and beliefs about our particular features become central to our overall self-image. For example, global self-respect might involve affirming one's general worth because of one's excellence as a physician, whereas specific self-respect is valuing oneself as a physician while hating oneself overall.

Perhaps some persons find an adequate sense of self-worth in appraisal self-respect that is global. Living up to our personal standards is indeed an important ingredient of all self-respect.[39] Appraisal self-respect, however, is unstable because it varies according to how well we meet our standards of excellence. Most of us need something more deeply rooted in our moral status as persons. We need *recognition self-respect,* which is the affirmation of our inherent moral worth.

Does recognition self-respect return us to Fromm's idea of self-love as one application of a general love for humanity? I do not think so. Self-respect implies caring for oneself, which is a highly particularized response rather than an instance of a universal affirmation of humanity. As Robin Dillon says, self-respecting persons value their "concrete particularity," including their "quirks and idiosyncrasies" and especially their personal relationships with others.[40] This self-affirmation is not based solely on self-appraisals, but it does imply caring for oneself in light of detailed self-knowledge. The expression *care self-respect* serves as a useful reminder that we are dealing with a particularized focus of recognition self-respect.

I propose to understand care self-respect in terms of four overlapping attitudes: self-acceptance, self-confidence, self-esteem, and self-responsibility. Each attitude applies to the self-respect thesis.

Self-Acceptance and Tolerance

Self-acceptance comes despite awareness of our limitations and flaws. It differs, however, from complacency and self-indulgence, which imply neglect of rather than care for oneself. An absence of self-acceptance is shown in chronically hostile attitudes toward ourselves, such as hate, anger, shame, guilt, and depression. These attitudes erode our capacity to love others by lowering tolerance for their weaknesses and increasing a tendency to blame them for our problems, as Nietzsche saw: "For one thing is needful: that a human being should *attain* satisfaction with himself. . . . Whoever is dissatisfied with himself is continually ready for revenge, and we others will be his victims."[41] Spouses are the most frequent victims simply because they are closest, physically and emotionally.

Freud, too, understood how self-loathing finds an outlet in harming others. Specifically, he described "projection" as the psychological defense of warding off anxiety, fear, and self-hate. In projection we transform negative attitudes toward ourselves into unwarranted negative attitudes toward others. Thus, self-hate is transformed into hating others whom we blame for our suffering. One's spouse is the most obvious scapegoat: If only she were more supportive, intelligent, richer. Conversely, the ability to accept a spouse's imperfections depends on our ability to accept our own imperfections. Self-acceptance removes self-righteous superiority over our spouse.

Self-Confidence and Helping

Self-confidence is faith in our ability to pursue and achieve goals. As such it is essential to pursuing endeavors with any degree of enthusiasm.[42] In particular, self-confidence helps sustain love relationships. We can most effectively help a lover or spouse, or anyone else for that matter, when we are confident in our ability to help. Conversely, the absence of self-confidence can lead to overzealous and misguided attempts to help. Suppose that a man is frustrated because he repeatedly attempts and fails to dominate his colleagues at work.[43] Lacking the confidence to explain to him what she suspects is the problem, his wife instead reassures him. The upshot is that she reinforces his domineering tendency. Greater confidence to speak freely might have yielded a sympathetic yet objective appraisal of the difficulty. In general, self-confidence enables us to feel at ease in expressing ourselves in ways that sustain intimacy, both in words and behavior.[44]

This example further illustrates the problem with the Romantic model of love. It is true that spouses have a common good so that when major events happen to one of them, they also happen to the other, but it does not follow that they should have identical reactions to those events. Having their own emotional and intellectual responses enables them to help each other by contributing alternative perspectives on problems and thereby strengthens their ability to solve problems together.

In addition, without self-confidence we easily become preoccupied with our problems and neglect the needs of people we love. Self-absorption takes innumerable forms, including harmful addictions and obsessions with work and social recognition. Self-confidence frees us to attend to a partner's needs.[45] Again, the absence of self-confidence can also generate excessive jealousy that threatens love. Normal or healthy jealousy strengthens relationships by serving as an emotional alarm, warning us of threats to our relationships.[46] It is compatible with and even manifests self-respect insofar as it affirms our worthiness to be in a particular relationship. Only excessive, obsessive jealousy damages love as well as outside friendships.

Self-confidence also affects our confidence about relationships. Lovers continually give off subtle cues to each other about faith in their love, thereby strengthening or weakening each other's faith. Lack of confidence and faith become self-fulfilling prophesies. Insofar as self-confidence contributes to a sense of purpose, it is one of the most important gifts we can offer a spouse.[47]

Self-Esteem and Being Loved

Self-respect and self-esteem are closely connected but not synonymous. "Self-respect" is a moral concept; it refers to the virtue of valuing oneself in appropriate ways according to justified standards. "Self-esteem" is a psychological concept; it means thinking well of and having a positive attitude toward oneself. Not all self-esteem is justified and desirable.[48] Its unjustified forms include arrogance (being rudely overbearing), excessive vanity (undue preoccupation with being praised), and egotism (self-absorption).[49] But here my interest is in justified self-esteem, which is an aspect of self-respect.

Self-esteem is emotionally richer than recognition self-respect, and it is more constant than appraisal self-respect. Joel Feinberg put the point this way: "I may (realistically) assign myself very low grades for physique, intellect, talent, even character . . . while still remaining steadfastly loyal and affectionate to myself."[50] Affectionate loyalty makes possible the kind of bedrock self-esteem possessed by Ursula and Birkin and absent in Gudrun, Gerald, and Werther.

Self-esteem enables us to feel worthy of being loved, worthy of having our love returned in ways essential to the reciprocity that makes love flourish. Nathaniel Branden pointed out, "No matter what our partner does to show that he or she cares, we do not experience the devotion as convincing [if we lack self-esteem] because we do not feel lovable to ourselves."[51] In turn, that can lead us to sabotage our relationships through excessive jealousy and possessiveness, depression caused by self-deprecation, or annoying demands for reassurance. Consider the last example. Low self-esteem generates overt and covert demands on a partner to provide constant verbal reassurance. Of course, bolstering a partner's sense of self-worth is part of love, but in healthy relationships it takes place implicitly and effortlessly. By contrast, low self-esteem requires constant and explicit reassurance that ultimately saps energy and deflects from more rewarding interactions. In general, how we regard ourselves influences how other people perceive us, in love as elsewhere. As Toni Morrison has a character ask rhetorically, "Could you really love somebody who was absolutely nobody without you? You really want somebody like that? Somebody who falls apart when you walk out the door?"[52]

Fromm noted that one-sided submission can be as harmful to love as dominance. In the long run, both are self-defeating strategies caused by low self-worth. The aim in sadistic domination is to make a partner value us by becoming subservient to us, but that very subservience evokes hostility that threatens love. The aim in masochistic submission is to make a partner value us because of our docile worship of them, but docility is ultimately repulsive to a partner.

Just as self-esteem contributes to love, healthy love promotes self-esteem.[53] One study confirmed that individuals with generally high self-esteem tend to experience romantic love more frequently, probably because they are more confident and adept in relationships.[54] In addition, highly defensive individuals who lack positive self-images tend to avoid intimate relationships, no doubt because they fear self-disclosure. The study also revealed, however, that once within romantic relationships, individuals with lower self-esteem (in general) tend to have more intense experiences of love and to appreciate them more (as was perhaps true of Tereza). Thus, low self-esteem prior to entering relationships is not always harmful to love, and high self-esteem is not a causal prerequisite for love. As a dimension of self-respect, self-esteem is a constituent rather than a cause of love.

Self-Responsibility and Happiness

Self-respect implies being responsible for our well-being. That means taking care of ourselves, physically and psychologically, guided by an attitude that we are worthy of such attention. This self-caring is an essential part of being equipped to help people we love. Love places demands on us to maintain our strength, optimism, courage, and intelligence. We can summon those resources only if we care about meeting our own needs too, including our need for happiness.[55]

Kant thought that our most important responsibilities are to ourselves—to maintain personal integrity and self-respect.[56] Meeting our responsibilities to ourselves implies appreciating our rights, not selfishly but in ways that contribute to fair, reciprocal, balanced relationships. Relationships become unbalanced when one partner feels that his or her interests are less significant and feels less claim on shared resources, such as money, time, and opportunities. In this connection consider Thomas Hill's description of the "Deferential Wife" who systematically subordinates her interests to her husband's, even to the point of humiliation and maltreatment: "She does not simply defer to her husband in certain spheres as a trade-off for his deference in other spheres. On the contrary, she tends not to form her own interests, values, and ideals; and when she does, she counts them as less important than her husband's."[57] As Hill suggests, the wife fails to understand and appreciate the importance of her rights.

Finally, self-respect implies that we have something to give and are able to give it.[58] Love flourishes when partners remain interesting. Developing their interests throughout a lifetime increases what they have to offer to each other. Love is threatened when partners grow too far apart, but it is also threatened when partners stop growing.

6

FAIRNESS

Genuine love ought to be founded on the mutual recognition
of two liberties; the lovers would then experience themselves
both as self and as other; . . . together they would manifest
values and aims in the world.

—*Simone de Beauvoir*[1]

Consider two spouses who freely agree on a marriage that provides
fewer benefits and greater burdens for the wife, at least as viewed by
an impartial observer. Suppose, for example, that the husband has
greater opportunities for education, a challenging career, and social
interactions, while the wife has greater burdens of housekeeping and
child care. Is the marriage fair?

No, if the criterion for fairness is a fifty-fifty distribution of benefits and burdens. Yes, if the criterion is free consent. Each answer
has some appeal, but accepting both answers leads to a contradiction. Call this the *fairness paradox:* Mutual consent and balanced
distributions are plausible but seemingly incompatible criteria for
fairness in marriages.[2]

I will defend a feminist theory of fairness that resolves the fairness
paradox by mitigating, without removing, the conflict between free
choice and balanced distributions. In my view neither mutual consent nor fifty-fifty distributions of benefits and burdens is adequate
for understanding fairness in love. Instead, the wider idea of *equal
autonomy* is the primary criterion.

The opening section subsumes mutual consent under equal autonomy and then shows how equal autonomy is supported by equal

105

patterns of basic goods. The second section examines how equal and shared autonomy enter into understanding balanced patterns of distribution.

PRIMARY EQUALITY

"All's fair in love and war." Playfully interpreted, this adage expresses a willingness to relax customary amenities during lovers' sometimes desperate pursuits. In a nineteenth century novel, for example, the phrase was used to justify opening someone else's mail to gain information concerning a lover and possible rivals.[3] Taken literally, it says that nothing is unfair, that everything is permitted, and hence that moral values are external and irrelevant to love. Today the adage has a sinister sound when we think of date rape, wife beating, child abuse, and family abandonment (not to mention the horrors of unrestrained warfare). In my view, by contrast, fairness is internal to love. Rather than disappearing or being suspended, fairness takes on enormous importance in defining, sustaining, and guiding love — love as a relationship in which two persons value each other as having singular importance.

The fairness paradox arises because fairness is a complex idea that blends potentially conflicting elements. Accordingly, a quick response to the paradox is to regard mutual consent and balanced distribution as pertaining to different aspects of fairness. Mutual consent concerns fair *procedures* for decision-making, whereas balanced distribution concerns resulting *patterns* in apportioning benefits and burdens. There is no contradiction in saying that a marriage is fair in one respect and unfair in another, just as a relationship might be honest in one regard and dishonest in another.

This quick response is unsatisfying. After all, more is at stake than simply avoiding a contradiction. We want to understand what fairness is, as a feature of persons and of relationships. Both consent and balance seem important, but they also seem to point in different directions. If we emphasize consent, we must accept as fair whatever imbalances partners freely agree upon. If we emphasize balance, we cannot fully affirm partners' freedom to shape their relationships as they choose. The paradox arises because mutual consent allows couples to upset balanced patterns,[4] and because insisting on balanced patterns restricts shared decision-making.

A feminist conception of fairness offers the best approach to the paradox. Historically, the feminist movement deserves credit for making fairness a central virtue in love. Prior to that movement, the notions of fairness, equality, and justice were largely restricted to the public sphere where interests compete, for example in business, the professions, politics, and legal disputes.[5] Marriage was viewed as a private sphere of affection and altruism, not competing interests. If fairness was mentioned at all, it was in asserting the "natural" right of men to exercise economic and political power and the responsibility of women for domestic work and child care.

Feminists unmasked this public-private dichotomy as a double ruse. On the one hand, it silences moral inquiry into personal relationships, thereby closing the door on violence and exploitation within families. On the other hand, it supports restrictions on women's access to public roles. In a famous phrase, "the personal is political": Power is an aspect of personal relationships; it influences the exercise of autonomy and the distribution of benefits within love relationships and families. As a result, fairness is a fundamental virtue needed to assure respect for persons, in love as elsewhere. As I suggest later, it is also a virtue that supports and furthers love.

What is the feminist position on the fairness paradox? There is no single position. Feminism encompasses a wide spectrum of views united by an affirmation of women—in the teeth of a long history of oppression—and a commitment to achieving equal opportunities for women. Interestingly, the feminist movement contains tensions that mirror the contrasting emphases on mutual consent and balanced distributions. Liberal feminists, for example, emphasize mutual consent as the foundation for a wide range of freely-chosen love relationships, including many conventional ones. By contrast, socialist feminists emphasize balanced patterns and reject conventional families as inherently unjust. For example, a Marxist economic perspective is central to Shulamith Firestone's analysis of love: Genuine love is a mutual and equal "exchange of selves" that "becomes complicated, corrupted, or obstructed by *an unequal balance of power*" generated largely by women's economic dependence.[6]

Most feminists, however, challenge the conventional understanding of free consent as the absence of overt external coercion. They agree that women's choices are subverted in subtle ways by discrimination embedded in institutions and social practices. In addition, most feminists argue that free choice is more than exercising one's rights in the absence of immediate external force; freedom needs to be understood as part of the wider concept of autonomy.

In my view, autonomy combines rights, capacities, competencies, and caring.[7] Rights-autonomy is possessing moral rights to pursue one's interests. Some rights are liberty rights: the rights to pursue our lives without interference by others. Others are welfare rights: the rights to receive certain minimum resources when we cannot earn them on our own and when society can afford to make them available, for example, aid for severely disabled individuals. Capacity-autonomy is possessing fundamental human capacities such as reasoning, self-control, feeling, and social participation. Competence-autonomy is exercising these capacities in guiding one's life rationally and responsibly. Moral-autonomy implies respect for persons, including sufficient care for oneself to exercise competence-autonomy in pursuing self-fulfillment.

Using this four-faceted concept, autonomy implies more than exercising one's rights without outside interference. It includes competent assertion of one's needs in morally responsible ways so as to secure primary goods. *Primary goods* are goods that rational persons recognize as valuable, as essential to their self-fulfillment.[8] They include self-respect, self-confidence, education, opportunities to develop talents, physical safety (which battered wives lack), economic security, power in making decisions about the use of such resources as money and time, and meaningful work (paid or unpaid).

Let us say that *primary equality* is achieved when both partners obtain the primary goods needed for rationally pursuing their self-fulfillment. Primary equality tends to promote equal autonomy in three ways.

First, to value autonomy is to value the conditions that promote competence-autonomy throughout a lifetime. Those conditions begin in childhood. The foundation for rights-autonomy is the right to be raised in a manner that respects one's "right to an open future," so that as an adult one can exercise capacity-autonomy and competence-autonomy.[9] It also means there is a presumption against women entering into or remaining in marriages that undermine the attitudes, skills, and resources for competence-autonomy.

Capacity-autonomy is often undermined long before a marriage begins. One way this occurs is through sexist role differentiation. In particular, until fairly recently (and continuing today in many places) girls and women have been systematically prevented or discouraged from preparing for challenging and well-paid careers on the grounds that their proper role was homemaking. This placed women at economic disadvantages which erode autonomy during and after marriages, both overtly and covertly.

Overtly, economic disparities leave women with fewer economic resources to pursue their interests. When marriages dissolve, they are left without the education and work experience needed to support themselves. In addition, they are often left with children who add to the financial demands on them. Wives know of this danger, explicitly or tacitly. Lacking the power to exit relationships without great hardship adds pressure on them to submit to abuses from husbands, including intimidation, physical violence, and mental cruelty.

Covertly, economic disparities tend to make women feel less than equal in making decisions about the use of shared resources. If the husband is the exclusive or primary income earner, he will be more likely to feel entitled to have greater influence in making decisions. According to a sociological study by Philip Blumstein and Pepper Schwartz, "in three out of four of the types of couples . . . studied, . . . the amount of money a person earns — in comparison with a partner's income — establishes relative power."[10]

Second, oppression is more than the external forces that mold women from infancy on. It is also the "internalized oppression" of women who are conditioned to hold negative attitudes toward themselves.[11] Internalized oppression violates the procedures that promote mutual autonomy through subtle forms of inner coercion, both from negative attitudes toward oneself and ignorance about one's possibilities.

Overcoming the self-deception and "false consciousness" involved in internalized oppression may take years or never occur. For example, Sonia Johnson reports, "For the seventeen years preceding my feminist awakening in 1978, during which I was consciously and otherwise excusing the inequities of patriarchy, I was living a sort of half life, in half light, a grayish, half-awake limbo of neither clouds nor sunlight, a gray, same numbness."[12] Her "half-life" made her largely oblivious to how her husband failed to carry his share of the burdens of housework and care of their four children. It also made her an easy dupe when he connived a plot to divorce her while minimizing his legal liabilities, the act that finally shocked her into feminist awareness.

The very real possibility of self-deception and internalized oppression suggests an important interplay between primary equality and autonomy. In identifying competence-autonomy, we must do more than ask a woman whether she has exercised her preferences. We also need to look at the overall pattern of benefits and burdens within a relationship. When that pattern is all too obviously askew, we reasonably suspect that autonomy is not being fully exercised. In this way, balanced patterns of distribution of benefits and burdens enter into identifying competence-autonomy.

Third, the wife-mother-homemaker role contains hidden burdens and reduced benefits that increase the difficulties for women who seek to participate in public roles. Unpaid work experience in the home is not viewed as qualifying a person for paid work, and hence entering the job market after raising children becomes increasingly difficult with age. In addition, the low social status of homemaking erodes self-esteem, self-respect, and self-confidence, primary goods that function as psychological prerequisites for exercising autonomy.

In traditional relationships, where the wife is homemaker and the husband is the sole income earner, both spouses may underestimate the burden of the steady drain in the energy required for "emotion work" in tending children, bolstering a husband's ego, and sustaining the relationship.[13] Both may be blind to the belittlement and subtle coercion when a woman constantly has to ask for money from her spouse, not to mention the low social recognition for doing unpaid work. A woman's dependent status can work to lessen her sense of having opportunities for self-development, while the couple's resources are directed primarily to educational and career opportunities for the man.[14]

All these ways in which primary equality supports equal autonomy are insightfully discussed by Susan Moller Okin in *Justice, Gender, and the Family*. Okin concludes that fundamental social changes are needed before mutual autonomy can be widely achieved in marriages. In stating her conclusion, however, Okin seems to me to go beyond primary equality to demand further fifty-fifty equalities. In my terms, she resolves the fairness paradox by opting for equal patterns over equal autonomy, especially with respect to sharing paid work and the unpaid work of child care and housekeeping.

> Any just and fair solution to the urgent problem of women's and children's vulnerability must encourage and facilitate the equal sharing by men and women of paid and unpaid work, of productive and reproductive labor. We must work toward a future in which all will be likely to choose this mode of life. A just future would be one without [institutionally-entrenched differences based on] gender. In its social structures and practices, one's sex would have no more relevance than one's eye color or the length of one's toes.[15]

In this passage Okin runs together two proposals. One recommendation is to abolish gender-linked roles, at least with regard to paid and unpaid labor. Laws, social policies, educational policies, and attitudes need to be changed so as to overthrow the assumption that women are best suited for a particular roles. I agree with this recommendation, of course. Not only is it the most widely shared theme in feminist literature; it also is rapidly becoming a backbone of public policy in this country.

The other proposal is to arrange society so that "all will be likely" to choose to share equally both paid work and the unpaid work of housekeeping and child rearing. I find this proposal problematic. How could it be achieved without limiting couples' autonomy to shape their relationships as they choose? Okin's proposal amounts to social engineering in one direction, attempting to abolish conventional family arrangements altogether, rather than opening up free choices among a range of nonconventional and conventional relationships. For example, it would reject conventional families in which a wife chooses to remain home with young children. And it would socially engineer away the "invisible careers" of upper-class women as civic leaders who, given their husbands' large income, choose to lead lives of homemakers and volunteer leaders.[16]

Fairness does require that whatever agreements couples work out must not be likely to disempower one partner from pursuing the primary goods needed for self-fulfillment; that is the constraint imposed by primary equality. Moreover, when one spouse is the primary or exclusive wage earner there are special (although not insurmountable) barriers to securing balance in a marriage. In order to assure equal autonomy, care must be taken to assure both partners equal access to how that money is used. Nevertheless, if we follow Okin in trying to standardize more fine-grained forms of fifty-fifty patterns, we run the risk of limiting equal autonomy.

Robert Solomon's conception of fairness goes too far in the opposite direction. He specifies a context of "mutual respect to one another as equal persons,"[17] but he gives few guidelines as to what that requires. Instead he emphasizes a couple's complete freedom to work out their arrangements for work and for all other "roles in or out of the home,"[18] including the freedom for one partner to forego all decision-making in large areas of the relationship, as long as that is done voluntarily: "Even if it is generally understood by both people that one of them will make all the decisions, *this* decision must be a mutual one."[19]

Whereas Okin stressed equal patterns at the expense of equal consent, Solomon comes down too hard on equal consent. He reminds us of the importance of consent as an expression of autonomy, but he does not take seriously how consent is skewed by inequalities in decision-making within a society that remains sexist. The upshot of his account is that power imbalances can easily arise in relationships and threaten the primary equality essential to ongoing equal autonomy.

SHARED AUTONOMY

The fairness paradox, which sets in opposition mutual consent and balanced benefits, is partly resolved by subsuming mutual consent under the wider idea of mutual autonomy as a criterion for fairness and by identifying how primary equality contributes to mutual au-

tonomy. Having noted how primary equality promotes equal autonomy, I turn now to how equal autonomy enters into understanding
balanced distributions.

It does so in two ways. First, the autonomy of spouses is expressed
in their personal preferences that partly define what counts as benefits and burdens for them and hence what counts as equal distributions of benefits and burdens. Second, the autonomy of spouses is
largely shared autonomy, autonomy exercised together and on the
basis of a conception of shared benefits.

I began this discussion with two spouses who freely agree on a
marriage that results in greater burdens and fewer benefits for the
woman, as viewed by an impartial observer. But who is that observer? Impartiality implies the absence of prejudices, including sexist biases, but it does not imply the presence of a canonical set of
preferences. There is no such set. By definition, rational persons desire primary goods, but this minimum conception of rationality does
not stipulate how much of each primary good or other goods are required for an individual's self-fulfillment. It is important for our impartial observer to be empathetic to individual needs as well as unbi-
ased in appreciating how spouses' preferences shape their individual
conceptions of benefits and burdens.

Primary equality requires that both partners' needs for primary
goods are taken seriously, but it does not require an exact division of
each primary good or other goods. For example, primary equality
implies economic security for both spouses, but it says nothing about
how that security is achieved or about disparities in income. It implies that both partners have meaningful work, but it does not stipulate how much of the work is paid. Again, primary equality demands that the educational needs of both partners are given
balanced attention, but it does not demand that an equal number
of years of education or dollars for education be allocated to each
partner. The significance of these and other benefits largely turns on
the autonomous preferences of each spouse.

In a nonsexist society, the unpaid work of homemaking and child
rearing would be valued and rewarded more than it is now. That social recognition would also promote the self-esteem of persons who
choose to concentrate their energy in that direction, and hence in a
nonsexist society we might want to keep unpaid homemaking work

as an option for both sexes. Even in our present society it would be patronizing to assume that an intelligent woman must be a conditioned robot if she finds more satisfaction in a traditional lifestyle as wife-mother-homemaker-volunteer than in achievement in a paid career. It would also be demeaning to look down on the (rare) man who chooses to give his wife's career priority.

Each partner's preferences constitute an important aspect of their autonomy. Hence, respect for their autonomy implies taking their interests and desires seriously. To be sure, reaching balanced distributions means more than tallying up actual preferences. For again, partners may overlook or misjudge what are clearly benefits and burdens from any reasonable point of view. A theory of benefits would refer to what individuals would want upon adequate reflection—reflection based on relevant information and emotional stability—although not endorsement of any single ideal moral theory.[20] In these ways, a fully adequate theory of benefits and burdens will take into account primary equality, actual preferences, and reflective preferences.

Personal preferences (partly) define benefits and burdens in marriages, but they do so within the context of shared autonomy within love and marriage.[21] Shared autonomy implies mutual decision-making based on ongoing negotiations, a conception of a shared good, and mutual commitments. Each of these elements complicates an understanding of balanced distributions.

Negotiations

Couples constantly negotiate trade-offs. That is why equal distributions do not imply sameness of benefits and burdens. Sameness would force each partner to spend exactly the same amount of time doing each type of work, thus undermining their (equal) autonomy by preventing them from reaching mutually agreeable allocations of tasks. Balanced patterns imply equivalent rather than identical benefits and burdens.

Equivalence in equal patterning takes into account both preference satisfaction and objective measures of benefits and burdens. Cleaning the cat's litter box may be roughly equivalent to taking out the garbage, in terms of objective measures like time, energy, and unpleasantness. But personal preferences also need to be weighed:

Partners may differ over which activities they prefer doing and hence the relative significance they attach to the activities. Partners, as well as impartial observers, would take both sorts of considerations into account in identifying fair distributions. Such judgments are rough, but couples often manage to make them cogently.

Fairness calls for equivalence at the macro level, not the micro level. *Macro-level equivalence* concerns general patterns of benefits and burdens over time, whereas the micro level concerns particular tasks, benefits, or burdens at a given moment. A universal demand for micro-level equality would subvert autonomy. For example, it would prevent agreements to have one partner do most of the cooking and the other do most of the housecleaning, even when that arrangement pleased both partners.

It is reasonable, however, for couples to start with the presumption that each undesired task and mutually desired benefit should be divided equitably until the partners autonomously negotiate task exchanges, based on compromises and adjustments. Their agreements may be explicit or, as is more common, tacitly developed through everyday interactions. The macro level also takes into account temporal variations so that short-term overall inequalities are balanced in the long run. If we demand a criterion beyond the expression of personal preferences, it will be the largely subjective criterion of each person's reported satisfaction with macro-level patterns.

Shared Good

Typically, spouses conceive of their good together. That shared good includes mutual love, intimacy, support, enjoyed activities (including sex), and self-fulfillment. Often these goods occur together or not at all. The idea of fair distributions does not apply directly to them, since they are not distributable quantities. Beyond these inseparable goods, however, a couple's conception of their shared good includes equal autonomy and balanced benefits. Hence fairness is itself an aspect of a couple's shared good.

Having a shared good does not imply a complete unity of interests. As noted in Chapter 2, Roger Scruton is exaggerating when he writes that in love "all distinction between my interests and your interests is overcome. Your desires are then reasons for me, in exactly the same way, and to the same extent, that my desires are reasons for me."[22] Even the best relationships tolerate frictions and areas in which couples' interests do not perfectly coincide.

Although love is never entirely selfless, love includes a willingness to make sacrifices on behalf of one's spouse. Fairness merely requires that the sacrifices are reciprocal and roughly balanced at the macro level. Nevertheless, spouses' good becomes so intimately interwoven that what would otherwise seem a self-sacrifice is actually a contribution to a shared good in which both partners benefit. As far as possible, couples seek to act in unison on behalf of common purposes.

As also noted in Chapter 2, Robert Nozick construes this shared agency as based on a transfer of rights: "Each [spouse or lover] transfers some previous rights to make certain decisions unilaterally into a joint pool; somehow, decisions will be made together about how to be together."[23] The process is rarely that formal, however, because mutual caring blends interests developed through a couple's shared history to yield the distinctive benefits of love.

Interdependencies take healthy and unhealthy forms. Morbid dependencies diminish one or both partner's overall self-fulfillment. Indeed, in masochistic versions they are motivated by that end.[24] In "co-dependencies," as that term is used in contemporary social science literature, one partner collaborates in supporting the other's self-destructive tendencies, such as alcoholism and drug abuse. There can be a destructive mutual exploitation in which partners demean each other for their own ends.[25] One point of fairness is to prevent these distortions: "Fair exchange indicates that the other person's interests have been sufficiently taken into account; exploitation suggests that this is not the case."[26] A more positive point of fairness is to promote the well-being of both partners.

Mutual Commitments

Feminist conceptions of love are often criticized as a threat to relationships. The demand for fairness, it is charged, results in selfish and legalistic preoccupations with allocating benefits and burdens, thereby eroding intimacy and reducing marriages to contractual arrangements involving duties rather than love. These criticisms neglect how fairness supports mutual commitments in love.

Fairness implies that both partners commit themselves to the marriage; that each assumes responsibility for it; that they both have time alone and time together; that they are mindful of each other's needs, interests, and self-development (where mindfulness means vigilance, not constant reflection). In all these ways, fairness supports love by strengthening patterns of mutual altruism.

Appeals to fairness do sometimes conceal selfishness, but then any moral concept can be abused.[27] Responsible concern for fairness takes into account the good of both partners — the "we" rather than "me" — and it avoids obsessive preoccupation with fifty-fifty distributions.[28] As a virtue, fairness implies a context-sensitive concern for fair play and only occasional deliberation on the relationship's overall fairness. It is fully consistent with the spontaneous aspects of caring.

Nor does the virtue of fairness reduce loving companionships to semi-legal contracts that erode intimacy. Marriages typically involve contracts but are not reducible to them, and most marriages are strikingly unlike business contracts.[29] One difference lies in the degree to which fairness can be formalized in rules. In business, contracts tend to be relatively explicit and firm, so as to generate formal rules (within a legal framework). In love, fairness is a largely a matter of good judgment based on a sense of fair sharing and fair play. It cannot be formalized in rules, and it leaves far greater flexibility for couples to work out their own "style" of fairness within the relationship.

The most striking dissimilarity with business contracts concerns the benefits and burdens at stake. Far more than business contracts, love intertwines benefits. In a business arrangement the ultimate benefits are separable. Thus, the profit sheets of two companies doing business together are separate, whatever the empirical connections between the goods and services they exchange. The companies are mutually dependent on each other for success in business, but the goods and benefits involved are not as extensively interdependent as in love.

These theoretical comments are complemented by historical observations. Is there any empirical evidence that a concern for fairness tends to harm relationships? In *Habits of the Heart*, Robert Bellah and his associates charged Americans with excessive individualism that damages love. Their sociological study warned that a new contractual way of thinking was rendering marriages unstable: "Faced with onogoing demands to work on their relationships as well as their jobs, separate and equal selves are led to question the contractual terms of their commitments to one another: Are they getting what they want? Are they getting as much as they are giving? As much as they could get elsewhere? If not, they are tempted to withdraw and look elsewhere for fulfillment."[30] The preoccupation with fairness described in this passage sounds selfish—it is exclusively focused on oneself, rather than oneself and one's partner. Surely that is only one type of relationship.

Sociologist Francesca M. Cancian challenges Bellah's conclusions. True, during the past two decades an "independence model" of relationships emerged, with "a strong emphasis on being self-sufficient and avoiding obligations. Developing an independent self and expressing one's needs and feelings is seen as a precondition to love."[31] During the same decades, however, a contrasting "interdependence model" emerged that emphasizes long-term mutual commitments in which couples "believe that they owe each other mutual support and affection, and that love is a precondition to full self-development."[32] Instead of viewing the relationship as a contractual exchange mechanism for deriving goods that might be achieved in other ways, couples affirm the relationship as an end in itself that provides meaning and a valued personal identity. As Cancian writes, "If self-development is seen as a process of internalizing relationships with others, especially loving relationships, then love and self-development are mutually reinforcing, not conflicting."[33]

No doubt a concern for fairness has contributed to the demise of one-sided marriages in which women are exploited and abused. (That demise, of course, is good.) Yet fairness will tend to support marriages fitting the interdependence model. Couples will understand their marriage not in terms of balancing my good versus yours, but in a spirit of our good being promoted through an integrated expression of selflessness, shared autonomy, and equal use of resources. They will also view fairness and equal autonomy as among the shared goods defining their relationship, and they will understand how macro-level balances tend to support equal autonomy. As a result, equal autonomy and balanced distributions emerge as largely complementary.

7

HONESTY

Real love wants to have a real object,
and to know the truth of it, and to
love it in its truth as it really is.
—*Simone Weil*[1]

How is honesty related to erotic love? According to the external view, the demands of honesty and love are independent and frequently in conflict. Sometimes honesty furthers love, as a means to an end, and other times it is an obstacle to love; either way, the two make separable claims. According to the internal view, honesty is an important constituent of love, at least of "true love"—the kind worth having. The demands of honesty are part of the demands of love, although of course honesty might on occasion conflict with other aspects of love.

In the first section I develop a rationale for the internal view, drawing attention to how truthfulness and trustworthiness manifest caring and contribute to intimacy. I also suggest that some of the conflicts identified by the external view are better understood as inherent in love itself—as internal to love, rather than as a conflict between love and other values. In the second section I explore some practical difficulties in pursuing the ideal of honesty.

INTIMACY

Most defenders of the external view regard honesty as a subordinate virtue that should give way whenever necessary to promote caring, community, and love. Thus, Molière in the *Misanthrope* argues (with laughter) that honesty threatens personal relationships unless it is constrained by kindness. Alceste's demand for complete honesty is unmasked to reveal his insensitivity, self-righteous narcissism, self-deceptive desires for dominance, and general misanthropy. Philinte defends the opposite extreme of remaining silent even at the cost of complacency about others' wrongdoing, but he also voices the sane moderation required for caring.

> It's often best to veil one's true emotions.
> Wouldn't the social fabric come undone
> If we were wholly frank with everyone?[2]

The external view has other variations, however. Rather than making honesty subordinate to love, it is possible to regard these virtues as equally valuable and in need of balancing. Alternatively, we could make honesty paramount, as Nietzsche did: "Honesty, supposing that this is our virtue from which we cannot get away, we free spirits — well, let us work on it with all our malice and love and not weary of 'perfecting' ourselves in *our* virtue, the only one left us."[3] In his early existentialist writings, Jean-Paul Sartre shared a similar outlook when the sole value he defended was authenticity, understood as a combination of honesty and courage in overcoming self-deception about human freedom. To embrace honesty as the paramount value, however, leads directly to the moral imbalance identified by Molière. Ironically, Sartre implies as much at the end of *No Exit,* after his characters have relentlessly stripped away each other's illusions: "Hell is — other people!"[4]

The external view expresses a valuable insight: Ruthless truth-telling inevitably conflicts with love. Yet it misstates the insight. The merciless pursuit and presentation of truth should not be equated with honesty. Honesty embodies some requirements of decency, and it is a far richer notion than simple truth-telling. Rather than standing alone, honesty is richly woven into a tapestry of many additional virtues.

To begin with, Molière discussed only one aspect of honesty: candor. Candor is frankness in communicating mental states (beliefs, attitudes, and emotions) that are immediately accessible to consciousness. It forbids deception and also calls for voluntary disclosure of sensitive, disturbing, or controversial information. Hence, candor is not identical to mere truth-telling, or even attempted truth-telling, in the sense of randomly stating things we happen to believe. When we call people honest or candid in their speech, typically we praise them for uttering appropriate truths — truths relevant to a situation — together with their heartfelt views on pertinent issues.

The standards for appropriateness are contextual. They include relevance to a topic, a sense of what is interesting, and sensitivity to the feelings of others. We do not praise people for honesty when they chatter about irrelevant matters, even if they state facts. Indeed, chatter can function as a dishonest evasion of truth.[5] Nor do we praise individuals as honest when they are utterly insensitive, callous, or cruel. (When we say that someone is "honest to a fault," typically we imply that they have exceeded the boundaries of honesty as a virtue, perhaps becoming foolishly, naively, or even viciously blunt.)

Fully truthful communication, especially within caring relationships, includes "metatruthfulness"— truthfulness about our attitudes of truthfulness toward our partners and relationships. Sociolinguists remind us of how subtly those attitudes are expressed in everyday discourse.[6] They point to our needs to communicate indirectly, whether in order to maintain a self-defensive reserve, to promote rapport without spelling out everything, or to protect relationships by guarding against corrosive bluntness. Cruel sarcasm may effectively convey the truth about someone's appearance, but it disregards metatruths about how honesty interweaves with collegiality, friendship, and love within a complex tapestry of virtues. This internal limit that caring places on honesty is the first connection between honesty and love.

As a value, honesty is not so robust that it requires always saying the right thing in the morally correct way. Nonetheless, as a character trait and as a feature of truthful communication, honesty is a prima facie moral good, even when other moral considerations sometimes override that good so as to make honesty undesirable on balance.

Attending to the limits that caring places on honesty does not resolve the issue between internal and external views. Both views can allow that truthful communication is not reducible to truth-telling, and both can allow that candor should be balanced and limited by caring. Still, appreciating how some degree of decency and caring enters into the very meaning of honesty is a first step toward making the internal view plausible. That view becomes increasingly compelling as we take account of additional facets of honesty in relation to love.

Honesty has two main dimensions, truthfulness and trustworthiness, and each has several facets.[7] *Truthfulness* is the general disposition to care about truth. It is manifested not only in candid statements, but also in inquiry, reasoning, belief formation, conduct, and personal relationships. Thus, *intellectual honesty,* or intellectual integrity, is the disposition to inquire and reason on the basis of concern for truth. It implies habits of clear thinking, cogent argument, and carefulness about evidence. *Genuineness* precludes hypocrisy and phoniness in emotions, attitudes, commitments, and conduct. More positively, it entails autonomy (self-determination) in developing and acting on our outlook rather than passively submitting to outside influences. That does not mean jettisoning tradition; it means exercising our judgment in deciding which aspects of tradition and convention to accept. *Self-honesty* is being truthful with ourselves. That rules out objectionable forms of self-deception, especially evading topics and truths pertinent to meeting moral responsibilities and gaining self-fulfillment. Finally, *self-disclosure* is voluntarily revealing ourselves, more intimately than is customary in society, in order to create and sustain personal relationships such as love and friendship. This self-revelation in words, emotions, and behavior overlaps with candor and genuineness, but it is worth distinguishing in thinking about intimacy.

Indeed, all the major aspects of truthfulness are overlapping and interwoven. In particular, being truthful with other people is not a simple matter of candidly expressing opinions and attitudes easily accessible to consciousness. Often we cannot be completely truthful with people without trying hard to get at the truth (intellectual honesty), to confront unpleasant but essential truths (self-honesty), to shape emotions and conduct autonomously (genuineness), and, within personal relationships, to reveal private aspects of our personality (self-disclosure). The intimacy of love is impossible or restricted insofar as these aspects of honesty are missing. That is what Dostoyevsky had in mind in the following passage.

> Above all, don't lie to yourself. The man who lies to himself and listens to his own lie comes to such a point that he cannot distinguish the truth within him, or around him, and so loses all respect for himself and for others. And having no respect he ceases to love. And in order to distract himself without love he gives way to passions and coarse pleasures and sinks to bestiality in his vices—all this from continual lying to other men and to himself.[8]

It is clear that Dostoyevsky has in mind continual dishonesty—habitual self-deception and disregard for truth—rather than isolated instances of untruthfulness. Nevertheless, he voices a general danger, especially given the tendency for isolated acts of dishonesty to grow into patterns of careless disregard for the truth.

In addition to truthfulness, honesty includes *trustworthiness*. Here we can distinguish two main aspects. *Fidelity* is keeping commitments and maintaining loyalties. *Probity* is uprightness in avoiding cheating, stealing, exploitation, and deception. With both aspects, motives are important. Trustworthy persons are motivated, at least in part, by respect and caring for the persons they interact with, rather than the mere fear of being caught. They also manifest self-mastery in keeping commitments and self-control in heeding moral rules about respect for property, fair play, and not deceiving. Once again, honesty functions as part of a tapestry of many interwoven virtues.

Trustworthiness and truthfulness are distinct but overlapping. We could be truthful but untrustworthy, as when a person is forthright about being unreliable and unable to keep commitments. Again, we could be trustworthy but not especially truthful about things unrelated to obligations. Nevertheless, usually truthfulness and trustworthiness go together. That is because both require avoiding objectionable forms of deception and because deception is usually involved in cheating, stealing, and other violations of trust. And both are valuable constituents of love.

Ours is a time of experimentation with different conceptions of love, yet honesty remains a key value for most couples. Honesty is given high priority by many couples who pursue nontraditional relationships. Sometimes it is elevated to supreme value in providing a framework for exploring greater intimacy than conventional relationships permit. Honesty also remains a crucial component of most traditional conceptions of love, those that center on lifetime commitments and caring. Indeed, honesty has quite literally become a matter of life and death, as when a husband who is dishonest about his extramarital affairs passes the AIDS virus to his wife.

Some persons embrace a traditional conception of love as an absolute and reject alternatives as illegitimate. Others embrace a traditional conception as one permissible ideal among others, supplementing it with tolerance of alternative conceptions within a pluralistic value perspective. They also acknowledge substantial flexibility in interpreting and implementing honesty and other virtues such as caring, fidelity, and fairness. Here I am especially interested in the latter attitude, which affirms traditional conceptions of love as valuable but not mandatory. What I say, however, is relevant to any conception that makes intimacy and caring central to love. Caring, as a special way to value the beloved as having extraordinary importance, implies honesty.

On the one hand, honesty as truthfulness, especially as truthful self-disclosure, is an essential constituent of intimacy, both intimate experiences and intimate relationships. *Intimate experiences* are episodes of closeness—cognitively (knowledge and understanding), emotionally (feelings of affection and identification with), and behaviorally (spontaneous self-expression). Intimate experiences occur when two (or more) people willingly reveal more of themselves than is socially customary and do so within a context of caring. Honest self-disclosure is built into intimacy, although many degrees of intimacy and reciprocation are possible. *Intimate relationships* are reciprocal interpersonal interactions over time that are characterized

by large numbers of intimate experiences, and they are also structured by a complex web of expectations, hopes, memories, caring,
and trust.

A primary aim in love is to create and sustain an intimate relationship valued for itself — precisely because we value the beloved for
himself or herself — as well as valued for how the relationship satisfies our needs and desires.[9] The needs include sex, personal expression beyond what is possible in other social roles (such as work and
citizenship), and the self-esteem that comes from being valued in a
wholesale way (if not unconditionally). Erotic love, like parental
love, has the potential to affirm our worth more than most other
forms of human interaction. It enriches the meaning (significance
and coherence) of a life and enables a fuller expression of aspects of
the self restricted within other social roles.

To value persons is to value them under some description and understanding of who they are. Genuine love is impossible when that
understanding goes too far awry. David Henry Hwang provides an illuminating, if extreme, example in *M. Butterfly*. The play is based
on the unlikely but actual event described in a 1986 *New York Times*
article: "A former French diplomat and a Chinese opera singer have
been sentenced to six years in jail for spying for China after a two-
day trial that traced a story of clandestine love and mistaken sexual
identity. Mr. Bouriscot was accused of passing information to China
after he fell in love with Mr. Shi, whom he believed for twenty years
to be a woman."[10] Bouriscot claimed that Shi was never naked during their sexual intercourse, as he assumed was Chinese custom, and
Mr. Shi avoided discovery by being the active partner during intercourse. Hwang dramatizes Bouriscot as obsessed by a fantasy stereotype of Asian women as shy and submissively eager to please.

Did Bouriscot love Shi? In retrospect, Hwang's fictionalized protagonist concludes that he loved a fantasy, not a person, even though
for twenty years he thought otherwise. That conclusion is plausible,
given the significance of gender to personal identity. More generally,
partners whose love for each other is based on gross illusions may
later conclude that they loved a fantasy rather than a person.

Relationships are superficially intimate when partners withhold
deeper aspects of themselves. This "depth" metaphor need not con-

jure up the picture of the self as an onion with neatly ordered circles moving toward some inner core that defines us. Some cognitive psychologists suggest that we are more or less loosely structured and display coherent patterns only within particular contexts.[11] Nevertheless, intimacy is limited when persons withhold key information or constrict the natural expression of emotions and attitudes.

On the other hand, honesty as trustworthiness promotes the trust essential to intimate and interdependent relationships. A con artist may succeed in evoking trust for a while, but the odds of sustaining it favor the trustworthy person. Trust is a prerequisite for undertaking the risks characteristic of love's emotional vulnerability. Those risks include fear for the safety of the beloved, agony when the beloved suffers, shame and guilt for failures in the relationship, devastating depression when a valued relationship ends, and corrosive hate when a relationship turns sour.[12] Trust is also needed to sustain the complex interdependence in which two persons must be able to coordinate and rely upon each other's conduct. Much is at stake here, especially in long-term relationships that involve mutual support for careers, economic survival, and nurturing children.

When combined, truthfulness and trustworthiness provide much of love's power to transform lives. That power is most often heralded during early stages of falling in love, with its sometimes mistaken sense of mutual understanding. Yet its main role is to promote the ongoing process of caring and mutual valuing, a process that requires self-disclosure and leads to self-discovery through the eyes of the beloved, a process that with luck can last a lifetime. Indeed, as Doris Lessing suggests in describing her heroine Martha Quest, honesty in loving need not be prefaced by falling in love:

> Some force, some power, had taken hold of them both, and had made such changes in her. . . . Though of course she had never been "in love" with Thomas; that particular fever, in its aspect either of sickness or of magic had had nothing to do with it. . . . [T]o be with Thomas was as natural as breathing. And even the long process of breaking-down—as they both learned to put it—for the other; of learning to expose oneself, was something they did together, acknowledging they had to do it.[13]

ILLUSION

I noted several internal connections between honesty and love: the caring that distinguishes candor from sheer cruelty, the honest self-revelation inherent in intimacy, the trustworthiness that sustains intimate and interdependent relationships. These connections were sketched with regard to ideals of honesty and love, ideals that are not reducible to obligations. Not only is erotic love morally optional, but the firm requirements of honesty compose only a minimum standard. The pejorative term "dishonesty" applies to failures to meet that minimum but not to the absence of honesty beyond the minimum. Goodness in intimate and supportive caring can be achieved by reaching beyond the minimum standard in pursuing the ideals of candor, self-honesty, and self-disclosure so as to achieve higher degrees of intimacy.

In moving from ideals to practice, we need to take account of several complexities that leave room for ignorance and illusion in love, which falls short of ideal honesty, without being dishonest by falling below the minimum standard. Otherwise, an internal view could lead to absolutism about honesty in love.

That absolutism occurs in George Graham and Hugh LaFollette's otherwise illuminating discussion.[14] Intimacy is possible, they argue, only when partners are habitually honest with one another in communicating a "correct" picture of themselves. By honesty they mean primarily candor (truthful communication), genuineness, and self-disclosure. They discuss a wife who gives in to the temptation for an extramarital one-night stand and then has to decide whether to tell her husband. Perhaps most of us would say it depends on the circumstances, but Graham and LaFollette insist the partner should always be told if an intimate relationship is to continue. Not to tell would violate the spouse's right to know and thereby coercively restrict decision-making based on that information concerning, for example, whether to continue in the relationship or how to strengthen it so that extramarital affairs do not recur. In addition, covering up the truth might require additional lies and generate a guarded attitude that threatens emotional closeness.

Graham and LaFollette add a caveat that identifies one complexity: timing. They recognize that the truth may need to be temporarily withheld as part of an effort to salvage a strained relationship, either to reveal it at a later time with the goal of strengthening the relationship or to prevent the partner's unnecessary pain during the transition out of a moribund relationship.

With this caveat, their view applies to many cases—to most, in my view. Yet it cannot be generalized to establish truthful self-disclosure as an absolute value. We need to allow exceptions, such as when a person's lover is likely to overreact, perhaps violently, to information about the one-night stand and destroy a relationship worth preserving.[15] Also, foregoing intimacy about some information may be necessary to sustain ongoing intimate relationships that overall contain desirable levels of intimacy, intellectual honesty, self-honesty, and genuineness.

Sometimes a conflict occurs between different aspects of honesty. Perhaps being completely truthful would destroy the possibility of ongoing trust, whereas trustworthiness implies a general concern for maintaining trust. Similarly, cognitive intimacy in revealing a particular truth may lessen overall emotional intimacy and the prospects for a continuing relationship based on truthfulness.

Graham and LaFollette are right about the need in love to reveal an accurate self-image, or at least a roughly accurate one. Yet they overlook another desire that should be balanced with that need: the desire to look good in the eyes of the beloved. To be sure, that impulse inclines us toward self-revelation in order to feel valued for who we really are. Thus, in *Cyrano de Bergerac* Christian ultimately insists that Roxane be told about how he relied on Cyrano's wit and poetry in courting her.

> I want her love
> For the poor fool I am — or not at
> all![16]

Nevertheless, the same impulse points toward accenting the positive and downplaying the negative, sometimes by using elements of deception. Christian was quite willing to use deception while courting Roxane rather than risk losing her. Even within the special intimacy of love, honesty does not require divulging every ugly nook and cranny of our past and present.

Love intertwines the good of two people, and it contains elements of benevolence without being a disinterested altruism.[17] Typically it leaves room for areas of privacy and individuality apart from the relationship. Honesty needs to be balanced by recognizing the mutual autonomy of each other, the right to keep some things private and to use discretion in divulging them. Indeed, intimacy is largely a product of individuals selecting some information as crucial in understanding them.[18] Hence a large complication arises: Two partners may have different assessments about what that information is, whether or not the assessments are warranted. Thus, for one partner information about extramarital affairs is absolutely essential in understanding each other; for another a brief affair is interpreted as "merely physical; it didn't mean anything."

Communication goes a long way toward dealing with alternative interpretations of the information that contributes to intimacy. Some differences can be settled through mutual agreements, reached through adjustments and compromises, about what to reveal. These agreements, however, introduce new complexities. Once beyond the minimum standard of mandatory honesty, couples are free to agree on different degrees of self-disclosure. Typically those agreements are highly nuanced and tacit understandings. Whether explicit or implicit, they reveal the need to balance the ideal of honesty with mutual respect for autonomy. That is Robert C. Solomon's insight.[19] He points out, for example, that many couples tacitly agree to selectively withhold their sexual fantasies from their partners, thereby setting requirements for honest self-disclosure.

However, Solomon embraces an external view that leads him to unduly minimize the value of honesty. He tells us that "honesty is overrated" in matters of love, that it is sometimes an obstacle to love and at other times just unimportant. He implies that even when a couple has an agreement of sexual exclusivity, an adulterous partner should keep quiet if it threatens to disturb their love. Room is allowed for differences among reasonable individuals about how far to embrace the ideal of honesty. Nevertheless, Solomon's de-emphasis on honesty will shape a different conception of love than an internal view that takes honesty more seriously. In addition to appreciating the importance of shared agreements to restrict honesty, we should recognize that when partners' agreements become too sweeping they may close off entire areas of intimacy worth seeking.

The final complexity I will mention concerns the positive contribution of illusions to love. Earlier I noted that when illusions become too extreme they call into question whether we love a person or a fantasy. Nevertheless, we should allow that genuine love, at least in some stages, can be based on what may seem to be superficial aspects of a person. Thus, someone might fall in love primarily because of a partner's money or ephemeral bodily features, and then fall out of love when those features change. Here the love may be genuinely for the person, although superficial. "Deeper" love is directed toward a person for reasons more central to who a person really is, and this "really" implies a value judgment about what features are essential in understanding a person. Still, love has its own way of understanding. Lovers accent their beloved's good qualities and downplay their flaws. In that process they are notoriously prone to illusions and self-deceptions that are commonplace in profound and superficial love alike.

Not all self-deception is objectionable, if we think of self-deception broadly as the evasion of disturbing topics and truths.[20] Positive illusions serve love by strengthening attraction through exaggerating the positive and downplaying the negative features of the beloved. Stendhal made this feature central to his theory of crystallization, which he defined as "that process of the mind which discovers fresh perfections in its beloved at every turn of events."[21] Just as leaving a bough of wood in the salt mines at Salzburg transforms it into a crystalline beauty no longer recognizable as a plain piece of wood, so imagination transforms the beloved into someone other than who a purely disinterested observer sees. Is the chemistry a result of illusions or of valuing what is there to be seen, if only we properly appreciated it? In different passages Stendhal gives both answers. Ultimately he rejects the question, since for him beauty, in his wide sense of appreciating perfections, is in the eye of the beholder who takes pleasure in what is seen. Instead, we might say that love intertwines appreciation for the good in the beloved with the lover's own illusions so that they become inextricable.

In addition to illusions about the beloved, there are fruitful illusions about ourselves, about our relationships, and about love itself. Illusions about ourselves may invigorate self-assertion in love by elevating self-esteem beyond what a disinterested observer might see as warranted. Illusions about our relationships can bolster the hope and faith so essential to their growth. And illusions about the nature and possibilities of love may intensify its pursuit in creative ways.

Many self-deceptive illusions are dual-edged, creative in some respects but harmful in others. Eugene O'Neill explored these ambiguities in *The Iceman Cometh,* a play that is often misread as a wholesale endorsement of self-deceptive "pipe dreams" or vital lies as life-giving. Hickey and Evelyn's marriage was sustained by their shared dream that Hickey would gain the self-control needed to end his periodic alcoholic binges and visits to prostitutes. It was an impossible dream, although it kept them together in a relationship that sustained them both. The dream had a darker side, however. In Evelyn it supported low self-esteem and an unhealthy form of dependence on Hickey. In Hickey it generated a cycle of guilt and hatred for Evelyn's ever-ready forgiveness for his weakness. The cycle eventually exploded in murder, albeit a murder covered by the further illusion that death was the only way to bring Evelyn peace. O'Neill adds to our understanding of how self-deception functions in codependent relationships to simultaneously sustain and erode mutual support.

To sum up, the internal view of honesty must take account of several complexities: the sometimes conflicting aspects of honesty; morally permissible differences in how far couples emphasize honesty in their relationship; couples' agreements and shared understanding about degrees of truthfulness; the interplay between intimate episodes and relationships; timing in disclosing truths; needs for self-esteem and personal privacy within intimate relationships; and the contributions of illusions to love. But none of these complexities overthrow honesty as a constituent of love that makes possible intimacy and trust. Instead, the complexities represent areas where honesty must be tempered to make it a realistic and realizable ideal. Like other valuable ideals defining love, including mutual caring, fidelity, constancy, and fairness, honesty is rarely achieved perfectly. Yet aspiring to it is part of the meaning of that love worth having.

8
WISDOM

What is . . . love's knowledge — and
what writing does it dictate in the heart?
—*Martha C. Nussbaum*[1]

Lovers' folly is commonplace, in literature as in life. Its many forms include silly games, ridiculous quarrels, absurd misunderstandings, misplaced trust, and foolhardy failures to trust. Janus-faced, it is portrayed in comedy as a charming playfulness and in tragedy as a fatal lack of perspective. The association of love with folly reinforces our tendency to approach love with simple dichotomies: duty and delight, head and heart, loving wisely and loving well. Thus we seem to understand Othello when he asks to be remembered as "one that loved not wisely, but too well" (5.2.354).[2]

Yet do we understand? I will argue that Shakespeare challenges rather than endorses any general opposition between loving wisely and loving well. For him, as for me, erotic love is a way to value persons morally, as well as sexually, aesthetically, and self-interestedly. Genuine love is guided, structured, and partly defined by virtues — by caring and faithfulness, respect and self-respect, honesty and fairness, gratitude and courage. Each of these virtues embodies at least a modicum of wisdom, and hence some degree of wisdom is inherent in love. Indeed, love itself can be a form of wisdom.

BETRAYAL AND EVASION

Othello is not a melodrama about Iago's villainy. Even by himself, Iago lifts the play above melodrama, captivating us with his envy, sadism, conjurer-like deception, and uncanny (albeit sociopathic) insight. In addition, Iago represents an aspect of Othello's personality, and his deceptions take root so easily because Othello is already prone to self-deception—about himself and about love.[3] When Othello demands an explanation of his treachery, Iago's reply is incisive although also elusive: "Demand me nothing. What you know, you know" (5.2.311).

What does Othello know and yet refuse to acknowledge to himself? Not merely that he has been irrationally jealous and an all-too-willing dupe. No doubt that is the knowledge Iago intended, but, like elsewhere in the play, his words carry additional meanings that as a moral cynic he cannot endorse. What Othello finds too horrifying to acknowledge is that he betrayed Desdemona and their love.

Recall the context in which Othello claims to have loved not wisely but too well. He is voicing his final reflections about his motives in the hope of shaping how others will remember him. There is no reason to think he is consciously trying to deceive others, but there is every reason to believe he is not being completely truthful with himself. When he killed Desdemona, only a short while earlier, he employed the monstrous rationalization that he was acting in "the cause" of justice to punish her for adultery and to prevent her from betraying other men, actions that she could hardly envision, let alone commit (5.2.1). Shortly thereafter, upon learning of Iago's deceptions, he claimed to be motivated by honor rather than hatred, even though it is all too clear how he gave himself over "to tyrannous hate" (3.3.464). These rationalizations remain unretracted when, moments before killing himself, he claims to have loved not wisely but too well. Are we to believe that his self-delusion instantly vanished? Perhaps we want to believe it. Doing so would mute the horror of a play in which "no one . . . comes to understand himself or anyone else."[4] Perhaps, like Cassio, we seek reassurance that Othello's suicide manifests greatness of heart (5.2.371). Nevertheless, although Othello may suspect his deeply rooted self-deceptions, there is no evidence he saw through them.

As minimal evidence, we would need an explicit sign of remorse for his cruelty to Desdemona. That sign is never given. Othello blames himself for imprudence, not immorality. He chastises himself for being a fool who "threw a pearl away / Richer than all his tribe" (5.2.357). If there is contrition, it is diluted and displaced into violence against himself. When Othello claims to lack wisdom, he merely offers another, quite commonplace rationalization to mitigate his guilt: ignorant, but not malicious; certainly not guilty of a failure to love. Othello's remark, and perhaps the suicide that follows, extends his self-deceiving evasion of how he betrayed Desdemona and their love.

Betrayed in what way? In murdering her he violates the minimal decency owed to everyone, but that is not the betrayal. The betrayal occurs much earlier and centers on his failure to love Desdemona. At the same time, not all failures in love amount to betrayals, and probably all spouses love imperfectly. What justifies us in speaking here of betrayal rather than just a (seriously) flawed love?

One familiar reading locates Othello's betrayal in his jealousy, but that reading is superficial. Within wide limits jealousy is natural and healthy. Notice it is the socipath Iago, echoed by his wife Emilia, who makes wholesale condemnations of jealousy: "O, beware, my lord, of jealousy! / It is the green-eyed monster which doth mock the meat it feeds on" (3.3.178-180; cf. 3.4.162-163). Contrary to this generalization, jealousy can be a valuable response that alerts us to the danger of losing something dear.[5] Few people confronted with Iago's ingenuity would escape all jealous anger and hurt, and for the most part Othello's jealous emotions (as opposed to his way of acting on them) are symptoms of his love rather than of betrayal. To be sure, his jealous conduct is excessive and unwarranted; as such, it is a failure in loving, in particular a failure to sufficiently respect and trust Desdemona. But again, not all failures in love constitute betrayals, and by itself jealousy is not a betrayal.

Nor does betrayal occur when Othello resolves to "loathe" Desdemona after he begins to believe in her infidelity: "She's gone. I am abused, and my relief / Must be to loathe her" (3.3.283-284). This resolution is formed against, but not to the exclusion of, the love he continues to feel. Love, after all, is not an uninterrupted feeling of affection. As an attitude, love embodies the full gamut of human emotions, including moments of depression, annoyance, anger, and even hate. If Othello's resolve were followed by an effort to understand Desdemona's point of view, we would dismiss it as a passing episode of bad temper and self-pity.

What, then, is Othello's betrayal? It is unfaithfulness—not in the sense of sexual infidelity, but in the sense of losing faith, of being inconstant in the marital love he once vowed, and in violating Desdemona's trust and loyalty. He also betrays himself and his own integrity, not only in distorting his honor into sheer vengeance but in violating his own heart—the emotions, desires, commitments, and values that enter into his love. Othello fascinates us precisely because he is capable of love, certainly more than any other man in the play, and because at some level he continues throughout to love Desdemona. Under Iago's influence he feels love even as he acts in unloving ways. His primary betrayal is his failure to value Desdemona in the way required by their love for each other.

The betrayal occurs as a four-part sequence of actions that transform a resolution to loathe into an intention to kill. First, Othello begins to view Desdemona impersonally and with misogynous stereotypes. He takes his cue from Iago, who claims that all women in Venice lack a conscience adequate to prevent them from committing adultery and that at most they exercise discretion in concealing their adultery (3.3.216–218). The stereotype is false, and it is also based on the double standard that adultery is detestable in women but permissible for men, an unfairness that Emilia insightfully criticizes (4.3.95–106). Accompanying the stereotype is Othello's self-indulgent complaint that great men are doomed to have adulterous wives, whereas commoners are more fortunate, presumably because their wives have fewer opportunities to commit adultery (3.3.290). Insofar as Othello perceives Desdemona through misogynist stereotypes, as merely another untrustworthy woman, he cannot appreciate her with eyes of love, as being unique and irreplaceably dear.

Second, after Iago leaves him alone "on the rack" to think through the implications of being made a cuckold, Othello concludes that his career is ended. No more "glorious war": "Othello's occupation's gone" (3.3.373). This is an astonishing and momentous conclusion, one he arrives at without Iago's help. Why does he think the (alleged) adultery will end his career? As a black man and an outsider to the Venetian society that hired him as a mercenary, Othello must have worked exceptionally hard to earn acceptance and respect. He believes the adultery will publicly humiliate him, making him a laughingstock of his men and hence no longer an effective leader. In this regard he echoes Cassio's despair in having lost "the immortal part" of himself — his reputation (2.3.256). In his mind, killing Desdemona in the cause of justice might not restore his authority, but at least it will show he retains his honor.

Third, Othello becomes infuriated when Iago recounts Cassio's sexual dream. Iago alleges that Cassio, while sleeping next to him, declared his love for Desdemona. Then, turning his leg over Iago's thigh, he kissed Iago passionately. The graphic description heightens Othello's sexual jealousy and compounds it with homophobic disgust. Even more important, since the (alleged) event involves Othello's two top subordinates it intensifies his fears that the adultery will ruin his military career and hence his livelihood. In a rage he swears to "tear her all to pieces" (3.3.447).

Fourth, Iago reports that Cassio wiped his beard with Desdemona's handkerchief. For his lieutenant to wipe his beard with one of Desdemona's ordinary handkerchiefs would have been an insult. Yet this is no ordinary handkerchief. It resonates with symbolic meaning. A deathbed gift from his mother, who earlier received it from an Egyptian sorceress, the handkerchief was said to have the magical powers of a love potion. To lose it or give it away would curse love (3.4.57–70). By using the charmed handkerchief as a common rag, Cassio insulted his mother and assaulted his ideals of purity and constancy in love — ironically, the very ideals Othello betrays. This is the decisive event that makes Othello erupt in violence.

> Arise, black vengeance, from the hollow hell!
> Yield up, O love, thy crown and hearted throne
> To tyrannous hate! (3.3.462–464)

Kneeling, and with a horrifyingly calm determination, he utters a "sacred vow" of vengeance. Iago kneels with him, creating the effect of a mock marriage ceremony centered on shared vows of hate. If a commitment to love is the foundation of love's faithfulness, this vow of hatred is its explicit betrayal. The murder that follows culminates a betrayal that has already taken place here.

This four-part sequence alludes to the social structures that partly explain why the betrayal occurs as easily as it does. The betrayal is facilitated by the misogynist assumption that men have the right to control and to punish women, if necessary using violence. Each of the four actions signals a move away from a world of love defined by such virtues as caring, faithfulness, and mutuality and toward a patriarchal world defined by honor in the eyes of other men. This explanation in terms of patriarchal social structures, however, is not the full explanation for Othello's betrayal, even though it might suffice by itself to explain most marital murders in Elizabethan society and our own. A full explanation must take account of his individual character. Here again we need to go beyond, or rather beneath, his excessive jealousy and sexual insecurity.

As Arthur Kirsch argues, Othello manifests a profound lack of self-respect.[6] His fragile self-worth comes entirely from outside him, from his public reputation and from Desdemona. When those external sources are threatened, there is no inner core to sustain him. That explains why Desdemona's (alleged) adultery with Cassio is so devastating. Simultaneously it shatters both foundations of Othello's self-respect: his men's respect and Desdemona's love. We believe Othello when he says he could bear public humiliation as long as he had the love of Desdemona, "the fountain from the which my current runs" (4.2.61). The problem is that he also believes his life lacks value to him without Desdemona's love. Undoubtedly Desdemona's alleged infidelity threatens his masculinity and middle-age sexual potency, which were already put at risk by marrying a woman half his age.[7] But deeper than this, it shows he lacks a sufficient sense of his worth as an independent human being.

Othello's fragile self-respect explains why he is an easy mark for Iago's deceptions, which make him feel unloved and unlovable as well as about to lose his reputation. It also explains his explosive hatred and his twisted sense of justice in killing Desdemona. He is not merely jealous; he is desperately attempting to salvage a sense of self-worth.[8] The attempt, of course, is both self-defeating and self-destructive. What manner of thinking about love supported such a demented strategy?

NOT WISELY, BUT TOO WELL?

Each element in Othello's claim to have loved not wisely but too well is ambiguous: love, love wisely, love too well. (We might expect as much in the final words of a desperate self-deceiver.) To begin with, what is meant by love? As a virtue-structured way to value persons, love means caring for Desdemona in desirable ways. That implies making a sustained effort to understand her, rather than being eager for revenge; respecting her and being willing to trust her (within reasonable limits), rather than falling prey to inordinate jealousy; engaging in honest communication and fair dealing, rather than becoming a self-righteous judge; making an effort to summon courage in confronting his crisis, rather than reacting to his fear with self-protective violence; being grateful for the joy she brought, instead of becoming her executioner.

From the moment he allows himself to be manipulated by Iago, Othello displays none of love's virtues. He is unwise, to be sure, but he is also uncaring, unjust, cruel, arrogant, cowardly, dishonest, disloyal, and ungrateful. It is Othello's view of love, however, that is most relevant to understanding his intentions, his betrayal of love, and his self-deceiving evasions concerning that betrayal. How does he conceive of love? His conception is multifaceted, and each facet combines valid ideals with dangerous idealizations.

In sorting out Othello's self-deceiving combinations of ideals and idealizations, it is helpful to invoke Jean-Paul Sartre's suggestion that self-deceivers often rely on "two-faced" concepts that yoke together unreconciled extremes.[9] The extremes are both inviting and repelling. Troubled by ambivalences, self-deceivers oscillate between extremes in confused and contradictory ways, thereby managing to avoid honest confrontation with the varied, ambiguous, and troubling aspects of their lives. For example, everyone has freedom — "transcendence"—in some respects, and in other respects they are limited by fixed realities — "facticity"— although they are always free to change their attitudes concerning those realities. Self-deceivers, however, tend to alternate between seeing themselves as wholly free or wholly determined, according to when they want to accept credit or avoid responsibility. In doing so, they employ a contradictory concept: "transcendence-facticity."

In Sartre's famous illustration, a woman on a date shifts between thinking of herself and the man she is dating as pure "transcendence" (completely free personalities) and as pure "facticity" (completely determined by facts).[10] The woman is ambivalent about the man's sexual intentions and her own sexual interests, owing, no doubt, to sexist conventions that Sartre fails to mention. She wants to be appreciated as sexually exciting by the man she is dating, and yet her sexuality threatens her complete control and freedom. As a result she postpones any recognition of the man's sexual intentions. Caught up in a platonic conversation, she "fails to notice" that the man takes her hand. In doing so, she relies on a quick-switch: The instant she attends to herself or the man as physical beings (as facticity) she quickly switches to viewing them as free and mutually respective personalities (as transcendence); then, since that attitude removes the charm of the occasion, she quickly reverts back to attending to their physical being. Rather than sustaining an integrated and balanced attention, she relies on an unstable and incoherent concept of transcendence-facticity to avoid responsibility for confronting the distressful aspects of her situation.

Othello also thinks with confused concepts and ambivalent attitudes that combine two extremes, this time concerning the values defining erotic love. In each case his concepts and attitudes stand in sharp contrast to the more realistic views held by Desdemona and Emilia.

Caring and Selflessness-Selfishness

Othello tends to think of love as selfless altruism in sharp opposition to selfishness, that is, unjustified instances of self-seeking. In practice, however, his seemingly grand gestures of selflessness are mixed with self-interest in ways he cannot acknowledge because doing so would reveal that he falls short of the ideals he treasures. For example, he grants Desdemona's request to forgive Cassio's drunken misconduct: "I will deny thee nothing" (3.3.82). The concession comes as an indulgence, however, rather than a careful weighing of her arguments (as Desdemona immediately points out to him). Perhaps the abrupt concession, accompanied by a request to be left alone, indicates a suppressed irritation in having to deal with an assertive wife, thereby increasing his vulnerability to Iago's deceptions that commence immediately.

Othello's selflessness-selfishness duality overlooks how love blends the self-interest of two persons so as to transcend the distinction between selflessness and selfishness. Quite simply, to help one's partner is usually to help oneself and vice versa. At the same time, there are always conflicts and rough edges in which two distinct individuals assert their self-interests while being sensitive to their partner's needs. Love is an ambiguous wedding of two shared and sometimes conflicting self-interests. Desdemona embraces this more realistic view of love as calling for mutuality, fairness, and reasoned give and take, rather than complete selflessness. She wants to have her views weighed and considered, not selflessly conceded. The irony is that Othello becomes wholly selfish, and Desdemona, when left only with the option of judging or forgiving, chooses selfless forgiveness.

We admire Othello for the deep caring he initially shows toward Desdemona. The caring is shown in his kindness, gentleness, and concern for her comfort when he is called away to war. It is unmistakable in his joy when they reunite after the fighting. It is clear even when mixed with vanity, as when he uses her as a mirror in viewing himself (1.3.170). Yet Othello's caring is quickly replaced by selfish hatred the moment his self-respect is threatened by suspicions of adultery. At no time does he attempt to see things from Desdemona's point of view, much less to forgive her. This rapid transformation is facilitated by his lack of a realistic understanding that love is neither wholly selfless nor selfish but instead intermingles caring and self-interest.

Respect and Freedom-Fusion

In his first extended speech Othello proclaims his love for Desdemona, but he also seems preoccupied by his lost freedom as a bachelor.

> But that I love the gentle Desdemona,
> I would not my unhoused free condition

Put into circumscription and confine
For the sea's worth (1.2.25–28)

Shortly thereafter, he admirably aspires to be "free and bounteous to her mind," revealing sensitivity to how love requires mutual respect between two individuals, each of whom remains autonomous in voluntarily seeking a shared intimacy (1.3.268). So far, we have signs of the usual and healthy ambivalence about the "bonds of matrimony" that demand adjustments and compromises. As becomes clear, however, Othello does not genuinely recognize that demand. Instead, he thinks of love as a complete, all-or-nothing merging of identity with the beloved. Without his love for Desdemona he is destroyed as a coherent moral being: "And when I love thee not, / Chaos is come again" (3.3.99–100). This desire for fusion easily shifts into a demand for control.

The shift from fusion to ownership is sufficiently familiar to be embedded as an ambiguity in the language of love. Lovers exclaim they are "one" and "possessed" by each other. These words may express caring and shared identity, but they easily slide into meaning ownership. Thus, Othello thinks of Desdemona as his property, as "the thing" which he loves, after bemoaning the "curse of marriage, / That we can call these delicate creatures ours / And not their appetites" (3.3.284–286).[11] Even at the end, when he is forced to confront how he misjudged Desdemona, he thinks of her as a precious "pearl" that he has foolishly thrown away. The ambiguous metaphor of the pearl acknowledges Desdemona's exceptional value, but it is the value of an inanimate object with a material price, thus reminding us of Iago's cynical suggestion that women can be bought with jewels (5.2.357).[12]

Jealousy and Trust-Distrust

The willingness to trust one's partner is an especially important aspect of caring and respect. Usually it requires an effort to control jealousy. Othello naively suggests that love is incompatible with jealousy: "Away at once with love or jealousy" (3.3.206). He is deluded, of course, in priding himself on being invulnerable to jealousy, but he also fails to recognize that jealousy is not by itself a threat to love. As noted earlier, jealousy can support love by functioning as an emotional indicator of possible threats. But the capacity for jealousy also expresses our vulnerability to loss. To feel hurt, fear, and anger based on suspicions that our beloved's attentions are directed to someone else reminds us that we cannot force another person to love us. Othello's refusal to acknowledge his vulnerability to jealousy is the other side of his unwillingness to trust Desdemona, of his distrust of trust in love.

Once again Othello's attitudes emerge from a false and dangerous dichotomy. For him it must be all or nothing: wholly trust that Desdemona would never consider adultery (his view up until Iago deceives him) or assume she is prone to adultery and thereby guilty until proven innocent. As Frank Kermode points out, there can be no conclusive proof of fidelity, only of infidelity, and hence this polarization generates a permanent pattern of demanding proof.[13] Most couples accept that sexual temptation is always a possibility, with varying degrees of likelihood, and take reasonable precautions to minimize it. Othello's polarized way of thinking does not give him the conceptual resources to do so.

A related dichotomy is an all or nothing view of fidelity and faithfulness. Othello has a constricted understanding of faithfulness that essentially reduces it to complete sexual fidelity, at least on the part of wives, perhaps together with honesty. In his view, the violation of sexual fidelity transforms a wife into a whore. Like Shakespeare in another context, Othello thinks of faithfulness as a personal loyalty that makes possible "the marriage of true minds" despite the numerous impediments to love that couples must confront.[14] A more nuanced understanding of faithfulness, as a matter of degrees and aspects, might have prepared Othello to listen to and talk with Desdemona rather than self-righteously condemning her.

Sex and Purity-Perversion

Othello's ambivalence about sex parallels those described by Sartre. He thinks of (erotic and marital) love as transcending sexuality. That conception is admirable insofar as it manifests a refusal to reduce love to sex, especially when viewed in contrast with Iago's view that love is merely lust camouflaged by illusion. It is also understandable that he prides himself on having grown beyond the passions of youth, thereby assuring his employers that marital commitments will not interfere with martial duties (1.3.266–267). But Othello goes further, idealizing love as separate from rather than integrated with sex. In contrast with Desdemona's candid and healthy affirmations of sexual "rites," Othello seems threatened and provoked into defensive idealistic statements about love as transcending sex (1.3.260).

How are we to explain his ambivalence about sex? A common-sense reading is that Othello faces the insecurities expected in marrying a much younger woman, combined with the pressures on a black man marrying a white woman (in the sixteenth century). Stanley Cavell's more provocative reading traces Othello's sexual fears to his association of sex with blood, violence, and death.[15] Marianne Novy agrees but also points out how sex threatens Othello's obsession with self-control, a preoccupation not surprising in a military leader who also aspires to lead an unblemished personal life.[16] Whatever the explanation, his sexual insecurity is tied to another dichotomy: Desdemona must be completely pure or wholly perverted. There is no middle ground, no recognition of how sexuality generates desires in many directions that most people routinely struggle to unify, usually with imperfect results. Thinking in terms of this polarization intensifies his anxieties. At the first suspicion that Desdemona may have strayed on one occasion, she is suspected of being promiscuous and a prostitute.

Women and Deifying-Demonizing

The preceding dualities are all related. Each represents part of Othello's polarized view of women. As feminists have insightfully argued, Othello's view of women contains valuable elements that become distorted and split into idealization and degradation.[17] How else can we make sense of his astonishingly quick transformation from deifying Desdemona as saintly wife to demonizing her as a witch? Rather than saying there are two Othello's in the play, a loving husband juxtaposed with a murderous lunatic, we need to understand that there is one man with a radically divided view of women. Either a woman is saintly or she is corrupt, and his attitude toward a particular woman is unstable and subject to quick reversals.

Othello's conception of love, then, is a volatile and morally ambiguous mixture of admirable ideals and dangerous idealizations. This mixture partly explains why he so quickly resorts to violence and why he is unwilling to consider other options such as disciplining Cassio and chastising Desdemona. Considering other options would mean overthrowing his romantic idealizations. It would mean loving in an imperfect but realistic and virtue-structured way. It would mean seeing the incoherence of his wish that she keep breathing when she is dead so he will be able to love her after he kills her — with a restored, ideal love (5.2.19).

Turn now to the culminating dichotomy: What does Othello mean when he claims to have loved "not wisely but too well"? "But too well" might mean three things. One, the phrase might construed as unfolding and clarifying, rather than contrasting with, "not wisely." Taken one way, loving too well might mean loving effectively in a situation where doing so was inappropriate, perhaps because it harmed others or oneself. Analogously, we speak of being "all too honest" or "too generous" (to a fault), reflecting how virtues are context-bound and require that we find an Aristotelian mean, the reasonable middle ground on a continuum of too much and too little. This interpretation would be flattering to someone like Othello, who is proud of his ability to love and who is defending the genuineness of his love. It would amount to saying that he intended only love toward Desdemona but pursued the intention in excess within a situation where other virtues were called for, such as prudence and caution. In another regard, however, such a meaning would not be suitable, since Othello knows at this point that his love for Desdemona was fully appropriate and justified.

Two, taken another way, while still construing "but too well" as elaborating "not wisely," Othello might mean that his lack of wisdom (partly) consisted in loving with unreasonable and inordinate passion. Whereas the previous interpretation understood the lack of wisdom as concerning the context in which he loved, this one focuses on the desires constituting his love, such as the desire to achieve complete fusion with Desdemona. This reading fits nicely with his obsession for self-control. However, it treats him as rejecting his love as unreasonable, whereas in this context he is more likely to be affirming his love, at least at a conscious level.

Three, even if Othello unconsciously intends his words to resonate with the first two meanings, most likely he consciously intends to draw a contrast with "not wisely." In this interpretation, "but too well" means "and yet so very well," thereby affirming the genuineness, wholeheartedness, moral purity, and certainly the appropriateness of his love for Desdemona, while contrasting it with his unfortunate lack of wisdom about how to successfully act on it. The idea is that he cherished Desdemona so deeply that the thought of losing her to Cassio caused him to go berserk in a frenzy of jealousy. This meaning is consistent with his immediately following self-portrayal as "one not easily jealous" but merely unwise in becoming "wrought, / Perplexed in the extreme" (5.2.355–356).

Although this is the most plausible (and usual) interpretation, it renders his words patently false and self-deceiving.[18] For one thing, we know he is very easily made jealous by Iago's manipulations, and, judging from the rest of his life as a military leader, he is also capable of controlling his passions. For another thing, his claim to have loved wholeheartedly is outrageous. Desdemona may love too well in this sense, but not Othello. Most husbands manage not to murder their wives. Othello fails to love with even minimal decency.

Turn now to his claim to have loved "not wisely." Once again at least three interpretations are possible. One, to admit one's lack of wisdom is a conventional sign of intellectual humility, reflecting the Socratic insight that the first stage of wisdom is knowing one is ignorant. Could Othello perhaps be self-congratulatory in suggesting that he has achieved self-understanding? Not likely. He is filled with despair and self-loathing rather than a conscious effort to deceive his hearers. Nevertheless, I have already suggested that his final words extend his self-deception about betraying Desdemona and about his guilt. Alleging a lack of wisdom may be as much a self-deceiving excuse as a self-indictment.

Two, most plausibly Othello is acknowledging that he failed to love wisely by failing to exercise good judgment in appraising Desdemona's character as well as Iago's and Cassio's. He is also alluding to his poor judgment in assessing facts and evidence connected with his marriage—facts about the handkerchief, Desdemona's intentions in asking for forgiveness of Cassio, and the customs about adultery in Venetian society. He is alleging a lack of discernment in knowing that certain beliefs are justified and in exercising caution in making inferences from those beliefs. This evidence-centered or evidential wisdom is what he repeatedly ascribes to Iago and also what Iago (insincerely) urges him to exercise.

Three, Othello loves unwisely, however, in a much deeper way that he cannot acknowledge without also acknowledging his betrayal of Desdemona and their love. He lacks normative or evaluative wisdom, which consists in understanding and applying the values that give life meaning. It involves knowing how to live well—both morally and prudentially well—so as to maintain moral integrity, achieve self-fulfillment, and lead a worthwhile life.[19] Evaluative wisdom implies discernment about facts as well as breadth and depth of understanding, but most important it implies interpretation and integration of knowledge so as to form sound value judgments in particular situations.

What is evaluative wisdom concerning love? Primarily it is understanding what love is, including love's requirements, constituent values, and contributions to meaningful life. Evaluative wisdom is not an abstract understanding in terms of psychological or philosophical theories. Instead it is knowing how to care for the person we love and putting that knowledge into practice. It incorporates evidential wisdom by requiring a detailed knowledge of the needs and temperament of the beloved, but it integrates that knowledge within morally desirable forms of caring. As Martha C. Nussbaum writes, "The lover can be said to understand the beloved when, and only when, (s)he knows how to treat him or her: how to speak, look, and move at various times and in various circumstances; how to give pleasure and how to receive it; how to arouse desire and how to satisfy it; how to deal with the loved one's complex network of intellectual, emotional, and bodily needs."[20]

In addition to caring, love's more specific virtues also imply some minimum degree of wisdom. Wisdom is shown in knowing how to respect one's partner, including the (usually wide) areas in which they deserve to be trusted. Othello's absence of (evaluative) wisdom is manifested in his very obsession with evidence and proof about Desdemona's trustworthiness before he is willing to trust her in the way required by love. Moreover, knowing how to love implies knowing how to be honest (both truthful and trustworthy), how to be faithful by establishing mutual commitments and arrangements reasonably designed to protect love, how to find the courage to confront dangers to relationships, how to be fair in balancing benefits and burdens, how to show gratitude for love. Insofar as love is structured by these virtues, it is a way to value persons morally. Lovers see and know each other as irreplaceably dear and cherish each other accordingly. From this perspective, love is not blind but instead a profound way of seeing.[21] Given that it is a virtue-guided way to affirm the value that other persons have, love itself can be a form of wisdom.

Cannot love be genuine in the absence of the (evaluative) wisdom needed to make it flourish? Yes, but genuine love at least implies a sustained effort to achieve evaluative wisdom in loving — by finding a compatible partner, by keeping love alive, by exercising love's virtues, and by integrating the love into other aspects of life. Othello has the capacity to love wisely, but he fails to exercise the capacity in ways required for loving well. Hence, his lack of wisdom is not separable from loving well, in the way he alleges. He fails to love well precisely because he fails to achieve the requisite wisdom. At least in some measure, to love well is to love wisely.

9

COURAGE

Courage, which seemed at first to be something
on its own, a sort of specialized daring of the
spirit, is now seen to be a particular operation
of wisdom and love.

—*Iris Murdoch*[1]

The virtues of caring, respect, honesty, fairness, and faithfulness are internal to love, and they partly define what love is. By contrast, courage seems to be an enabling virtue that helps love flourish under difficult circumstances, but not a constitutive virtue that enters into the definition of love. As I argue in the first section, however, courage is sometimes a decisive manifestation of caring, as well as of faithfulness, honesty, and other virtues defining love. To that extent, courage is part of the meaning of love.

Courage also appears to be a simple and easily understood virtue: Dangers appear and courage consists in admirably confronting them. But matters are not so straightforward. Exactly which dangers call for courage and which responses count as "confronting" them courageously? The answers turn in part on practical wisdom exercised within particular contexts, in part on our responsibilities to others and in part on our personal aspirations, integrity, and ideals. I develop these ideas in the second section by discussing Janie Crawford's search for her "voice and vision" through love, in Zora Neale Hurston's novel *Their Eyes Were Watching God*.

149

COURAGE AS CARING

What is courage? As a virtue, it is a feature of persons: *Agents* are courageous to the extent they engage in courageous actions. *Actions* are courageous when agents have good reasons for believing the actions are substantially dangerous and also the means to achieving a significantly valuable goal. "Substantially" and "significantly" are vague terms, but they suffice to capture the paradigmatic cases of courage, in terms of which less clear-cut cases need to be understood. As with most important concepts, it is impossible to state precise, necessary, and sufficient conditions for courage.

With minor disagreements, I adopt the above definitions from Douglas N. Walton, who says that "a courageous action is one in which, based on the good intentions of the agent in attempting to realize a worthy goal, he or she overcomes great danger or difficulty — whether afraid or not."[2] One disagreement is that the adjective "great" seems to make this a definition of exceptional courage, whereas I would emphasize that courage comes in many degrees. A second disagreement is that Walton's definition applies to confronting formidable difficulties without danger being involved,[3] whereas I would describe those confrontations as strength, determination, or perseverence but not courage. The disagreement is minor, however, because formidable difficulties tend to pose dangers — namely, the dangers of losing valuable goods, perhaps through emotional or physical collapse — and hence difficulties often call for courage as well as determination. Also, Walton's definition says the danger must actually be "overcome," whereas in my view courage can also be shown in unsuccessful attempts to overcome dangers.

Both Walton's and my definitions recognize that actions can be courageous even when they turn out to be neither dangerous nor a means to a valuable goal, as long as the person reasonably believes they are. To be sure, we tend to admire courage more when it is based on accurate assessments of dangers, goods to be achieved, and the means necessary for achieving the goods. The most admirable courage embodies good judgment and wisdom. Nevertheless, a person might manifest courage in trying to save someone, even though in fact the apparent victim was not drowning and there was no serious risk to the would-be rescuer. At the same time, the person must have some good reason for believing that valuable goods are at stake. Otherwise the action is simply foolish and rash, such as when teenagers "play chicken" by driving recklessly. In this way, all courage embodies some degree of reasonable judgment and wisdom about the goals and means to those goals.

Note that courage is defined in terms of confronting dangers, where dangers are liabilities of harm to ourselves or others. It is not defined in terms of fearlessness, that is, the mere absence of fear. Fear may or may not be experienced, and fearlessness may reveal foolhardiness or naiveté rather than courage. Whatever their emotional state at the time, individuals are courageous because of their skillful conduct in response to perceived danger. Of course, fear itself can be a danger, especially when it threatens to cause panic or paralysis, unless we react to it with courage. In Franklin D. Roosevelt's memorable phrase, sometimes we have nothing to fear but fear itself, although only Roosevelt's courageous hyperbole as a leader could have led him to describe World War II as such a situation.

Different types of courage correspond to different kinds of dangers. Physical courage confronts dangers to life, limb, or health. Social courage confronts hazards from society, such as social disapproval or economic penalties. Intellectual courage is acting on one's convictions when faced with perils that threaten to undermine intellectual integrity. Moral courage is acting on moral principles, including principles of self-respect and integrity, in the presence of dangers that threaten moral integrity. Love may require all types of courage.

What are the primary dangers in love? They include the major risks confronting two people separately combined with a host of new risks generated by love itself. Perhaps it is no coincidence that the word "passion" originally meant suffering and only later came to mean strong sexual desire. In creating interdependencies, love makes us vulnerable to a multitude of emotional, physical, intellectual, economic, and social risks. The following categories sample only a few of these risks.

Reciprocity risks concern the danger that our love will not be returned, or at least not returned in the way we hoped for or need. Erotic love is not wholly selfless and almost always embodies a fervent desire to be loved back, to be valued in return by the person we value as singularly important. Hence the agony of unrequited love and the devastation from losing love once it has been granted. Associated liabilities include jealousy, doubt, fear, anger, and anxiety about whether we are loved in the way we want to be.

Commitment risks center on the danger that our commitments to love may not prove beneficial to ourselves and to the person we love. They include dangers that we will not be able to keep the commitments we make, thereby causing harm to the beloved. Failed commitments also generate painful emotions of guilt and shame (whether warranted or not). Love is an act of faith and hope—in the beloved, in ourselves, and in the world whose contingencies can support or threaten relationships. It can be frustrated by our own failures to summon the necessary strength and integrity or by bad luck.

Empathy risks refer to the suffering we feel when our partner is harmed. In love the good of two individuals is interwoven so that typically when something bad happens to one partner, it happens to both. Moreover, the deeper our caring and the greater the bad experience, the deeper the suffering to which we are vulnerable. Empathy risks include, in Annette Baier's words, "paralyzing grief or reckless despair at the loss or death of loved ones, retreat into a sort of psychic hibernation when cut off from 'news' of them, crippling anxiety when they are in danger, helpless anguish when they are in pain."[4]

Dependency risks arise from emotional, economic, and other forms of dependence. Baier also draws attention to these risks, including "the danger of overprotection, of suffocation, of loss of independence, toughness and self-reliance."[5] Through love, two persons forge a new, shared identity, but the identity can be confining rather than expansive. At its worst, love is distorted into wife battering, marital rape, and many more subtle forms of spouse abuse. There is also the emotional trauma in "co-dependent" relationships with a spouse who is an alcoholic or drug abuser.[6]

External risks are threats to the relationship from outside. They include religious, racial, or cultural prohibitions, financial obstacles, hostile relatives, and threats to the educations and careers that provide necessary resources for relationships. Many of these risks are unforeseeable, especially when relationships endure for decades.

Others are obvious and perhaps eagerly embraced: The forbidden can be an aphrodisiac that also satisfies desires for rebellion and radical change, familiar accompaniments of erotic love.

Third-party risks arise from the possibility of harm to persons a couple cares for. Most important is harm to children caused through poor parenting, traumatic divorce, and tragic accidents. There are also threats to friendships, professional relationships, or family relationships that may become difficult to maintain after new loves, whether because of limited time or personality conflicts.

Taken together, these dangers explain some of our ambivalence about love. Love is bittersweet or "sweetbitter" as Sappho wrote:

> Eros once again limb-loosener whirls me
> sweetbitter, impossible to fight off, creature stealing up.[7]

Indeed, sometimes the risks become so extreme that we must wrench ourselves away from the beloved, whether for our sake, for the sake of the beloved, or in order to respect already established valuable relationships. Other times love is well worth the risks. As with life itself, love "shrinks or expands in proportion to one's courage."[8]

This brings me to my first main thesis: Courage not only furthers but also partly constitutes love insofar as courage is a decisive sign of caring. Very often, courage is required by, embodies, and manifests deep caring and commitment. That explains why so many legends celebrate lovers who are willing to undergo great risk on behalf of the person they love: Paris and Helen, Abelard and Heloise, Tristan and Isolde, Guinevere and Lancelot, Romeo and Juliet. In all these legends, the primary test for commitment, caring, and faithfulness is the willingness to take risks. This willingness is a test for love itself, not just a promising indicator for successful marriage and parenting. Indeed, in the courtly romances, there is no prospect for marriage, since the beloved is already married or otherwise forbidden. As a decisive indication of deep caring, courage is internal to love.

Legends about premarital feats are one thing; the demands of marriage are something else. Elisabeth and Paul Glaser provide a remarkable example. In 1981, during the cesarean delivery of their first child, Ariel, Elizabeth Glaser needed a blood transfusion. Four years later, Ariel began to experience unusual symptoms that after months of testing were diagnosed as caused by AIDS. During the cesarian delivery Elizabeth had received HIV-contaminated blood, and the virus was passed to Ariel during breast-feeding. To compound the tragedy, their second child, Jake, was infected in utero with the AIDS virus.

For the next three years the Glasers tried to save Ariel and also to give her as normal a life as possible. They suffered with her through repeated medical procedures and recurring pain, knowing the odds against them. They coped with social isolation as terrified friends would no longer allow their children to play with Ariel. And they struggled to maintain their privacy in order to keep their children in school at a time when other parents were pressuring school officials to expel children with AIDS. The privacy issue faced by all AIDS victims was compounded by Paul Glaser's celebrity status because of his starring role (as Starsky) in the television show "Starsky and Hutch."

Ariel died in 1988. Shortly thereafter, the tabloids' intrusiveness forced the Glasers to go public with their story. In writing about their ordeal, Elizabeth Glaser wrote, "My life is not a lesson about AIDS; my life is a lesson about love."[9] The same could be said of her husband. Their courage expressed, embodied, and partly constituted their love. It enabled them to hold together during a crisis, both as a couple and as individuals.

There are distinctive styles of courage, different ways of admirably confronting dangers. Paul Glaser relied on his buoyant humor and his ability to throw himself into work, although later he also gave talks and testified at congressional hearings on AIDS. Earlier, Elizabeth Glaser became a social activist. Using whatever time she had left after caring for Ariel, she crusaded for increased funding for pediatric AIDS research. She told her story to politicians, including then president Ronald Reagan, who listened sympathetically but did nothing. She also created and raised funds for a private foundation for AIDS research, remaining actively engaged until her own death from AIDS in 1995.

The Glasers illustrate how courage is especially admirable when it embodies caring. In general, courage is admirable according to the degree of caring and commitment shown in overcoming obstacles and dangers, as well as according to its good results. As Douglas

Walton writes in another context, "the depth of that commitment [to the intended good] is indicated by the time, effort, ingenuity, and sacrifice the agent is willing to put into the carrying out of his good intention."[10] More fully, we admire courage for four reasons: (1) the good intention acted upon; (2) the goodness of the actual results; (3) the degree of commitment to the intended good; and (4) additional virtues revealed in that commitment, such as wisdom, intelligence, self-control, self-sacrifice, honesty, personal integrity, patience, perseverence, faith, and hope.

The fourth reason deserves special comment. As I have emphasized, virtues are interconnected within a complex tapestry, and this is especially true of courage. For example, honesty may require enormous courage in confronting problems whose solution is essential for the marriage to survive. Again, in addition to being guided by wisdom, courage can be needed to achieve the wisdom in solving problems. As a fuller illustration consider hope, which, as we saw with the Glasers, typically accompanies courage. Hope is an active attitude rather than a passive feeling. It means desiring something that is believed to be both desirable and possible, although not certain, together with the readiness to act on that desire.[11] As a virtue, hope is the tendency to have and to act on justified attitudes about what is worthwhile and reasonable beliefs about what is possible. Courage requires hope: We will not courageously pursue a goal unless we desire it as well as believe it is desirable and possible. In particular, we will not courageously pursue a love unless we hope that a valuable relationship can be established. At the same time, it may take courage to maintain hope in the first place. The chances of achieving a desirable goal, such as finding or maintaining a valuable love, may seem so slight that courage is needed to sustain the active desire to seek tha goal.

I have argued that courage partly constitutes love when it embodies caring and other constitutive virtues in love. But consider an objection raised by Alasdair MacIntyre. Isn't it possible to care even though we lack the courage to confront dangers to the person we care for? MacIntyre agrees that courage is a virtue because of its role in caring, but he contends that caring does not imply courage in confronting risks to people we care for. If someone says that he cares for some individual, community, or cause,

but is unwilling to risk harm or danger on his, her or its own behalf, he puts in question the genuineness of his care and concern. Courage, the capacity to risk harm or danger to oneself,
has its role in human life because of this connection with care
and concern. This is not to say that a man cannot genuinely
care and also be a coward. It is in part to say that a man who
genuinely cares and has not the capacity for risking harm or
danger has to define himself, both to himself and to others, as a
coward.[12]

In MacIntyre's view, the lack of courage calls into question the genuineness of caring, but the question can be answered. Persons who
lack a capacity for courage can genuinely care as long as they are
willing to admit they are cowards.

This view needs to be modified. Of course, if individuals literally
lack a "capacity" for courage in the sense of being physically or psychologically unable to act courageously, then they can care without
being courageous. But in that case it is not clear they are cowards.
Cowardice implies blameworthiness for failing to act appropriately,
and we are not blameworthy for what is impossible to do. Lack of
courage does not entail cowardice. If, however, we are able to act
courageously but (voluntarily) fail to do so, there is a presumption
that our caring was not as deep as it might have been.

Perhaps my disagreement with MacIntyre turns partly on the
word "genuine," which in this context seems to mean all or nothing
(authentic versus fake). But caring is not all or nothing; it has degrees. Let us grant MacIntyre that some degree of caring can be
shown in the absence of courage. Strong or deep caring, however,
does imply the courageous willingness to confront threats to what we
care about. In this way, courage enters into the meaning of caring,
and courage enters into the meaning of love.

VOICE AND VISION

Courage appears to be a simple and straightforward virtue: A danger is perceived and courage means confronting it. Admittedly,
courage may be difficult to summon, but that is a practical, psycho-

logical difficulty concerning self-control, firm resolve, and steadiness under pressure. Whatever practical difficulties in mustering courage, there seems little difficulty in understanding what courage means, whether in love or elsewhere.

This appearance of simplicity is an illusion. It is caused by restricting attention to situations that require one obvious response: the soldier attacks rather than flees; the rescuer helps rather than walks away; the dissident speaks up against abuses rather than remains silent. Even in these cases, however, it is only after courage is exercised that the precise course of conduct seems obviously the correct one. The nuances in how the soldier attacks, how the rescuer proceeds, and how the dissident speaks up are often what matter most.

Moreover, exactly when do dangers call for us to "confront" them rather than to avoid or bypass them? Each moment we are surrounded by actual and potential dangers, most of which do not "confront" us for the simple reason that we avoid endeavors that would make us directly vulnerable to them. (I avoid hang gliding, driving on the wrong side of the road, and drinking Clorox.) Moreover, even when it is evident that we must directly confront a danger, how do we know when the appropriate response is courage rather than prudent withdrawal? (Discretion is the better part of valor.) Which results are worth courageous risk-taking? Which actions will best surmount ambiguous dangers whose severity is unclear or unknowable?

Wisdom and good judgment enable us to answer these questions. Wisdom is not an abstract understanding of universal truths. Instead, it is a contextual response in which we have skill in achieving good ends by exercising nuanced sensitivity to exigencies, others' needs, and our own commitments and ideals, including those of love. In part, our commitments and ideals define the harms to which we are vulnerable and hence define what counts as courage. We cannot assume that the courageous action is the one that surmounts the greatest dangers to which we are exposed, if only because there may be equal dangers in several directions.

In particular, a person might be courageous in either staying with or leaving a marriage. As Erica Jong points out, "being miserable in your marriage for another year and *another* year and *another* year is a *big* risk too — only you don't *see* the risk. The risk is your life. Wasting it, I mean. It's a pretty big risk."[13] Staying with a marriage can be courageous caring or foolish self-denigration. To complicate matters further, the same action can be courageous or not depending on an individual's personality, aversion to risks, and personal evaluation of the goal to be achieved. Asking someone for a date can be a routine act for one person but a courageous act for someone else.

These personal dimensions of courage, especially as they concern authenticity in pursuing love ideals, are explored by Zora Neale Hurston in *Their Eyes Were Watching God*. The novel's protagonist is Janie Crawford, an intelligent although uneducated black woman, who engages in a search, through love, to find her own "voice and vision" (11).[14] In telling her story to her friend Pheoby, Janie invites us to judge her love, "to look into me loving Tea Cake and see whether it was done right or not!" (6). Stated in my terms, Janie invites us to assess whether her relationship with Tea Cake embodied love's virtues — caring and courage, respect and self-respect, faithfulness and sexual fidelity, honesty and fairness, gratitude and morally creative wisdom.

As an adolescent, Janie felt a sense of mystery about erotic love, a mystery symbolized in the image of a blossoming pear tree being pollinated by bees. Later, in talking to her friend Pheoby, she uses a contrasting image of her life as "a great tree in leaf with the things suffered, things enjoyed, things done and undone" (8). The shift in images reflects her growth throughout three marriages. The first marriage with Logan Killicks is coerced and proves disastrous; the second marriage with Joe Starks is chosen under duress and proves exploitive; the third is autonomously chosen and becomes the fulfilling relationship with Tea Cake.

Janie is raised in Florida by her grandmother, a former slave who believes that the best a woman can hope for is to be cared for by a wealthy man. As for romantic love, "Dat's de very prong all us black women gits hung on" (22). When the grandmother sees sixteen-year-old Janie kiss a boyfriend, she immediately arranges her marriage to Logan Killicks, a prosperous local landowner. Janie finds Killicks physically repugnant, but she submits to the marriage (after being slapped hard by her grandmother) with a naive expectation that marriage will magically generate love. Soon her repulsion deepens as she discovers that the marriage lacks all intimacy and that she is little more than a mule working for Killicks. She runs away with Joe Starks, a passing stranger who speaks confidently of developing an all-black town in southern Florida where he will become "a big voice" (27).

Is leaving her first marriage an act of cowardly flight or courageous confrontation? Would she have shown greater courage in trying to work things out with Killicks? In fact she did try. While agonizing over whether to leave, she asked Killicks what her leaving would mean to him. He reacted with hurt pride and a desperate effort to control her. At that point, when caring for Killicks became impossible and when her self-respect was placed in jeopardy, her only reasonable hope for happiness was with Starks who "spoke for change and chance" (28). Her ideals and needs, understood in light of her situation, enter into our assessment of her choice as courageous rather than cowardly.

Unlike Killicks, Starks has many attractive qualities. Janie takes pride in his appearance and his power as an entrepreneur to organize and become the first mayor of the all-black town of Eatonville. Almost immediately, however, he begins to dominate her. He forces her to work in his store, demands that she tie up her hair with a rag to appease his jealousy over how men look at her, and makes her "class off" by not socializing with their poorer neighbers. Worst of all, he silences her voice in public. In his view, women can't think for themselves (67), and Janie should be content to bask in his glory as "Mrs. Mayor Starks" (43). The tensions in their marriage finally erupt when Starks slaps her for failing to cook a satisfactory dinner. After seven years of Starks's dominance, it is clear to Janie that the marriage is doomed.

Does courage require leaving Starks, as it required leaving Killicks? The answer must take into account her situation. This time there is no better place to go, and running off would be foolish rather than courageous. Instead of fleeing, Jamie survives by living in a private world of thought and feeling: "She had an inside and an outside now and suddenly she knew how not to mix them" (68). Is this turning inward a courageous compromise, given her circumstances, or a cowardly failure to assert herself by challenging Starks's authority? Given her strength, it seems clear she could have shown greater courage, and hence she is responsible for at least some of her suffering during the second decade of her marriage.[15]

The aging Starks grows increasingly critical of Janie. One day, projecting his insecurities onto her, he ignites a round of derisive laughter in the store by making a derogatory comment about her figure. Janie defends herself with a stinging repartee about Starks's physical unmanliness (74). In Starks's eyes, this public humiliation is tantamount to emasculation. He severs all ties with Janie, isolates himself, and fails to attend to his serious kidney ailment. Only on his deathbed does Janie force him to confront how he had "squeezed and crowded out" her mind (82).

Was this deathbed confrontation an act of courage or cruelty? The answer depends in part on Janie's motives and intentions. She was not being vindictive, and she had every right to assert her self-respect with "firm determination" to a husband who for twenty years bullied her. But the answer turns also on the moral ambiguity surrounding her earlier failures to show greater courage in confronting Starks. In my view, the confrontation is morally ambiguous.

When Janie inherits Starks's substantial fortune she is freed at age forty to live independently for the first time. She finds the courage to be honest with herself, to acknowledge the emotions she had kept submerged, including hatred toward her grandmother who had "twisted her so in the name of love" (85). We would admire Janie more if her hatred were mixed with compassion, as perhaps it is later. Nevertheless, acknowledging her anger about being oppressed by people who loved her is an important and courageous step in refinding her own voice and vision.

Janie has no intention to remarry, but before long Vergible ("Tea Cake") Woods enters the store and gets her laughing, something she had not done for years. He is fifteen years younger, charming and handsome, but also poor and a drifter—a perfect profile for a con artist seeking her money. Nevertheless she falls deeply in love for the first time in her life. The romance is joyous, replete with whimsical moments of midnight fishing and commonplace pleasures of playing checkers, a game that Starks had said she was too stupid to learn. She feels as if she has known Tea Cake all her life, and they agree to marry (94).

This time she enters marriage with her eyes wide open, fully aware of the risks. Marriage "always changes folks, and sometimes it brings out dirt and meanness dat even de person didn't know they had in 'em theyselves" (108). Her friends caution against the relationship, but Janie persists. She also takes precautions, however, by carrying two hundred dollars as emergency money that she conceals from Tea Cake. Confirming her worst fears, Tea Cake discovers the money and loses most of it gambling before he returns a day later. His excuse, although hardly a justification, is a humble acknowledgement that he never had the chance to impress his friends with big money.

Janie indulges Tea Cake's other flaws. Perhaps the worst is revealed after they resettle in the Everglades—he hits her. "He just slapped her around a bit to show he was boss" (140). To be sure, there are mitigating circumstances. The "showing" was aimed less at Janie than at the local community that praised such behavior, and it was an isolated act. Janie understood that the slap relieved an "awful fear inside him" about his masculinity at a time when another man had expressed a sexual interest in her. Tea Cake overheard the man criticizing him during a conversation with Janie in which Janie failed to vigorously defend Tea Cake. Moreover, the slap is unlike other episodes in the novel in which woman battering is used to silence and subdue, including occasions when Nanny and Starks hit Janie. Finally, reciprocity plays a role: Earlier Janie had hit Tea Cake in a fit of jealousy over a woman whom she believed Tea Cake was attracted to. Taken together, do these circumstances excuse Janie for acquiescing, or is she guilty of cowardice?[16] If the answer is not altogether clear, we are again reminded of the highly personal dimension of courage that depends in part on personal ideals and perceptions of danger.

Despite his flaws, Tea Cake shares a "self-crushing love" with Janie that makes it possible for her to be herself: "Her soul crawled out from its hiding place" (122). She participates as an equal in the relationship and within the Everglades community. At his invitation, she voluntarily chooses to work alongside him in the fields. She also learns to shoot, hunt, and engage in other activities traditionally reserved for males. When their life together ends, the cause is from outside, not from anything internal to their love.

In fleeing from a deadly hurricane, they protect each another as best they can until they become separated in the churning floodwater. Janie escapes drowning by holding on to the tail of a swimming cow, on top of which rides a rabid dog. Tea Cake rescues Janie but he is bitten by the dog, and within a month he is dying from rabies. Berserk and hallucinating, he tries to shoot Janie. Janie shoots back and kills him in a spontaneous act of self-defense.[17] The town puts her on trial for murder. Despairing but driven by the fear that her love for Tea Cake was being misunderstood, she convinces a jury that she could not possibly have killed Tea Cake in malice.

The novel ends with a return to the conversation between Janie and Pheoby. Janie is at peace with her memories of Tea Cake, who remains with her as a ghostly but palpable presence (184). She offers Pheoby two final reflections on love. First, every love is unique in some ways, precisely because it involves two persons creatively adjusting to each other: "Love ain't somethin' lak uh grindstone dat's de same thing everywhere and do de same thing tuh everything it touch. Love is lak de sea. It's uh movin' thing, but still and all, it takes its shape from de shore it meets, and it's different with every shore" (182).

Second, everyone must do two things for themselves: "They got tuh go tuh God, and they got tuh find out about livin' fuh theyselves" (183). In terms of the novel, God represents fate, which love must accept, rather than a personal deity. God is the hurricane whose power over life and death is absolute and arbitrary and could only be observed by its potential victims who watch the hurricane approach: "They seemed to be staring at the dark, but their eyes were watching God" (151). After the hurricane took its death toll, Janie comments that "luck is uh fortune" (165). Later, after learning of Tea Cake's disease, Janie only asks questions of God, without pleading with him. She accepts that God cannot make the world perfect: "God would do less than He had in His heart" (169).

In the end, did Janie courageously find her voice and vision, or did she rely too much on Tea Cake to shape her identity? If we find Janie too eager to attune her voice to his, we may temper our ascription of courage.[18] If instead, we see her accommodations as acts of caring that are compatible with self-respect, we will admire her as a convincing hero.[19] Either way, we understand her courage in terms of both her ideals of love and our own.

To turn from fiction to biography, Hurston wrote the novel at a time when she was in love with a man who combined the qualities of Starks and Tea Cake.[20] Most of the emotions in the novel were autobiographical, including the overwhelming passion, the sense of belonging together, and the jealousy. Unlike Janie and Tea Cake, however, Hurston and her lover were well educated professionals struggling to balance two careers. Her lover wanted Hurston to abandon her career as an anthropologist and author. She writes, "I really wanted to do anything he wanted me to do, but that one thing I could not do. . . . I had things clawing inside of me that must be said."[21] They were unable to work things out—he would not compromise any more than Starks would. Janie's killing of Tea Cake in self-defense foreshadowed Hurston's own separation from the person she most loved during her life. At the same time, Janie's loving memories of Tea Cake parallel the love Hurston sustained following the breakup of her love affair. For both, love "seems to be the unknown country from which no traveler ever returns," that is, returns the same as when she enters.[22] Hence the promise—and peril—of love.

Courage seems the most public of virtues, the subject of social admiration and awards. I have argued that it is also a personal virtue whose requirements depend on individual ideals and commitments within intimate relationships. In both roles, courage can be a decisive indicator of deep caring and commitment. As such, it enters into the understanding of what love is.

10
GRATITUDE

> But above all, above respect and esteem, there was
> a motive within her of good will which could not
> be overlooked. It was gratitude. —Gratitude, not
> merely for [his] having once loved her, but for
> loving her still.
>
> —*Jane Austen*[1]

Gratitude enters into love in complicated ways. On the one hand, we would be deeply hurt to learn that our lover or spouse cared for us primarily because of gratitude for the benefits we provide.[2] That is because we want to be loved for who we are, rather than merely for things we have to offer. On the other hand, we would be equally hurt by our partner's ingratitude toward us. We need to be appreciated, especially by people we love. In addition, our indignation at ingratitude suggests there are obligations of gratitude. Yet we are keenly sensitive to how appeals to these obligations, whether explicitly or implicitly, can be used to manipulate us.

Gratitude is an enabling virtue, one that sustains love between partners who cherish their shared history and identity. It is also a constitutive virtue that partly defines love as a relationship based on mutuality and reciprocity. Given its intimate connection with joy, gratitude is one of love's crowning virtues. At the same time, gratitude blends joy with responsibility, much like love itself. In the opening section, I explore this union of joy and obligation, delight and duty, in the course of clarifying what gratitude is. In the following section I turn to how love merges into a wider appreciation of a

164

shared life, drawing on Alice Walker's conception of love as appreciation in *The Color Purple*.

OBLIGATION AND JOY

Most traditional discussions of gratitude are restricted to three topics: duties of children to their parents, duties of citizens to their countries, and duties of humans to God.[3] For example, probably the majority of philosophical discussions have been inspired by Socrates' argument in the *Crito* that he should not flee punishment, even unjust punishment, because there is an obligation of gratitude to obey the laws, an obligation that he compares to the duty to honor one's parents. Notice that these topics center around authority relationships involving unequal power. Each also concerns duties attached to roles, the roles of family members, citizens, or "children of God." This narrow focus on role-attached duties and attitudes toward authority constricts our understanding of gratitude. It neglects, or rather distorts, how the virtue of gratitude supports love and friendship within reciprocal relationships between equals.

For example, only a preoccupation with authority relationships could have led Kant to disparage gratitude among adults: "If I accept favours, I contract debts which I can never repay, for I can never get on equal terms with him who has conferred the favours upon me; . . . if I do him a favour I am only returning a *quid pro quo;* I shall always owe him a debt of gratitude, and who will accept such a debt? For to be indebted is to be subject to unending constraint."[4] Kant's quid pro quo approach distorts both gratitude and love, each of which involves pleasurable appreciation more than onerous duties to reciprocate. Moreover, in ongoing personal relationships there is always the possibility of initiating new gifts so that one partner is not eternally indebted for the initial gift. Most important, gratitude within love is a positive, reinforcing motive for caring, not a constraint that unbalances relationships.

Recently, several philosophers have discussed gratitude among equals, in particular among friends. Their accounts provide a helpful starting point for thinking about gratitude in love, albeit with one qualification. Most of these accounts focus on isolated acts of gift-giving, whereas in love (and deep friendships) what matters most are ongoing cycles of mutual giving within long-term relationships.

As a virtue, gratitude is the disposition to have and express emotions and attitudes of gratefulness, in desirable ways and on appropriate occasions. As an expression of emotions and attitudes, gratefulness is defined in terms of three characteristic objects: what we respond to with gratitude; responses to the objects; and reasons for the responses.[5] First, we are grateful *to* persons *for* gifts they provide us with (or provide to people, animals, or causes we care for). Thus, in one sense the object of gratitude is the person or persons who provide a benefit. (Occasionally there is no donor, as when a person feels grateful for winning the lottery). In another sense the object is a gift, where a gift is an unearned benefit or intended benefit that was provided voluntarily and intentionally. In love, the most important unearned good is love itself. Second, the response to the benefit is welcoming or pleasure combined with a desire to make a return, if only a thank you, by way of showing one's appreciation. Third, the reason for the desire to make a return is goodwill toward the donor.

As this three-part definition makes clear, gratitude is primarily a matter of desires and attitudes, not obligations. Nevertheless, there are obligations or "debts" of gratitude, and we should take account of them before returning to gratitude as a virtue.[6] Roughly speaking, an obligation is created when we accept a benefit offered by someone who acts voluntarily, intentionally, and without trying to manipulate us. Precisely why this principle of obligation is justified is a question for ethical theory.[7] I believe that gratitude generates very basic obligations, but ones that can be grounded in all major ethical theories. Indeed, any ethical theory that failed to make room for obligations of gratitude would on that ground alone be seriously flawed. For example, utilitarians highlight how showing gratitude contributes to social ties, civility, and other good consequences. And duty ethicists (like Immanuel Kant) argue that gratitude is an aspect of showing respect for persons by recognizing their good intentions in helping us.

Exactly what is owed by way of gratitude? It is impossible to say in the abstract. Appropriate ways of showing gratitude are a function of many factors: social customs about showing appreciation, the needs of individuals to whom the gratitude is owed, our personal resources, and our personality and tastes. Even with regard to specific contexts, rules may not specify what is owed. In particular, we do not always owe the same or an equal benefit. The demand for equality reduces gratitude to tit-for-tat exchanges. Morever, equal returns may be impossible, if only because our benefactor dies before we have an opportunity to reciprocate. Terrance McConnell suggests that we owe a "commensurate benefit," provided on occasions suitable in terms of the needs of the person to whom gratitude is owed, and provided willingly and because we previously received a benefit from the giver.[8] If "commensurate" means comparable in value, however, this condition will not do. For example, even as adults most of us can never return to our parents anything comparable to the loving care we received from them. If "commensurate" means appropriate or fitting, then we have an accurate account, but the problem of vagueness returns. Appropriate ways of meeting obligations of gratitude are matters of good judgment, sensitivity, and sometimes creativity, but not precise rules.

Is there perhaps an obligation to *feel* grateful, as well as to show gratitude? It would seem not. "Ought implies can": Obligations imply opportunity and freedom to meet them. Gratitude, however, is an emotion, and emotions are not under our direct voluntary control. Nevertheless, we do have some control. For one thing, gratitude is an attitude as well as an emotion, and we have some control over our attitudes through rational reflection and through the experiences we seek or avoid. For another thing, since attitudes influence emotions, the control over our attitudes provides some indirect control over our emotions. Of course, we cannot create attitudes at will. When gratefulness does not arise spontaneously in appropriate circumstances, it may be evoked by reflecting on the caring expressed in a gift, the sacrifice involved in making it, and the importance to us of both the caring and the gift. In short, it is coherent to speak of obligations to be grateful as well as to show gratitude. As Roslyn Weiss concludes, when gratitude does not come spontaneously there is a "duty to 'cultivate' the grateful attitude under appropriate circumstances."[9] This duty, I would emphasize, is prima facie: It can be overridden by other more pressing obligations in particular situations.

If we can intelligibly speak of obligations of gratitude, what role do those obligations play in love? Lovers and spouses are continually providing each other with "unearned benefits" motivated by caring—at least in part, remembering that in love caring and self-interest are inextricably interwoven. Love itself is the greatest unearned benefit. One aspect of cherishing the beloved is feeling and expressing gratefulness for his or her love, as well as for all the other unearned benefits the love makes possible. Nevertheless, spouses often lapse into taking each other for granted. When that happens, and when gratitude remains appropriate, there is an obligation to cultivate the attitude and expression of gratitude.

In this way, obligations provide backup motives that contribute to reciprocal caring and ongoing cycles of mutual helping and giving. For the most part, however, these feelings of obligations of gratitude play a minor role in love, especially feelings of onerous duties. Even expressions of gratitude are typically joined with expressions of the wider, caring, defining love. Obligations of gratitude tend to surface when love has gone awry. With this in mind, we might say the important obligation in love is *not* to be *un*grateful, not to be guilty of *in*gratitude.

For example, Samuel Taylor Coleridge failed to meet this obligation.[10] His marriage to Sara Fricker was loving and happy for a number of years until his opium addiction began to wreak havoc. A vicious cycle ensued. In addition to its harm to him, Coleridge began to blame Sara—"blame the victim"—for the problems caused by his addiction. As Sara responded with quite justifiable resentment, additional marital problems followed, which Coleridge in turn used to rationalize his continued use of opium. With extraordinary self-deception, he charged Sara with ingratitude for failing to appreciate what he gave her. Taking advantage of his reputation as a major literary figure, he successfully promulgated the view that Sara was callous and unsuited to him, a distortion that took historians nearly two centuries to overturn.

As this example illustrates, wholesale ingratitude not only violates specific obligations of gratitude, but it betrays one's spouse and betrays love. The example also illustrates how a partner's ingratitude can justify withholding one's own gratitude. Sara would have been fully warranted in refusing to allow gratitude to be abused by Samuel when he used it as a manipulative device for getting her to feel guilt and to bend to his wishes. Gratitude can be misplaced and harmful.[11] Most abuses of gratitude occur within power imbalances that threaten reciprocity between equals, whether within authority relationships or within marriages. Of course, many traditional marriages involve patriarchal authority relationships. That makes it easy for a manipulative husband with superior power to demand gratitude in order to arouse guilt and to sustain an image of being unappreciated, one of many emotional ruses in maintaining dominance.

Having noted the extent and limits of obligations of gratitude in love, I reemphasize that obligations are secondary. In love, friendship, and other caring relationships, gratefulness should be an appreciative response of delight, not a felt burden. This "should" refers to a desirable ideal, not to a further obligation. As a virtue, gratitude embodies desirable emotions and attitudes that are not reducible to obligations.[12]

Why are emotions and attitudes of gratitude desirable, beyond their roles in meeting obligations? Part of the answer is that gratitude is a crucial aspect of respecting persons.[13] To feel (appropriate) gratitude is to recognize the benevolence of the person who helps and cares for us. It shows we do not view the person as a mere means to getting things for ourselves. In addition, expressing gratitude is important because it reciprocates the giver's respect and caring for us, thereby maintaining ties of mutual respect.

Of course, far more than mutual respect is involved in love (and friendship). Gratefulness for the love received from one's partner is an essential aspect of caring for the other, singling him or her out as having special importance in one's life. We acknowledge that love is the most important gift a partner bestows on us, and to be indifferent or blind to it is to devalue the partner. It amounts to disloyalty as well as dishonesty. And it undermines one of the essential contributions of gratitude to successful love: a spirit of overlooking or forgiving a partner's peccadilloes, the very opposite of Samuel blaming Sara for his own faults.

Perhaps most important, joy is the primary contribution of gratitude to love. As Paul F. Camenisch points out, relationships of gratitude ideally involve a "free and joyous coming together of two persons in a mutually enriching and caring relationship."[14] Within caring relationships "a grateful response is, by definition, more spontaneous, more autonomous than an act constrained by a sense of being under an obligation."[15]

In exploring the role of joy in gratitude, Camenisch is preoccupied with specific gifts, but he draws an interesting distinction between initiating gifts and sustaining gifts. Initiating gifts are bestowed with the hope of creating a new or deepened relationship with the recipient. Sustaining gifts express and reaffirm an already existing relationship involving caring, love, or friendship. Furthermore, caring relationships reshape the standards for what counts as grateful responses to sustaining gifts. What Camenisch says about friendship applies even more to marriage: "Gifts between friends of long standing fit comfortably into the give and take of the relation and neither immediate nor specific response is expected. Even verbal expressions of gratitude will often be appropriately restrained. But between relative strangers such casualness could well be an affront to the donor."[16]

To be sure, even within marriage there is a place for explicit expressions of gratitude, both as responses to special favors and as ritualized expressions, for example on birthdays and anniversaries. For the most part, however, expressions of gratitude take more subtle forms in marriages, including simple enjoyment, felt and manifested in the presence of one's partner. Because enjoyment is integral to the mutual caring embodied in love, feelings of gratitude are typically interwoven with other experiences of love. To find and convey joy in living with one's spouse is itself the most satisfying sign and expression of gratitude.

What is joy? As an emotion, it is a relatively brief and intense feeling of elation in which we affirm the world as wonderful.[17] It seems to be a simple emotion, but the psychologist Chris M. Meadows identified some complexities.[18] When he asked his subjects to describe their feelings of joy, most reported a general affirmation of their lives or of the world. In addition, however, there were several interesting juxtapositions of feeling. Many experiences of joy involve these four combinations: feelings of excitement (energy, enthusiasm) and serenity (contentedness, peacefulness); self-potency (inner power, personal worth) and affiliation (affection, connection with others); heightened perception (alertness, celebration of immediate experience) and a sense of ecstasy (as if one were in another world); and passivity (about the events leading up to the joy and in undergoing the joy) and productiveness (motivation and ease in functioning in the world). These juxtapositions reflect the wider unions created by successful love.

Nel Noddings suggests that joy "is the special affect that arises out of the receptivity of caring, and it represents a major reward for the one-caring," that is, for the person who cares.[19] Recognition of caring relationships induces joy, at least when the focus is on caring and being cared for rather than on responsibilities. As such, the biological and social function of joy is to reinforce and sustain our capacities to care. It motivates us to strengthen social bonding.[20] Specifically, the joys of gratitude strengthen relationships and ingratitude weakens them.

The role of gratitude in strengthening relationships is illustrated in Robb Forman Dew's novel *Dale Loves Sophie to Death*. Martin Howells undergoes a midlife crisis that threatens his marriage. Separated for the summer from his wife and three children in order to work on editing a journal, he feels adrift. He also feels tempted to have an affair with a friend for whom he has no deep affection. At first the temptation is overshadowed by a need for his family: "He had a heartsick need for that quiet and continual celebration of the spirit when it is bound fast by the expectations and wants and demands of other people whom one desires above all else to please and cherish and be nurtured by in turn."[21] The need is not sufficient, however, to prevent him from drifting into the affair by convincing himself that it means nothing more than pleasurable sex.

A longtime friend forces him to realize that his wife, Dinah, would be deeply hurt to learn about the affair, and that his infidelity has already caused moral damage by violating their shared commitment against outside affairs. Shortly thereafter, a call from his youngest child, who mistakenly thinks he is dying, reunites him with his family. Driving home with them, he is filled with a quiet but joyful gratitude. He thinks of Mies van der Rohe's remark that in architecture "God hides in the details," and he finds reassurance in "the adhesive intricacy of this domestic life. Each moment was . . . an affirmation of his own existence that kept him tethered safely to the earth."[22] Gratitude's joy, not obligation, restores the marriage.

APPRECIATION AND WONDER

So far the focus has been on episodic feelings of joy, but we also speak of entire marriages and lives as joyous. What does that mean? It does not mean that spouses experience uninterrupted bliss, and yet in happy marriages feelings of joy suffuse the mundane details of everyday life. Moments of joy tend to reverberate throughout the relationship.[23] Those moments are varied: ecstatic joys of sex, quiet joys of companionship, proud joys of parenting, and reassuring joys of mutual support. Unlike routine pleasures, joys leave deep impressions that, as memory revives them, structure meaningful life. In addition, anticipated joys form a thread from present to future. Remembered and anticipated joys are integral to the shared history for which couples are grateful.

At the end of his essay Camenisch moves beyond specific gifts and introduces the idea of a "comprehensive sense of gratitude" in which gratitude becomes "the dominant mood or theme of a total way of life" and in which one lives "with a joyful sense of the interrelatedness of things."[24] He has in mind religiously based gratitude, but there is a secular analogue to the comprehensive or global gratitude he describes. In happy marriages, gratitude for love becomes gratitude for an entire life together. Spouses live with an ongoing sense of joyous gratitude for their shared life, including its past, present, and hoped-for future.

This link between gratitude in love and comprehensive gratitude for (a shared) life is a central theme in Alice Walker's *The Color Purple*. Walker suggests that gratitude for love and the benefits it provides contributes to a wider appreciation of life and vice versa.

As used in the novel, the word "appreciate" has several meanings.[25] To appreciate can mean to be grateful for, to enjoy, cherish, and find joy in, or to discern the value or excellence of. These meanings are closely related, especially with regard to love. Usually, feeling grateful implies discerning the value of a benefit received and enjoying the benefit as well as finding pleasure in the recognition received from our benefactor. Appreciation is grateful cherishing that brings delight.

The Color Purple is structured as a series of letters. Most are written by Celie and record her development from an uneducated and sexually abused fourteen-year-old girl to an astute and autonomous woman. Because her stepfather warned that it would kill her mother if she told anyone but God about how the stepfather had raped her and twice made her pregnant, Celie addresses her early letters to God. There are also letters to Celie from her sister Nettie. Celie's husband Albert prevents her from knowing about the letters in retribution for Nettie resisting his attempt to rape her. Those letters explain how Celie's two children were adopted by Samuel and Corrine, the local minister and his wife, whom Nettie accompanies on an African mission. After discovering Nettie's letters, Celie addresses subsequent letters to Nettie rather than to a God who could allow Albert's ultimate cruelty in preventing love from being expressed. The final letter records the sisters' joyous reunion after thirty years and is addressed to a pantheistic deity who symbolizes her awakened sense of joy in life.

The marriage between Celie and Albert is without love. As Celie observes, it was never really—morally—a marriage at all (261).[26] From the outset, Celie was a piece of property exchanged between her stepfather, who was eager to remove the visible reminder that he was a rapist, and Albert, who wanted a caregiver for his children by a previous marriage. Albert's cruelty overshadows but also accentuates his ingratitude. Quite apart from love, he owes Celie gratitude for raising his children as well as for cooking, cleaning, and providing numerous other benefits to him without any reciprocation on his part. The point is made abundantly clear: Ingratitude makes love impossible. In order to be worthy of caring, spouses must respond gratefully to each other, rather than one partner treating the other as a possession to be taken for granted.

To be sure, Celie's marriage to Albert is doomed not only by Albert's violence and ingratitude but also by her passivity and her unwillingness to assert herself. Does this remark suggest blaming the victim? I have in mind taking responsibility for one's life, not blaming. There are ample reasons for excusing Celie's passivity as a survival device in her savage circumstances, a passivity that even Sofia adopts in order to cope when she is unjustly imprisoned (93). At the same time, being a victim of racist and sexist oppression does not always fully excuse moral passivity.[27]

Despite the salience of Albert's failures as a husband, the novel is not cynical about marital love. The marriage between Samuel and Corrine is sympathetically portrayed, as is the marriage between Samuel and Nettie following the death of Corrine. Those relationships are grounded in mutual appreciation of a shared life. The primary example of how gratitude supports mutual caring, however, is the lesbian love between Celie and Shug Avery, a honky-tonk singer who since adolescence had been Albert's lover. After seeing Albert's picture of her, Celie became infatuated with Shug long before they met. Their mutual love develops gradually from their friendship as Celie nurses Shug after alcoholism nearly kills her. Grateful, Shug listens sympathetically to Celie, writes a song in her honor, and bolsters her self-respect to the point where she can leave Albert. She also encourages her to sew pants and to develop a talent that eventually enables her to start her own clothing company.

Shug's gratitude is sufficiently strong to overcome her jealousy of Celie for marrying Albert. Gratefulness, however, is neither the primary motive in her love for Celie nor enough to keep them together. Shug eventually runs off with a young man, although in the end Shug, Celie, and Albert reunite. Nevertheless, grateful appreciation serves as a supportive motive for their mutual caring, and their gratitude for each other is linked to their wider appreciation of life.

Throughout her life Celie depended on Nettie's love. When Celie learns that for years Albert had hid Nettie's letters from her, she leaves him, as does Shug. Celie also rejects, as racist and sexist, her conventional belief in God as a white male. She listens sympathetically to Shug's expression of faith in a pantheistic deity. The theological details are left vague. Roughly, God is a personified spirit of love (although not a person) which "wants" to be gratefully admired for "its" gifts of love and beauty: "I think it pisses god off if you walk by the color purple in a field somewhere and don't notice it" (203). We express gratitude to God by properly using the gift of life, if only by being happy and enjoying what life has to offer (200, 203). This sounds like self-centered hedonism, and sometimes Shug does move too far in that direction, especially when she loses contact with the children she had with Albert. Yet Shug emphasizes pleasures that are tied to love for individuals, communities, and nature. In doing so, she overthrows the preoccupation with gratitude toward God as an obligation and replaces it with gratitude as joy in loving and living. By attending to the good in life she gradually develops a joyous gratefulness that removes her anxious self-preoccupation and the hatred that threatens to overwhelm her. She learns to see the bad in perspective, as only part of life.

The connection between joy in love and the wider joy in life is highlighted in the experiences of both Nettie and Albert. After they are married, Nettie and Samuel undergo a religious conversion much like Celie's conversion to pantheism (264). In part, the conversion results from their sympathetic responses to the Africans' nature worship; in part, it results from contact with a woman missionary who urges that they learn to appreciate people as they are rather than trying to impose one's own religious beliefs on them. The conversion also occurs simultaneously with their marriage and their love for each other. And it leads them to return home with an attitude of encouraging all people to have their own personal relationship to God as a spirit within themselves.

Albert's transformation is less religious and more philosophical, but it closely parallels the experiences of Celie and Nettie. Provoked by his suffering after Shug and Celie leave him, he comes to feel genuine remorse. He sends Nettie's remaining letters to Celie, and he also learns, in Celie's words, to "appreciate some of the things God was playful enough to make" (267). In his own words, he learns "to wonder . . . bout the big things," about love, suffering, race, and gender (290). He learns to wonder, to appreciate life, and thereby to love: "The more I wonder . . . the more I love" (290).

Spouses cannot appreciate each other without mutual acceptance and support. For this to occur, gender-based role restrictions must be removed because they paralyze personal growth, as both Albert and his son Harpo discover. Some roles concern sex: Celie is liberated through a lesbian relationship outside customary sexual roles. Other roles pertain to work: Celie's friend Sofia, who is married to Harpo, is physically stronger than most males and enjoys outdoor labor, whereas Albert and Harpo become willing to do housework at the same time they stop domineering their wives. Still other roles are linked to personality traits: Both Shug and Sofia are independent in a way traditionally associated with men and can "hold they own" more than most men (276). In each case, appreciation as grateful cherishing implies overcoming conventional gender roles that threaten fulfillment and happiness.

Albert learns how to understand, listen to, and talk sympathetically with Celie. More remarkably, Celie finds herself able to care for him, not sexually but as a companion with whom she can talk. By the end of the novel, Celie and Albert have become "two old fools left over from love, keeping each other company under the stars" (278). Celie is able to forgive him, at least in part, not only because of his transformation but also because he loves Shug and Shug once loved him. If we think of Shug as a symbol of religious love, this reconciliation represents a secular analogue to loving persons through God.

As an expression of his remorse and his awakened gratitude, Albert gives Celie a purple frog. The gift is self-mocking: Celie once expressed her sexual preference by saying that with their pants down men look like frogs. The gift is also richly symbolic: As Celie's favorite color, purple symbolizes the wonder of the natural world, the dignity earned in transcending suffering and blue-black beatings, Celie's love for Shug, Shug herself, and in general the joy of erotic love.[28]

Finally, the novel takes into account how gratitude can be abused, especially by exploiters who are in positions of power and authority. The exploitation of Celie by her stepfather, whom she mistakenly believes to be her biological father, was facilitated in part by her lack of self-respect together with her faith in the biblical commandment to honor one's parents (43). Sofia, by contrast, is fully aware of how racism is expressed and supported by white people's attitude that black people are ungrateful (111). That awareness, together with her self-respect, enables her to resist being exploited by disingenuous appeals to gratitude. Also, Nettie and Samuel discern the covert desire of missionaries to gain recognition by evincing gratitude from converts (243).

Despite being vulnerable to abuse, gratitude plays essential roles in love. It provides motives that help sustain love. It brings joys that enter into the meaning that love creates. And it is interwoven with the celebration of shared lives in which persons value each other within virtue-structured relationships.

EPILOGUE

> For the uncle, love was control. Respect was
> obedience. For Prakash, love was letting go.
> Independence, self-reliance. I learned the litany
> by heart. But I felt suspended between worlds.
> —*Bharati Mukherjee*[1]

In thinking about love, as in loving, we confront two temptations. One is to engage in the excessive, and usually self-righteous, moralism that suffocates love with rigid universal duties. The other is to de-moralize love altogether by reducing it solely to a matter of personal happiness and happenstance. I have tried to avoid both temptations. Love is internally connected with morality, but primarily in terms of virtues and ideals rather than duties. As virtue-structured ways to value persons, love opens new possibilities for morally valuable relationships.

Within a pluralistic framework, I have celebrated diversity in how ideals are embraced, interpreted, and applied so as to achieve different kinds of valuable relationships. Nevertheless, multiculturalists might object that I have not gone far enough. We live in a multicultural society amidst a world of other such societies. Haven't I set forth a liberal Western conception that is ultimately ethnocentric rather than genuinely pluralistic?

This is an interesting objection that provides a challenge for further work. Toward that end, I offer a few concluding comments. First, multiculturalism comes in many varieties. In its unsavory form, it reduces morality to whatever values a group happens to en-

178

dorse. I have rejected that view, not only on the general grounds that it amounts to a form of moral skepticism that could be used to justify any insidious practice, but also on grounds directly related to my conception of love. As a feminist committed to both fairness and basic decency between spouses, I am committed to cross-cultural dialogue that leaves room for strong condemnation of violence against women, in all its forms. Similarly, pluralism implies rejecting those versions of multiculturalism that protect a society's predominant outlook as canonical. Cross-cultural moral dialogue, of course, should be contextually sensitive, taking into account the moral relevance of particular exigencies and social traditions.

Second, my version of pluralism is consistent with desirable versions of multiculturalism that celebrate a wide range of moral outlooks. In particular, I have emphasized that love's virtues can be interpreted and applied by couples in many different ways so as to create morally valuable relationships. How wide are those permissible differences? For example, I focused on monogamous relationships grounded in commitments to love one partner, but what about polygamy and arranged marriages? Given different cultural circumstances than our own, polygamy opens options for valuing persons in ways structured by the virtues of caring, respect, honesty, gratitude, and so on. Again, many arranged marriages permit and invite commitments to love, sometimes more so than the hasty Hollywood-type romances in Western societies, at least where the participants (including the arrangers) exercise wisdom and sensitivity.

Third, part of the multicultural challenge can be turned on its head. The very fact that our world is composed of increasingly diverse cultural traditions makes it inevitable that individuals will have to make new choices about love. Those choices require that clashing value perspectives be understood and evaluated together. I have in mind not only interracial and intercultural marriages, although they will become increasingly common and important, but how individuals must struggle with mixed elements within their own traditions, as those traditions interact with and are modified by other traditions.

In *Jasmine*, Bharati Mukherjee portrays a Hindu woman who must choose between different conceptions of marital love. One conception is traditional: Not only are marriages arranged, but a woman is regarded as a man's property, so much so that she is expected to engage in ritual suicide (*sati*) by throwing herself on her husband's funeral pyre to show her devotion to him. Another conception is modern: A woman's happiness and freedom matter as much as a man's. These clashing views of love epitomize radically different ways of life. The traditional conception is undergirded by a metaphysics of fatalism and karma, whereas the modern conception is tied to a belief in personal freedom. Living in the United States as an illegal immigrant, Jasmine gradually comes to believe in the freedom to choose relationships, regardless of how structured the context in which those choices are made.

These choices can be difficult: "There are no harmless, compassionate ways to remake oneself. We murder who we were so we can rebirth ourselves in the images of dreams."[2] Yet there is also continuity of identity as we undergo the transformations so characteristic in love. Jasmine must choose between the security of caring for a tragically disabled man and a riskier marriage to a man whom she loves in a deeper way. "I am not choosing between men. I am caught between the promise of America and old-world dutifulness."[3] Both lives can be good ones. The agony is not in choosing between good and bad, but in choosing between different goods. When she decides, she seems to herself self-seeking, "greedy with wants and reckless from hope." Yet her decision is morally resonant: She acts with courage, honesty, and wisdom in pursuing a relationship that promises greater fairness and mutual caring.

Fourth, I acknowledge that my conception of love is a Western liberal conception—"liberal" in a sense that cuts across left-and right-wing politics. It is a conception that embraces diversity as the inevitable and desirable by-product of freedom while retaining a conviction that the core values of caring and respect for persons limit what we can count as desirable relationships. In addition to the great diversity within Western liberal perspectives on love, there are differences among the conceptions of love produced by other world cultures. In general, these conceptions will be linked by various family resemblances. At some point, of course, cultural differences concerning sexual relationships will be so great that questions will arise about whether we are talking about the same thing. Nevertheless, with regard to paradigmatic cases of love I am confident that the virtues I have discussed will play prominent roles, and that hence my conception of love has cross-cultural significance.

Affirming a liberal Western conception of love need not imply ethnocentrism in the pejorative sense of culture-bound narrowness and bigotry. We can appreciate and learn from other cultures in ways that help us deal with our increasingly troubled society. Nevertheless, we need to understand the values to which we are legitimately committed, explicitly or tacitly, as individuals and as a society. My faith is that those values include the virtue-structured relationships of love.

NOTES

INTRODUCTION: EROTIC FAITH

1. Isak Dinesen, *On Marriage and Other Observations,* trans. Anne Born (New York: St. Martin's Press, 1986), p. 56.

2. In using virtues as a framework for exploring love, I am not claiming that virtues are more fundamental in justifying moral claims than are principles of duty, rights, or utility. I believe that an adequate theory of morality will integrate all these moral considerations.

3. Nicholas Rescher, *Ethical Idealism: An Inquiry into the Nature and Function of Ideals* (Berkeley: University of California Press, 1987).

4. Elizabeth Barrett Browning, *Sonnets from the Portuguese,* sonnet 43, reprinted in Jon Stallworthy, ed., *A Book of Love Poetry* (New York: Oxford University Press, 1974), p. 51.

5. Julia Markus, *Dared and Done: The Marriage of Elizabeth Barrett and Robert Browning* (New York: Alfred A. Knopf, 1995).

6. Leo Tolstoy, *Anna Karenina,* trans. David Magarshack (New York: New American Library, 1961), p. 17.

7. John Bayley, *Tolstoy and the Novel* (New York: Viking Press, 1967), p. 284.

8. A. N. Wilson, *Tolstoy* (London: Hamish Hamilton, 1988), p. 196.

9. Tolstoy, *Anna Karenina,* p. 150.

10. Robert M. Polhemus, *Erotic Faith: Being in Love from Jane Austen to D. H. Lawrence* (Chicago: University of Chicago Press, 1990), p. 1.

11. As applied to romantic love in general, this is a central theme in Ethel Spector Person's *Dreams of Love and Fateful Encounters: The Power of Romantic Passion* (New York: W. W. Norton, 1988).

12. Robert N. Bellah, Richard Madsen, William M. Sullivan, Ann Swidler, and Steven M. Tipton, *Habits of the Heart: Individualism and*

Commitment in American Life (Berkeley: University of California Press, 1985), p. 93.

13. Ibid., p. 109.

14. Cf. Jeffrey Stout, *Ethics After Babel: The Languages of Morals and Their Discontents* (Boston: Beacon Press, 1988), pp. 193-200.

15. Bellah et al., *Habits of the Heart,* p. 105.

16. Ibid. Bellah and his colleagues do hear in the man's remarks a sense of a "deeper sharing relationship" but fail to elucidate what sharing might mean for the man they are interviewing.

17. Ibid., p. 5.

CHAPTER 1. LOVE AND MORALITY

1. Esther Tusquets, *Love Is a Solitary Game,* trans. Bruce Penman (New York: Riverrun Press, 1985), p. 85.

2. The image comes from C. S. Lewis, *The Four Loves* (San Diego: Harcourt Brace Jovanovich, 1960), pp. 163-164.

3. Harry S. Broudy, *Enlightened Cherishing* (Urbana: University of Illinois Press, 1972), p. 57. In a similar vein, Robert C. Roberts says love involves a disposition to feel a range of emotions; see "What an Emotion Is: A Sketch," *Philosophical Review* 97 (April 1988): 203.

4. Cf. Annette Baier, "Unsafe Loves," in Robert C. Solomon and Kathleen M. Higgins, eds., *The Philosophy of (Erotic) Love* (Lawrence: University Press of Kansas, 1991), p. 444.

5. John Wilson, *Love, Sex, and Feminism* (New York: Praeger, 1980), pp. 16-17.

6. Dorothy Tennov, *Love and Limerence* (Chelsea, MI: Scarborough House, 1979), pp. 23-24.

7. John Alan Lee, *The Colors of Love* (Englewood Cliffs, NJ: Prentice-Hall, 1976); and "Love-Styles," in Robert J. Sternberg and Michael L. Barnes, eds., *The Psychology of Love* (New Haven: Yale University Press, 1988), pp. 38-67.

8. Ibid., p. 41.

9. Ibid., p. 46.

10. Plato, *Symposium,* trans. Alexander Nehamas and Paul Woodruff (Indianapolis: Hackett, 1989), p. 17. Another part of Pausanias's conception of "higher" love is expressed in the ancient Greeks' preference for homosexual love and—something quite distinct—their misogyny.

11. Robert J. Sternberg, "Triangulating Love," in Sternberg and Barnes, *The Psychology of Love,* pp. 119-138.

12. Lee, "Love-Styles," pp. 64–66.

13. Parenthetical page references are to Ingmar Bergman, *Scenes from a Marriage,* in *The Marriage Scenarios,* trans. Alan Blair (New York: Pantheon Books, 1983).

14. Iris Murdoch, *The Sovereignty of Good* (Boston: Routledge and Kegan Paul, 1985), p. 46; first published in 1970.

15. Irving Singer, *The Nature of Love,* vol. 1, *Plato to Luther,* 2d ed. (Chicago: University of Chicago Press, 1984), p. 11; emphasis in original.

16. Ibid.

17. Cf. Steven Seidman, *Embattled Eros: Sexual Politics and Ethics in Contemporary America* (New York: Routledge, 1992). Also see James Davison Hunter, *Culture Wars: The Struggle to Define America* (New York: Basic Books, 1991).

18. John Kekes, *The Morality of Pluralism* (Princeton: Princeton University Press, 1993), pp. 178 and 161.

19. John Stuart Mill, *On Liberty* (Indianapolis: Hackett, 1978), p. 54. The spirit of Mill's *On Liberty* is celebrated by Isaiah Berlin in "The Pursuit of the Ideal," in *The Crooked Timber of Humanity,* ed. Henry Hardy (New York: Vintage Books, 1992), pp. 1–19. On Mill's relationship with Harriet Taylor see his *Autobiography* (Garden City, N.Y.: Doubleday, 1873); and Phyllis Rose, *Parallel Lives: Five Victorian Marriages* (New York: Vintage Books, 1984), pp. 95–140.

20. A notable exception is Roger Scruton, who grounds his canonical perspective in an Aristotelian conception of a univocal pathway for human self-fulfillment. Scruton argues, for example, that traditional marital love "generates a sense of the irreplaceable value, both of the other and of the self, and of the activities which bind them. To receive and to give this love is to achieve something of incomparable value in the process of self-fulfilment" (*Sexual Desire* [New York: Free Press, 1986], p. 337); cf. pp. 250–251. I agree that marital love makes possible special ways of valuing persons, ways that promote the self-fulfillment for many persons—but all? Scruton is insensitive to the diversity of fulfilling lives. For example, he rejects gay sexuality and love because he thinks it encourages promiscuity and discourages long-term monogamous commitments (306–310). Oddly, he traces these alleged tendencies to the lessened "mystery" and "risk" involved in loving someone of the same sex, while admitting that the tendencies do not occur in lesbian love. He never confronts the role of social oppression in actively discouraging long-term gay relationships.

21. Socrates asked, "Is what is holy holy because the gods approve it, or do they approve it because it is holy?" (Plato, *Euthyphro,* trans. Lane Cooper, in Edith Hamilton and Huntington Cairns, eds., *The Collected Di-*

alogues of Plato [Princeton: Princeton University Press, 1961], 10a). Paraphrasing: Are moral values the products of the directives of a capricious God, or does God approve of them because (like us, but more accurately) God discerns good reasons for those values? Most religious thinkers reject the simple versions of "Divine Command Ethics" that understand right conduct as defined by God's commands because such a view implies that God does not have good moral reasons for making particular commands and hence is a morally irrational or whimsical being.

22. For these and other criticisms of marriage from a Marxist perspective see John McMurtry, "Monogamy: A Critique," *The Monist* 56 (1972); reprinted in Robert Baker and Frederick Elliston, eds., *Philosophy and Sex*, rev. ed. (Buffalo, NY: Prometheus Books, 1984), pp. 107–118. For an incisive reply see David Palmer, "The Consolation of the Wedded," in Baker and Elliston, *Philosophy and Sex*, pp. 119–129.

23. Marilyn Friedman, "The Social Self and the Partiality Debates," in Claudia Card, ed. *Feminist Ethics* (Lawrence: University Press of Kansas, 1991), p. 170. For a review of some of the problems with traditional intimate relationships, see Irene Diamond, ed., *Families, Politics, and Public Policy* (New York: Longman, 1983).

CHAPTER 2. CARING

1. George Eliot, *Daniel Deronda* (New York: Penguin Books, 1967), p. 868; first published in 1876.

2. Cf. Jeffrey Blustein, *Care and Commitment* (New York: Oxford University Press, 1991), chap. 2. Also see Nel Noddings, *Caring: A Feminine Approach to Ethics and Moral Education* (Berkeley: University of California Press, 1984), chap. 1.

3. Owen Flanagan, *Varieties of Moral Personality* (Cambridge: Harvard University Press, 1991), p. 202; and Blustein, *Care and Commitment*, p. 40.

4. Irvin D. Yalom, *Love's Executioner* (New York: Harper Collins, 1989), pp. 15–67.

5. Émile Zola, *Thérèse Raquin*, trans. Leonard Tancock (New York: Penguin Books, 1984), p. 135.

6. Scott Kraft, "Murderous Affair Shocks Kansas Town," *Los Angeles Times* (March 17, 1986), pp. 1, 14–15.

7. Plato, *Symposium*, trans. Alexander Nehamas and Paul Woodruff (Indianapolis: Hackett, 1989), 179A.

8. Ibid., 191D.

9. For an important caveat about interpreting Plato's views as those voiced by Socrates, see Martha C. Nussbaum, "The Speech of Alcibiades: A Reading of Plato's *Symposium,*" *Philosophy and Literature* 3 (1979): 131–169; reprinted in Robert C. Solomon and Kathleen M. Higgins, eds., *The Philosophy of (Erotic) Love* (Lawrence: University Press of Kansas, 1991), pp. 279–316.

10. Plato, *Symposium,* 203C-D. Portraying Love's father as resourceful and his (!) mother as needy reflects the sexism in the *Symposium.* At the same time, the myth portrays Penia, the mother of Love, as creating the plan to "relieve her lack of resources" by making love with Poros, the father of Love. Note too that Socrates' insights on love come from the wise *woman* Diotima.

11. Ibid., 206A. Although Plato offers an egoistic theory of love, one that emphasizes the lover over the beloved, his focus is also outward, on how one relates to ideals of beauty and goodness. See Gregory Vlastos, "The Individual as an Object of Love in Plato," in *Platonic Studies,* 2d ed. (Princeton: Princeton University Press, 1973), pp. 3–34; reprinted in Alan Soble, ed., *Eros, Agape, and Philia: Readings in the Philosophy of Love* (New York: Paragon House, 1989), pp. 96–128. Also see Elisabeth Young-Bruehl's illuminating comments in *Creative Characters* (New York: Routledge, 1991), pp. 19–26.

12. Plato, *Symposium,* 206B, 208E.

13. Gerasimos Santas, *Plato and Freud: Two Theories of Love* (New York: Basil Blackwell, 1988), pp. 58–72.

14. Vlastos, "The Individual as an Object of Love in Plato," in Soble, *Eros, Agape, and Philia,* p. 110.

15. See Gregory S. Kavka, *Hobbesian Moral and Political Theory* (Princeton: Princeton University Press, 1986), pp. 64–80.

16. Singer sometimes portrays appraisals as judgments or decisions about worth, by contrast with the attitudes of caring involved in bestowal; see, for example, *The Nature of Love,* vol. 1, *Plato to Luther,* 2d ed. (Chicago: University of Chicago Press, 1984), pp. 4–5. In the main, however, he portrays appraisals as including both judgments and attitudes of positive regard (what I call caring).

17. Singer, *The Nature of Love,* vol. 3, *The Modern World* (Chicago: University of Chicago Press, 1987), p. 393.

18. Ibid., p. 403. Indeed, all values are created through bestowal: "All appraisals must ultimately depend on bestowal since they presuppose that human beings give importance to the satisfying of their needs and desires. Without such bestowal nothing could take on value of any sort" (393).

19. Paul Gooch, "A Mind to Love: Friends and Lovers in Ancient Greek

Philosophy," in David Goicoechea, ed., *The Nature and Pursuit of Love: The Philosophy of Irving Singer* (Amherst, NY: Prometheus Books, 1995), p. 89.

20. Singer might try to defend his view by contrasting individual bestowals with community-wide bestowals that "make" people valuable. Yet communities too can be tragically mistaken in their standards — witness Nazi Germany, Stalinist Russia, and Christian crusades. This problem might be solved by hypothesizing an imagined community of ideally rational agents who bestow value on persons. But that seems a roundabout way of saying that persons have inherent value, and our bestowals and appraisals respond to that value. I share the more objectivist view of the unique worth of persons defended by Jeffrey Blustein in *Care and Commitment,* pp. 203–216.

21. Alan Soble provides a full and insightful discussion of how love is reason-dependent in *The Structure of Love* (New Haven: Yale University Press, 1990). See especially pages 4, 112–117, 281–283, 314–320.

22. Blustein, *Care and Commitment,* p. 194.

23. See Neera Kapur Badhwar, "Friends as Ends in Themselves," in Soble, *Eros, Agape and Philia,* pp. 165–187, and Blustein, *Care and Commitment,* chap. 17.

24. George Eliot, *The Mill on the Floss* (New York: New American Library, 1965), p. 521; quoted by Carol Gilligan, *In a Different Voice* (Cambridge: Harvard University Press, 1982), p. 148.

25. Flanagan, *Varieties of Moral Personality,* p. 258.

26. Jean Grimshaw, *Philosophy and Feminist Thinking* (Minneapolis: University of Minnesota Press, 1986), p. 245.

27. Marilyn Friedman, "Beyond Caring: The De-Moralization of Gender," *Canadian Journal of Philosophy,* supplementary vol. 13, *Science, Morality and Feminist Theory* (1987): 100–104. Also see Lawrence A. Blum, *Moral Perception and Particularity* (Cambridge: Cambridge University Press, 1994), esp. pt. 3.

28. Michael Slote, *Goods and Virtues* (Oxford: Clarendon Press, 1983).

29. Cf. Simone de Beauvoir, *The Ethics of Ambiguity,* trans. Bernard Frechtman (Secaucus, NJ: Citadel Press, 1980), pp. 103–104; Margaret Adams, "The Compassion Trap," in Vivian Gornick and Barbara K. Moran, eds., *Woman in Sexist Society* (New York: New American Library, 1972), pp. 555–575; and Mike W. Martin, *Virtuous Giving: Philanthropy, Voluntary Service, and Caring* (Bloomington: Indiana University Press, 1994), p. 151.

30. Robert R. Ehman, "Personal Love," in Soble, *Eros, Agape and Philia,* p. 256.

31. Michael D. Bayles, "Marriage, Love, and Procreation," in Robert Baker and Frederick Elliston, eds., *Philosophy and Sex*, 2d ed. (Buffalo, NY: Prometheus Books, 1984), p. 137.

32. Elizabeth Barrett Browning, *Sonnets from the Portuguese*, Sonnet 43, in Jon Stallworthy (ed.) *A Book of Love Poetry* (New York: Oxford University Press, 1986), p. 51.

33. Roger Scruton, *Sexual Desire* (New York: Free Press, 1986), p. 230.

34. Marvin Kohl discusses the issue of paternalism in love in "Caring Love and Liberty: Some Questions," in Goicoechea, *The Nature and Pursuit of Love*, pp. 221-228.

35. Robert Nozick, *The Examined Life* (New York: Simon and Schuster, 1989), p. 71.

36. Cf. Peter French, "The Corporation as a Moral Person," in French, *Collective and Corporate Responsibility* (New York: Columbia University Press, 1984).

37. Robert C. Solomon, *About Love* (New York: Simon and Schuster, 1988), pp. 24-25. Also see "The Virtue of (Erotic) Love," in Solomon and Higgins, *The Philosophy of (Erotic) Love*, pp. 492-518.

38. Solomon attempts to drive a wedge between love and relationships (*About Love*, pp. 82-88). Love is an emotional process of redefining oneself in terms of the beloved (although he also refers to love as an emotion); relationships, by contrast, are social arrangements (such as marriage). Even in Solomon's own terms this wedge is mistaken, as the kinds of redefinition of identity are inseparable from the types of relationships into which people enter.

39. Solomon, *About Love*, p. 243.

40. John Kekes, "Good Lives and Happiness," in Kekes, *The Examined Life* (Lewisburg, PA: Bucknell University Press, 1988), pp. 161-173. Also see Elizabeth Telfer, *Happiness* (New York: St. Martin's Press, 1980).

41. Joel Feinberg, "Absurd Self-Fulfillment," in Tom L. Beauchamp, Joel Feinberg, and James M. Smith, eds., *Philosophy and the Human Condition*, 2d ed. (Englewood Cliffs, NJ: Prentice-Hall, 1989), pp. 586-605.

42. Adolf Guggenbuhl-Craig, *Marriage: Dead or Alive*, trans. Murray Stein (Dallas: Spring Publications, 1977), p. 41.

43. Cf. Søren Kierkegaard, *Either/Or*, trans. Walter Lowrie, 2 vols. (Princeton: Princeton University Press, 1959), 2:267.

44. Ibid., p. 152.

45. As an adjective, the word "creative" applies to many things, including creative products, persons, activities, and supportive environments like organizations and families. Conceptually, the central idea is creative products (or the results of activities). Products are creative when they are new in

a valuable way, when they are valuably new. In turn, creative individuals are people who make creative products, creative activities lead to creative products, and creative environments support creative activities. See Jack Glickman, "On Creating," in M. K. Munitz, ed., *Perspectives in Education, Religion, and the Arts* (Albany: State University of New York Press, 1970), pp. 262-265. Cf. D. N. Perkins, *The Mind's Best Work* (Cambridge: Harvard University Press, 1981), p. 245. Standards for measuring creativity can be set high or low, depending on our practical interests. Do we want to encourage and appreciate everyone's capacities for development, in which case our criteria will be more inclusive, or do we want to single out a few of the most influential geniuses as "truly" creative? I use inclusive criteria in an effort to draw attention to neglected areas of everyday creativity in relationships. Cf. Abraham H. Maslow, *Toward a Psychology of Being* (New York: Van Nostrand Reinhold, 1968), pp. 135-145, and Carl R. Rogers, *Becoming Partners: Marriage and Its Alternatives* (New York: Dell, 1972).

46. See A. S. Cua, *Dimensions of Moral Creativity: Paradigms, Principles, and Ideals* (University Park: Pennsylvania State University Press, 1978); and Mary Midgley, "Creation and Originality," in Midgley, *Heart and Mind: The Varieties of Moral Experience* (New York: St. Martin's Press, 1981), pp. 43-58.

47. Jean-Paul Sartre, "Existentialism Is a Humanism," trans. Philip Mairet, in Walter Kaufmann, ed., *Existentialism from Dostoevsky to Sartre*, rev. ed. (New York: Meridian Books, 1975), p. 364. According to Sartre's subjective view of moral values, "my freedom is the unique foundation of [my] values and . . . *nothing*, absolutely nothing, justifies me in adopting this or that particular value, this or that particular scale of values" (*Being and Nothingness*, trans. Hazel E. Barnes [New York: Pocket Books, 1966], p. 76). Sartre's skepticism about values, or rather cynicism, also applies to love, which Sartre defines pejoratively as an ongoing struggle to dominate (sadism) or submit to domination (masochism). Love is the project of "making oneself be loved," with the deep affection and exclusive devotion of the beloved, without reciprocating (*Being and Nothingness*, p. 488). Later Sartre himself rejected this outlook as omitting the "positivity in love" ("Interview with Jean-Paul Sartre," in Paul Arthur Schilpp, ed., *The Philosophy of Jean-Paul Sartre* [La Salle, IL: Open Court, 1981], p. 13).

48. A better analogy is between moral creativity and creative art criticism that illuminates values which are "out there" to be discovered and appreciated. Cf. Eliot Deutsch, *Personhood, Creativity and Freedom* (Honolulu: University of Hawaii Press, 1982), p. 130. We might also consider an analogy between creative marriages and collaborative art projects, such as

making movies, which introduce an element of intersubjective agreement about values.

49. Caroline Whitbeck explores connections between moral agency and engineering practice in "The Trouble With Dilemmas: Rethinking Applied Ethics," *Professional Ethics* 1 (1992): 119–142.

50. John Dewey, *Human Nature and Conduct* (New York: Modern Library, 1930), p. 183.

51. James D. Wallace, *Moral Relevance and Moral Conflict* (Ithaca, NY: Cornell University Press, 1988), pp. 93–94.

52. Quoted by Deirdre Bair, *Simone de Beauvoir: A Biography* (New York: Simon and Schuster, 1990), pp. 414–415. Also see Kate Fullbrook and Edward Fullbrook, *Simone de Beauvoir and Jean-Paul Sartre: The Remaking of a Twentieth-Century Legend* (New York: Basic Books, 1994).

53. Diana Souhami, *Gertrude and Alice* (San Francisco: Pandora, 1991), p. 208.

54. Ibid., p. 153.

55. Ibid., p. 15.

56. Ronnie Scharfman, "Significantly Other: Simone and Andre Schwarz-Bart," in Whitney Chadwick and Isabelle de Courtivron, eds., *Significant Others: Creativity and Intimate Partnership* (New York: Thames and Hudson, 1993), p. 209.

57. Ibid., p. 221.

CHAPTER 3. FAITHFULNESS

1. Alison Lurie, *Love and Friendship* (New York: Macmillan, 1962), p. 295.

2. *The Book of Common Prayer* (1549), reprinted in part in Helge Rubinstein, ed., *The Oxford Book of Marriage* (Oxford: Oxford University Press, 1990), pp. 83–84.

3. Two illuminating (and contrasting) discussions of the rationale for traditional links between lifetime marital commitments and sexual fidelity are Edmund Leites, *The Puritan Conscience and Modern Sexuality* (New Haven: Yale University Press, 1986), and Roger Scruton, *Sexual Desire* (New York: Free Press, 1986). Also see Chapter 4.

4. Leo Tolstoy, *Kreutzer Sonata,* in *Great Short Works of Leo Tolstoy,* trans. Louise and Aylmer Maude (New York: Harper and Row, 1967), pp. 361–362. Also see Paul Gilbert's discussion in *Human Relationships* (Oxford: Blackwell, 1991), pp. 9ff.

5. George Eliot, *The Mill on the Floss* (New York: New American Library, 1965), p. 499.

6. John Wilson, "Can One Promise to Love Another?" *Philosophy* 64 (1989): 560. Also see Edward Sankowski, "Responsibility of Persons for Their Emotions," *Canadian Journal of Philosophy* 12 (1977): 829-840.

7. Amélie Oksenberg Rorty argues that the core of some emotions is a pattern of attention rather than the more common beliefs and attitudes in "Explaining Emotions," in Amélie Oksenberg Rorty, ed., *Explaining Emotions* (Berkeley: University of California Press, 1980), pp. 103-126.

8. Cf. Martin E. P. Seligman, *Learned Optimism* (New York: Alfred A. Knopf, 1991).

9. J. F. M. Hunter, *Thinking About Sex and Love* (Toronto: Macmillan of Canada, 1980), p. 59.

10. Except when it inspires individuals to do more than they could have otherwise. On this, and on the entire topic of "ought implies can," see Nicholas Rescher, *Ethical Idealism: An Inquiry into the Nature and Function of Ideals* (Berkeley: University of California Press, 1987).

11. Cf. P. E. Hutchings, "Conjugal Faithfulness," in Godfrey Vesey, ed., *Human Values* (Atlantic Highlands, NJ: Humanities Press, 1978).

12. J. F. M. Hunter, *Thinking about Sex and Love*, p. 59. Cf. Derek Parfit, "Later Selves and Moral Principles," in A. Montefiore, ed., *Philosophy and Personal Relations* (London: Routledge and Kegan Paul, 1973).

13. Susan Mendus, "Marital Faithfulness," *Philosophy* 59 (1984): 246.

14. Ibid., p. 247.

15. Alan Soble, *The Structure of Love* (New Haven: Yale University Press, 1990), pp. 166-167.

16. Robert C. Solomon, *Love: Emotion, Myth and Metaphor* (Garden City, NY: Anchor Press, 1981), p. 224.

17. Ibid., p. 227.

18. Cf. Lawrence A. Blum, *Friendship, Altruism and Morality* (London: Routledge and Kegan Paul, 1980).

19. Robert C. Solomon, *About Love* (New York: Simon and Schuster, 1988), p. 134.

20. Ibid., p. 134.

21. Mary Midgley, *Beast and Man* (New York: New American Library, 1980), p. 303.

22. Michael Slote, *Goods and Virtues* (Oxford: Clarendon Press, 1983), pp. 62ff.

23. Martha C. Nussbaum, *The Fragility of Goodness* (Cambridge: Cambridge University Press, 1986), pp. 359-61.

24. Bernard Williams, *Moral Luck* (New York: Cambridge University Press, 1981), pp. 26ff.

25. Bertrand Russell, *The Autobiography of Bertrand Russell,* vol. 1 (New York: Bantam Books, 1968), pp. 195-196.

26. Quoted by Barbara Strachey in *Remarkable Relations* (London: Victor Gollancz, 1980), p. 216.

27. Mary Midgley, *Wisdom, Information and Wonder* (New York: Routledge, 1989), p. 157.

28. Anaïs Nin, *Henry and June* (New York: Harcourt Brace Jovanovich, 1986), p. 29.

29. Ibid., p. 229.

30. Slote, *Goods and Virtues,* p. 77ff.

31. Sonnet 116, in William Shakespeare, *The Sonnets* (New York: New American Library, 1964), p. 156.

32. Dorothy Day, *The Long Loneliness* (New York: Harper and Row, 1952), pp. 147-148.

33. Friedrich Nietzsche, *The Gay Science,* trans. Walter Kaufmann (New York: Vintage Books, 1974), p. 232.

CHAPTER 4. SEXUAL FIDELITY

1. George Eliot, *The Mill on the Floss* (New York: New American Library, 1965), pp. 520-521

2. R. J. Connelly, "Philosophy and Adultery," in Philip E. Lampe, ed., *Adultery in the United States* (Buffalo, NY: Prometheus Books, 1987), pp. 131-164.

3. Denis de Rougemont, *Love in the Western World,* rev. ed., trans. Montgomery Belgion (New York: Harper and Row, 1974), p. 16. Two illuminating literary studies are Tony Tanner, *Adultery in the Novel: Contract and Transgression* (Baltimore: Johns Hopkins University Press, 1979) and Donald J. Greiner, *Adultery in the American Novel: Updike, James, and Hawthorne* (Columbia: University of South Carolina Press, 1985).

4. Cf. Owen Flanagan, *Varieties of Moral Personality* (Cambridge: Harvard University Press, 1991).

5. Matt. 5:27-28 (New International Version). In targeting males, this scripture presupposes that husbands are the primary adulterers. That presupposition is not surprising given a long history of indulging profligate husbands while severely punishing wayward wives, based in part on the view that wives are their husbands' property, duty-bound to maintain male lines of progeny, and in part on the view that women are chaste creatures

who can be held to a higher standard than males. Today, husbands continue to lead in adultery statistics—well over half of them have extramarital affairs—although wives are catching up. Annette Lawson cautiously estimates that somewhere between 25–50% of wives have at least one extramarital lover during any given marriage, and 50–65% of husbands engage in adultery by the age of forty (*Adultery: An Analysis of Love and Betrayal* [New York: Basic Books, 1988], p. 75). More conservative statistics (perhaps owing to the increased prudence resulting from the AIDS epidemic) are reported by Robert T. Michael, John H. Gagnon, Edward O. Laumann, and Gina Kolata, *Sex in America: A Definitive Survey* (Boston: Little, Brown, 1994). A humanistic approach regards male and female adultery as on a par and also proceeds without invoking religious beliefs that condemn all adultery as sinful.

6. Morton Hunt, *The Affair* (New York: World Publishing, 1969), p. 9.

7. This is not an imaginary case. See ibid., p. 80.

8. Michael J. Wreen plausibly widens the term "adultery" to apply to nonmarried persons who have sex with married persons, ("What's Really Wrong with Adultery?" *Journal of Applied Philosophy* 3 [1986], 45–49), but since my focus is spouses I will not widen the definition.

9. Richard Wasserstrom, "Is Adultery Immoral?" *Philosophical Forum* 5 (1974): 513–528. Wasserstrom's preoccupation with rules explains why the most interesting part of his essay—the discussion of the connections between sex, love, and sexually exclusive loving relationships—is approached so indirectly, in terms of "deeper deceptions" that violate the rule against deception, rather than directly in terms of violating moral ideals embedded in love.

10. Ibid., p. 518. In one passage, on p. 522, he hints at the value-laden meaning of love: "the issues are conceptual, empirical and normative all at once: What is love? How could it be different? Would it be a good thing or a bad thing if it were different?"

11. Roger Scruton, *Sexual Desire* (New York: Free Press, 1986), p. 339.

12. For an illuminating historical study of changing attitudes see Peter N. Stearns, *Jealousy* (New York: New York University Press, 1989).

13. Janet Z. Giele, as quoted by Philip E. Lampe, "The Many Dimensions of Adultery," in Lampe, *Adultery in the United States*, p. 56.

14. Cf. H. J. N. Horsburgh, "The Ethics of Trust," *The Philosophical Quarterly* 10 (1960): 343–354; Annette Baier, "Trust and Antitrust," *Ethics* 96 (1986): 231–260; and Laurence Thomas, "Trust, Affirmation, and Moral Character: A Critique of Kantian Morality," in Owen Flanagan and Amélie Oksenberg Rorty, eds., *Identity, Character, and Morality: Essays in Moral Psychology* (Cambridge, MA: MIT Press, 1990), pp. 235–257.

15. Michael Slote, *Goods and Virtues* (Oxford: Clarendon Press, 1983), pp. 49, 65.

16. Bonnie Steinbock, "Adultery," in Alan Soble, ed., *The Philosophy of Sex*, 2d ed. (Savage, MD: Rowman and Littlefield, 1991), p. 191.

17. See Russell Vannoy, *Sex Without Love* (Buffalo, NY: Prometheus Books, 1980).

18. I am assuming that the consent involved in agreements between couples is fully voluntary and that a dominant partner does not exert pressures that make consent "intellectual" rather than emotionally wholehearted. Cf. J. F. M. Hunter, *Thinking About Sex and Love* (Toronto: Macmillan of Canada, 1980), p. 42. To be sure, autonomy is not the sole value governing the making of marital commitments. There are reasons that need to be weighed in deciding what kind of commitments to make. Are partners being realistic in choosing between an exclusive relationship (with its element of sexual restriction) or an open relationship (with its risks of jealousy and new loves) as the best way to promote their happiness and love for each other? And would permitting extramarital affairs negatively affect third parties (perhaps children)?

19. These are not the only factors—a book would be needed to discuss all relevant factors. For example, what about the effects on third parties: not just children and other family but the extramarital lover? Ellen Glasgow describes the joys of her affair with a married man as "miraculous" in *The Woman Within* (New York: Hill and Wang, 1980), p. 156. Again, there are factors about how affairs are conducted, including the risk of contracting AIDS and giving it to one's spouse.

20. The mutual renegotiation of relationships is a central aspect of marital equality, as argued by Robert C. Solomon, *About Love* (New York: Simon and Schuster, 1980), pp. 283–300.

21. Lawson, *Adultery*, pp. 72–73.

22. Nigel Nicolson, *Portrait of a Marriage* (New York: Atheneum, 1973), p. 188.

23. Ibid., p. 231.

24. Philip Blumstein and Pepper Schwartz, *American Couples* (New York: William Morrow, 1983), pp. 286–287.

25. Cf. J. E. Barnhart and Mary Ann Barnhart, "Marital Faithfulness and Unfaithfulness," *Journal of Social Philosophy* 4 (April 1973): 10–15.

26. E.g., Herbert S. Strean, *The Extramarital Affair* (New York: Free Press, 1980); and Frank Pittman, *Private Lies: Infidelity and the Betrayal of Intimacy* (New York: W. W. Norton, 1989).

27. Cf. Martha C. Nussbaum, *The Fragility of Goodness* (New York: Cambridge University Press, 1986), pp. 259–362.

28. An interesting example of deciding *against* adultery is the subject of Lotte Hamburger and Joseph Hamburger in *Contemplating Adultery* (New York: Fawcett Columbine, 1991).

29. Robert Nozick develops a slightly different argument based on the intimate mutual identification involved in forming a couple or a "we"; see *The Examined Life* (New York: Simon and Schuster, 1989), pp. 82, 84.

30. Richard Taylor, *Having Love Affairs* (Buffalo, NY: Prometheus Books, 1982), pp. 67–68.

31. Ibid., pp. 59–60.

32. Ibid., pp. 70, 72–73. The possible frustrations of monogamy are discussed by Edmund Leites in his illuminating book, *The Puritan Conscience and Modern Sexuality* (New Haven: Yale University Press, 1986).

33. Ibid., p. 48; emphasis in original. For these and other ambiguities of "rights" see Ronald Dworkin, *Taking Rights Seriously* (Cambridge: Harvard University Press, 1977), pp. 188–189.

34. Taylor, *Having Love Affairs,* p. 12.

35. Steinbock, "Adultery," in Soble, *The Philosophy of Sex,* p. 192.

36. For an interesting example, see Janice Rosenberg, "Fidelity," in Laurie Abraham, ed., *Reinventing Love* (New York: Plume, 1993), pp. 101–106.

37. Lynn Atwater, *The Extramarital Connection* (New York: Irvington Publishers, 1982), p. 143. The same theme is developed in Dalma Heyn, *The Erotic Silence of the American Wife* (New York: Signet, 1993). The power of this theme is also reflected in Robert James Waller, *The Bridges of Madison County* (New York: Warner Books, 1992), which sold over eight million hardback copies by 1995, before the movie (starring Clint Eastwood and Meryl Streep) pushed sales even higher.

38. Dalma Heyn (*The Erotic Silence*) urges that not confessing adultery to one's spouse is especially justified for women whose adultery is likely to provoke physical abuse or a divorce that would leave them and their children impoverished. Others argue that even when the adultery is immoral, confession wreaks more harm than the benefits of restoring full honesty in the relationship. (E.g., Laura Green, "Never Confess," in Abraham, *Reinventing Love,* pp. 192–197.) The case for promoting honesty by confessing an infidelity to one's spouse is made by Frank Pittman in *Private Lies.*

CHAPTER 5. RESPECT

1. Toni Morrison, *Song of Solomon* (New York: New American Library, 1977), p. 310.

2. Carol Gilligan, *In a Different Voice* (Cambridge: Harvard University Press, 1982), p. 63.

3. Stephen L. Darwall, "Two Kinds of Respect," *Ethics* 88 (1977): 36–49. More cautiously, recognition-respect is owed to almost all people, since there is a question about whether full recognition-respect is owed to sociopaths.

4. Robin S. Dillon, "Care and Respect," in E. B. Cole and S. Coultrap-McQuin, eds., *Explorations in Feminist Ethics* (Bloomington: Indiana University Press, 1992), p. 73. Dillon's conception of care-respect is inspired in part by Carol Gilligan, *In a Different Voice* (Cambridge: Harvard University Press, 1982).

5. Cf. A. I. Melden, *Rights and Persons* (Berkeley: University of California Press, 1979), esp. chap. 5.

6. Percy Bysshe Shelley, "Love's Philosophy," reprinted in Jon Stallworthy, ed., *A Book of Love Poetry* (New York: Oxford University Press, 1974), p. 80.

7. Plato, *Symposium,* trans. Alexander Nehamas and Paul Woodruff (Indianapolis: Hackett, 1989), 192D–E.

8. Gottfried von Strassburg, *Tristan,* trans. A. T. Hatto (New York: Penguin Books, 1960), p. 262.

9. Denis de Rougement, *Love in the Western World,* rev. ed., trans. Montgomery Belgion (New York: Harper and Row, 1956).

10. Irving Singer, *The Nature of Love,* vol. 2, *Courtly and Romantic* (Chicago: University of Chicago Press, 1984), p. 298.

11. E.g., Stendhal, *Love,* trans. Gilbert Sale and Suzanne Sale (New York: Penguin Books, 1975).

12. Johann Wolfgang von Goethe, *The Sorrows of Young Werther,* trans. Michael Hulse (New York: Penguin Books, 1989), p. 53.

13. Ibid., p. 115.

14. Thomas J. Scheff and Suzanne M. Retzinger, *Emotions and Violence: Shame and Rage in Destructive Conflicts* (Lexington, MA: Lexington Books, 1991), pp. 108–111.

15. D. H. Lawrence, *Women in Love* (New York: Penguin Books, 1982), p. 506.

16. Ibid., p. 542.

17. Ibid., p. 215.

18. Ibid., p. 210.

19. Ibid., p. 343.

20. Cf. Irving Singer, *The Nature of Love,* vol. 3, *The Modern World* (Chicago: University of Chicago Press, 1987), pp. 223–224.

21. Better than a single circle, the traditional image of the heart retains an outline of two distinct personalities while otherwise blending them. Cf.

Robert Nozick, *The Examined Life* (New York: Simon and Schuster, 1989), p. 73.

22. Milan Kundera, *The Unbearable Lightness of Being,* trans. Michael Henry Heim (New York: Harper Perennial, 1991), p. 8.

23. Ibid., p. 195.

24. Ibid., pp. 238–239.

25. Ibid., p. 298. Also see Fred Misurella, *Understanding Milan Kundera* (Columbia: University of South Carolina Press, 1992), pp. 105–133.

26. Irving Singer, *The Pursuit of Love* (Baltimore: Johns Hopkins University Press, 1994), pp. 25–26.

27. Erich Fromm, *The Art of Loving* (New York: Harper and Row, 1956). Earlier Fromm developed the self-respect thesis in "Selfishness and Self-Love," *Psychiatry* 2 (1939): 507–524, and *Man for Himself* (New York: Holt, Rinehart and Winston, 1947), chap. 4, sec. 5. Although Fromm prefers to speak of self-love, it is clear he means self-respect. As examples of Fromm's influence in the self-help literature on love, see Stanton Peele, *Love and Addiction* (New York: New American Library, 1975), p. 83; M. Scott Peck, *The Road Less Traveled* (New York: Simon and Schuster, 1978), p. 82; and Ethel Spector Person, *Dreams of Love and Fateful Encounters: The Power of Romantic Passion* (New York: W. W. Norton, 1988), p. 191.

28. Fromm, *The Art of Loving,* p. 50.

29. Ibid., p. 49.

30. Ibid., p. 19.

31. Ibid., pp. 21–22.

32. Ibid., pp. 23–24.

33. Ibid., p. 17; emphasis in original.

34. Ibid., p. 23.

35. Ibid., pp. 38–39; italics removed.

36. Ibid., p. 50.

37. Cf. Singer, *The Nature of Love,* 3:418.

38. As can self-esteem; see L. T. Sanford and M. E. Donovan, *Women and Self-Esteem* (New York: Penguin Books, 1984), p. 9.

39. Thomas E. Hill, Jr., in *Autonomy and Self-Respect* (New York: Cambridge University Press, 1991), pp. 19–24.

40. Robin S. Dillon, "Toward a Feminist Conception of Self-Respect," *Hypatia* 7 (1992): 60.

41. Friedrich Nietzsche, *The Gay Science,* trans. Walter Kaufmann (New York: Vintage Books, 1974), p. 233. The same insight is developed by Fyodor Dostoevsky in *Notes from the Underground,* trans. Ralph E. Matlaw (New York: E. P. Dutton, 1960).

42. John Rawls, *A Theory of Justice* (Cambridge: Harvard University Press, 1971), p. 440.

43. Lawrence A. Blum, Marcia Homiak, Judy Housman, and Naomi Scheman, "Altruism and Women's Oppression," *Philosophical Forum* 5 (1975): 231.

44. Nathaniel Branden, *The Psychology of Romantic Love* (New York: Bantam Books, 1981), p. 141.

45. Milton Mayeroff, *On Caring* (New York: Harper and Row, 1971), p. 13.

46. Jerome Neu, "Jealous Thoughts," in Amélie O. Rorty, ed., *Explaining Emotions* (Berkeley: University of California Press, 1980); Nancy Friday, *Jealousy* (New York: William Morrow, 1985), p. 390; and G. Clanton and L. G. Smith, eds., *Jealousy* (Lanham, MD: University Press of America, 1986).

47. Cf. Robin Dillon, "How to Lose Your Self-Respect," *American Philosophical Quarterly,* 29 (1992): 135.

48. Stephen J. Massey, "Is Self-Respect a Moral or a Psychological Concept?" *Ethics* 93 (1983): 246–261, and David Sachs, "How to Distinguish Self-Respect from Self-Esteem," *Philosophy and Public Affairs* 10 (1981): 346–360.

49. Richard Taylor, *Ethics, Faith and Reason* (Englewood Cliffs, NJ: Prentice-Hall, 1985), pp. 100–102.

50. Joel Feinberg, "Absurd Self-Fulfillment," in Feinberg, *Freedom and Fulfillment* (Princeton: Princeton University Press, 1992), p. 326.

51. Branden, *The Psychology of Romantic Love,* p. 124.

52. Morrison, *Song of Solomon,* p. 310.

53. Robert C. Solomon, *About Love* (New York: Simon and Schuster, 1988).

54. K. L. Dion, and K. K. Dion, "Romantic Love: Individual and Cultural Perspectives," in Robert J. Sternberg and Michael L. Barnes, eds., *The Psychology of Love* (New Haven: Yale University Press, 1988).

55. Nel Noddings, *Caring: A Feminine Approach to Ethics and Moral Education* (Berkeley: University of California Press, 1984), p. 100.

56. Immanuel Kant, *The Doctrine of Virtue,* trans. M. J. Gregor (Philadelphia: University of Pennsylvania Press, 1964).

57. Hill, *Autonomy and Self-Respect,* p. 5.

58. Rollo May, *Love and Will* (New York: Dell, 1974), p. 145.

Chapter 6. Fairness

1. Simone de Beauvoir, *The Second Sex,* trans. H. M. Parshley (New York: Vintage Books, 1974), p. 741.

2. For some examples of fairness in heterosexual marriages, see Gayle Kimball, *The 50/50 Marriage* (Boston: Beacon Press, 1983). For an intriguing case study of a lesbian marriage—"marriage" in a moral rather than a legal sense—see Diana Souhami, *Gertrude and Alice* (San Francisco: Pandora, 1991). And for insights into negotiating tasks within lesbian relationships see Sue Cartledge and Joanna Ryan, eds., *Sex and Love: New Thoughts on Old Contradictions* (London: Women's Press, 1983).

3. Francis Edward Smedley, *Frank Fairlegh* (London: George Routledge and Sons, 1850), p. 446. Somewhat more somberly, in the eighteenth century Susanna Centilivre applied a precursor of the maxim—"All Policy's allow'd in War and Love"—to a rogue who used deception as a weapon of seduction and exploitation (*Love at a Venture,* in *The Plays of Susanna Centilivre,* ed. Richard C. Frushell. [New York: Garland Publishing, 1982], p. 12; first published in 1706).

4. Robert Nozick discusses how liberty upsets distribution patterns in the different context of economic transactions in *Anarchy, State, and Utopia* (New York: Basic Books, 1974), pp. 160-164.

5. Michael Walzer, *Spheres of Justice: A Defense of Pluralism and Equality* (New York: Basic Books, 1983), p. 227.

6. Shulamith Firestone, *The Dialectic of Sex* (New York: William Morrow, 1970), p. 146; emphasis in original.

7. Lawrence Haworth, *Autonomy* (New Haven: Yale University Press, 1986); and Diana T. Meyers, *Self, Society, and Personal Choice* (New York: Columbia University Press, 1989).

8. The concept of primary goods, although not this list, comes from John Rawls, *A Theory of Justice* (Cambridge: Harvard University Press, 1971). It is used in a different form by Susan Moller Okin, *Justice, Gender, and the Family* (New York: Basic Books, 1989), esp. chap. 7.

9. Joel Feinberg, "The Child's Right to an Open Future," in William Aiken and Hugh LaFollette, eds., *Whose Child?* (Totowa, NJ: Littlefield, Adams, 1980). For a discussion of the covert ways in which women's autonomy is subverted by upbringing see Margaret Adams, "The Compassion Trap," in Vivian Gornick and Barbara K. Moran, eds., *Woman in Sexist Society,* (New York: New American Library, 1972).

10. Philip Blumstein and Pepper Schwartz, *American Couples* (New York: William Morrow, 1983), pp. 52-53.

11. Sandra Lee Bartky, *Femininity and Domination* (New York: Routledge, 1990), p. 77; and Cass R. Sunstein, *Feminism and Political Theory* (Chicago: University of Chicago Press, 1990), p. 9.

12. Sonia Johnson, *From Housewife to Heretic* (Garden City, NY: Anchor Books, 1983), p. 161. For a more subtle case in which a wife comes to

feel that her autonomy is distorted within a seemingly equal relationship, see Molly Haskell's engaging memoir, *Love and Other Infectious Diseases* (New York: Citadel Press, 1992).

13. Arlie Russell Hochschild, "Emotion Work, Feeling Rules, and Social Structure," *American Journal of Sociology* 85 (1979): 551–575; and *The Managed Heart* (Berkeley: University of California Press, 1983).

14. Lawrence A. Blum, Marcia Homiak, Judy Housman, and Naomi Scheman, "Altruism and Women's Oppression," *Philosophical Forum* 5 (1975): 231.

15. Okin, *Justice, Gender, and the Family,* p. 171.

16. Arlene Kaplan Daniels shows the value of nonpaid work in *Invisible Careers: Women Civic Leaders from the Volunteer World* (Chicago: University of Chicago Press, 1988).

17. Robert C. Solomon, *About Love* (New York: Simon and Schuster, 1988), p 297.

18. Ibid., p. 298.

19. Ibid., p. 297.

20. Sharon Bishop, "Love and Dependency," in Sharon Bishop and Marjorie Weinzweig, eds., *Philosophy and Women* (Belmont, CA: Wadsworth, 1979), p. 152.

21. See, e.g., Carol Gilligan, *In a Different Voice* (Cambridge: Harvard University Press, 1982), and Jean Grimshaw, *Philosophy and Feminist Thinking* (Minneapolis: University of Minnesota Press, 1986).

22. Roger Scruton, *Sexual Desire* (New York: Free Press, 1986).

23. Robert Nozick, *The Examined Life* (New York: Simon and Schuster, 1989), p. 71.

24. Bishop, "Love and Dependency," in Bishop and Weinzweig, *Philosophy and Women,* pp. 153–154.

25. Irving Singer, *The Nature of Love,* vol. 3, *The Modern World* (Chicago: University of Chicago Press, 1987), p. 412.

26. Judith Farr Tormey, "Exploitation, Oppression and Self-Sacrifice," *Philosophical Forum* 5 (1975): 212.

27. Edmund L. Pincoffs, *Quandaries and Virtues* (Lawrence: University Press of Kansas, 1986), pp. 112–114.

28. Cf. Lawrence C. Becker on reciprocity as a virtue in *Reciprocity* (New York: Routledge and Kegan Paul, 1986), pp. 186–188.

29. For a discussion of some similarities see Lenore J. Weitzman, *The Marriage Contract* (New York: Free Press, 1981).

30. Robert N. Bellah, Richard Madsen, William M. Sullivan, Ann Swidler, and Steven M. Tipton, *Habits of the Heart: Individualism and*

Commitment in American Life (Berkeley: University of California Press, 1985), p. 130.

31. Francesca M. Cancian, *Love in America: Gender and Self-Development* (New York: Cambridge University Press, 1987), p. 40. For an interesting study of these themes in nineteenth-century relationships see Phyllis Rose, *Parallel Lives: Five Victorian Marriages* (New York: Vintage Books, 1984).

32. Cancian, *Love in America,* p. 40.

33. Ibid., p. 110.

CHAPTER 7. HONESTY

1. Sian Miles, ed., *Simone Weil: An Anthology* (London: Virago, 1986), p. 93; quoted by Peter Winch, *Simone Weil: "The Just Balance"* (New York: Cambridge University Press, 1989), p. 201.

2. Molière, *The Misanthrope,* trans. Richard Wilbur (New York: Harcourt, Brace and World, 1954), act I, scene 1.

3. Friedrich Nietzsche, *Beyond Good and Evil,* trans. Walter Kaufmann (New York: Vintage Books, 1966), sec. 227.

4. Jean-Paul Sartre, *No Exit and Three Other Plays* (New York: Vintage Books, 1955).

5. Martin Heidegger, *Being and Time,* trans. John Macquarrie and Edward Robinson (New York: Harper and Row, 1962), pp. 211-214.

6. Deborah Tannen, *That's Not What I Meant!* (New York: Ballantine Books, 1986); and *You Just Don't Understand* (New York: Ballantine Books, 1990).

7. Mike W. Martin, "Honesty with Oneself," in Mary I. Bockover, ed., *Rules, Rituals, and Responsibility* (La Salle, IL: Open Court, 1991), pp. 115-136; and Annette C. Baier, "Why Honesty Is a Hard Virtue," in Owen Flanagan and Amélie Oksenberg Rorty, eds., *Identity, Character, and Morality* (Cambridge, MA: MIT Press, 1990), pp. 259-282.

8. Fyodor Dostoyevsky, *The Brothers Karamazov,* trans. Constance Garnett (New York: New American Library, 1957), p. 49.

9. Robert R. Ehman, "Personal Love," *The Personalist* 49 (1968): 116-141. Also see Valerian J. Derlega, Sandra Metts, Sandra Petronio, and Stephen T. Margulis, *Self-Disclosure* (Newbury Park, CA: Sage Publications, 1993).

10. David Henry Hwang, *M. Butterfly* (New York: Penguin Books, 1989).

11. Owen Flanagan, *Varieties of Moral Personality* (Cambridge: Harvard University Press, 1991).

12. Annette Baier, "Unsafe Loves," in Robert C. Solomon and Kathleen M. Higgins, eds., *The Philosophy of (Erotic) Love* (Lawrence: University Press of Kansas, 1991), pp. 433-450.

13. Doris Lessing, *Landlocked* (New York: Plume, 1970), pp. 218-219.

14. George Graham and Hugh LaFollette, "Honesty and Intimacy," in George Graham and Hugh LaFollette, eds., *Person to Person* (Philadelphia: Temple University Press, 1989), pp. 167-181. I benefited from this essay in several ways, including the emphasis given to the distinction between intimate experiences (or "encounters") and intimate relationships, as well as their discussion of metahonesty.

15. David Wood, "Honesty," in Alan Montefiore, ed., *Philosophy and Personal Relationships* (London: Routledge and Kegan Paul, 1973), p. 192.

16. Edmond Rostand, *Cyrano de Bergerac,* trans. Brian Hooker (New York: Bantam Books, 1950), p. 165.

17. Robert Nozick, "Love's Bond," in Nozick, *The Examined Life* (New York: Simon and Schuster, 1989), p. 68.

18. Ferdinand D. Schoeman, "Privacy and Intimate Information," in Ferdinand D. Schoeman, ed., *Philosophical Dimensions of Privacy* (Cambridge: Cambridge University Press, 1984), p. 406.

19. Robert C. Solomon, *Love: Emotion, Myth, and Metaphor* (Garden City, NY: Anchor Press, 1981), pp. 232-245.

20. Mike W. Martin, *Self-Deception and Morality* (Lawrence: University Press of Kansas, 1986); Joan S. Lockard and Delroy L. Paulhus, eds., *Self-Deception: An Adaptive Mechanism?* (Englewood Cliffs, NJ: Prentice-Hall, 1988); and Shelley E. Taylor, *Positive Illusions* (New York: Basic Books, 1989).

21. Stendhal, *On Love,* trans. H. B. V. Scott-Moncrieff and C. K. Scott-Moncrieff (New York: Liveright, 1983), p. 6.

CHAPTER 8. WISDOM

1. Martha C. Nussbaum, *Love's Knowledge: Essays on Philosophy and Literature* (New York: Oxford University Press, 1990), p. 4.

2. Parenthetical references—by act, scene, line—are to the Bantam edition of Shakespeare's *Othello,* ed. David Bevington (New York: Bantam Books, 1988).

3. F. R. Leavis, "Diabolic Intellect and the Noble Hero," *Scrutiny* 6 (1937), pp. 264, 270. Leavis, however, mistakenly dismisses Othello as not loving at all, a conclusion incisively criticized by Arthur Kirsch, *Shake-*

speare and the Experience of Love (Cambridge: Cambridge University Press, 1981), pp. 27-28.

4. John Bayley, *The Characters of Love: A Study in the Literature of Personality* (New York: Basic Books, 1960), p. 146.

5. Jerome Neu, "Jealous Thoughts," in Amélie O. Rorty, ed., *Explaining Emotions* (Berkeley: University of California Press, 1980), pp. 454-455.

6. Kirsch, *Shakespeare and the Experience of Love*, p. 32, and Evelyn Gajowski, *The Art of Loving: Female Subjectivity and Male Discursive Traditions in Shakespeare's Tragedies* (Newark: University of Delaware Press, 1992), pp. 53-54.

7. Coppelia Kahn, *Man's Estate: Masculine Identity in Shakespeare* (Berkeley: University of California Press, 1981).

8. On this general psychological response see Thomas J. Scheff and Suzanne M. Retzinger, *Emotions and Violence: Shame and Rage in Destructive Conflicts* (Lexington, MA: Lexington Books, 1991).

9. Jean-Paul Sartre, *Being and Nothingness*, trans. Hazel E. Barnes (New York: Washington Square Press, 1966), pp. 86-116. Hegelians might prefer to speak in terms of a thesis and antithesis that are never synthesized.

10. Ibid., pp. 96-97. The sexism in how Sartre describes the example is ironic since he borrowed the example (without acknowledgment) from George Gordon Byron, who had placed the woman in an assertive sexual role *Don Juan*, 105-117, in Russell Noyes, ed., *English Romantic Poetry and Prose* [New York: Oxford University Press, 1956], pp. 870-871). See Mike W. Martin, *Self-Deception and Morality* (Lawrence: University Press of Kansas, 1986), p. 151, n. 28.

11. Martin Elliott, *Shakespeare's Invention of Othello: A Study in Early Modern English* (New York: Macmillan, 1988), p. 24, and H. A. Mason, *Shakespeare's Tragedies of Love* (London: Chatto and Windus, 1970), p. 101.

12. Marianne Novy, *Love's Argument: Gender Relations in Shakespeare* (Chapel Hill: University of North Carolina Press, 1984), p. 143, and John Bayley, *The Characters of Love*, p. 145.

13. Frank Kermode, "Introduction to *Romeo and Juliet, Othello*, and *Anthony and Cleopatra*," in G. Blakemore Evans, ed., *The Riverside Shakespeare* (Boston: Houghton Mifflin, 1974), p. 1201.

14. William Shakespeare, sonnet 116, *The Sonnets* (New York: New American Library, 1964), p. 156. Danny L. Smith discusses this sonnet in connection with Othello in *"To Be Once in Doubt": Certainty and the Marriage of Minds in Othello* (New York: Peter Lang, 1989), pp. 179-192.

15. Stanley Cavell, "Othello and the Stake of the Other," in Cavell, *Disowning Knowledge, in Six Plays of Shakespeare* (New York: Cambridge University Press, 1987), pp. 125-142.

16. Novy, *Love's Argument*, pp. 131–132.

17. Carol Thomas Neely, "Women and Men in *Othello*," in Carolyn Ruth Swift Lenz, Gayle Greene, and Carol Thomas Neely, eds., *The Woman's Part: Feminist Criticism of Shakespeare* (Urbana: University of Illinois Press, 1983), pp. 216–217. Norman Council provides an insightful study of patriarchal honor in *When Honour's at the Stake: Ideas of Honour in Shakespeare's Plays* (London: George Allen and Unwin, 1973).

18. Elliott, *Shakespeare's Invention of Othello*, p. 228–229.

19. Robert J. Sternberg, ed., *Wisdom: Its Nature, Origins, and Development* (New York: Cambridge University Press, 1990).

20. Martha C. Nussbaum, "The Speech of Alcibiades: A Reading of Plato's *Symposium*," in Robert C. Solomon and Kathleen M. Higgins, eds., *The Philosophy of (Erotic) Love* (Lawrence: University Press of Kansas, 1991), p. 304.

21. Max Scheler, "Love and Knowledge," in Harold J. Bershady, ed., *On Feeling, Knowing, and Valuing* (Chicago: University of Chicago Press, 1992), pp. 147–165.

CHAPTER 9. COURAGE

1. Iris Murdoch, *The Sovereignty of Good* (Boston: Routledge and Kegan Paul, 1985), p. 95; first published in 1970.

2. Douglas N. Walton, *Courage: A Philosophical Investigation* (Berkeley: University of California Press, 1986), p. 14.

3. Ibid., pp. 93–94.

4. Annette Baier, "Unsafe Loves," in Robert C. Solomon and Kathleen M. Higgins, eds., *The Philosophy of (Erotic) Love* (Lawrence: University Press of Kansas, 1991), pp. 433–434.

5. Ibid., p. 434.

6. Cf. Robin Norwood, *Women Who Love Too Much* (New York: Pocket Books, 1986).

7. Sappho, quoted and translated by Anne Carson, *Eros the Bittersweet* (Princeton: Princeton University Press, 1986), p. 3.

8. Anaïs Nin, *The Diary of Anaïs Nin*, ed. Gunther Stuhlmann (New York: Harcourt Brace Jovanovich, 1969), vol. 3, p. 125.

9. Elizabeth Glaser and Laura Palmer, *In the Absence of Angels* (New York: Berkley Books, 1991), p. 276.

10. Walton, *Courage*, p. 191.

11. See James L. Muyskens, *The Sufficiency of Hope* (Philadelphia: Temple University Press, 1979), pp. 18–19.

12. Alasdair MacIntyre, *After Virtue,* 2d ed. (Notre Dame: University of Notre Dame Press, 1984), p. 192.

13. Erica Jong, *How To Save Your Own Life* (New York: New American Library, 1977), p. 265.

14. Parenthetical page references are to Zora Neale Hurston, *Their Eyes Were Watching God* (New York: Harper and Row, 1990).

15. Cf. Missy Dehn Kubitschek, "Tuh de Horizon and Back: The Female Quest in *Their Eyes Were Watching God,"* in Harold Bloom, ed., *Zora Neale Hurston's Their Eyes Were Watching God* (New York: Chelsea House, 1987), p. 23.

16. Alice Walker suggests that "the real reason . . . Hurston *permits* Janie to kill Tea Cake in the end" is that "Janie knows she has been publicly humiliated" (*In Search of Our Mothers' Gardens* [New York: Harcourt Brace Jovanovich, 1983], pp. 305–306). That seems off the mark, but I agree with Walker that the present episode teaches Janie that even Tea Cake cannot be completely trusted to always act for her good.

17. As she cradles him moments before he dies, Tea Cake bites her, presumably infecting her with rabies. It is thus possible that Janie is dying from rabies at the end of the novel, although it seems more likely to me that she would seek adequate medical attention.

18. Robert B. Stepto, in "Ascent, Immersion, Narration," questions whether Janie ever really achieves her voice; this essay and rejoinders are in Bloom, *Zora Neale Hurston's Their Eyes Were Watching God.* Mary Helen Washington also questions whether Janie achieves authenticity, in " 'I Love the Way Janie Crawford Left Her Husbands': Emergent Female Hero," in Henry Louis Gates, Jr., and K. A. Appiah, eds., *Zora Neale Hurston: Critical Perspectives Past and Present* (New York: Amistad Press, 1993), pp. 98–109.

19. Alice Walker says that Hurston's novel is "perhaps the most authentic and moving black love story ever published" (*In Search of Our Mothers' Gardens,* p. 35).

20. Cf. Michael Awkward, ed., *New Essays on Their Eyes Were Watching God* (New York: Cambridge University Press, 1990), p. 21.

21. Zora Neale Hurston, *Dust Tracks on a Road* (New York: Harper Perennial, 1991), p. 186.

22. Ibid., p. 192.

Chapter 10. Gratitude

1. Jane Austen, *Pride and Prejudice* (New York: Penguin Books, 1972), pp. 284–285.

2. Patricia S. Greenspan, *Emotions and Reasons* (New York: Routledge, 1988), p. 59. Also, on the insufficiency of gratitude to motivate love see Robert M. Polhemus, *Erotic Faith: Being in Love from Jane Austen to D. H. Lawrence* (Chicago: University of Chicago Press, 1990), pp. 52-53.

3. See, e.g., John A. Simmons, *Moral Principles and Political Obligations* (Princeton: Princeton University Press, 1979).

4. Immanuel Kant, *Lectures on Ethics*, trans. Louis Infield (New York: Harper and Row, 1963), p. 118. Cf. Kant, *The Doctrine of Virtue*, trans. M. J. Gregor (Philadelphia: University of Pennsylvania Press, 1964), p. 123.

5. A. D. M. Walker, "Gratefulness and Gratitude," *Proceedings of the Aristotelian Society* 81 (1980-1981): 39-55. I use the words "gratitude" and "gratefulness" as rough synonyms, whereas Walker restricts the word "gratitude" to matters of conduct toward others and presents his definition as an analysis of gratefulness.

6. Cf. Claudia Card, "Gratitude and Obligation," *American Philosophical Quarterly* 25 (1988): 115. Card recommends that the model of debtor be replaced by the model of a trustee or guardian. Debts and loans imply rights of benefactor to get something back, whereas in trustee relationships and gratitude there are no such rights. "Owing gratitude is more like having accepted a deposit, than like having taken out a loan. . . . As a beneficiary, I can regard myself as the 'trustee' of another's good will or concern. I cannot literally return another's good will, but I can reciprocate it" (121). Yet many instances of entrusting someone with something do involve rights to receive back what is entrusted, either upon request or as stipulated in agreements.

7. See Terrance McConnell, *Gratitude* (Philadelphia: Temple University Press, 1993), pp. 44, 148-179. Within an ethical theory that regards love's virtues as fundamental, Lawrence C. Becker attempts to subsume gratitude under a wider virtue of reciprocity, which is the disposition to return good for good in a fitting way (*Reciprocity* [New York: Routledge and Kegan Paul, 1986]).

8. McConnell, *Gratitude*, p. 56.

9. Roslyn Weiss, "The Moral and Social Dimensions of Gratitude," *The Southern Journal of Philosophy* 23 (1985): 494.

10. Molly Lefebure, *The Bondage of Love: A Life of Mrs. Samuel Taylor Coleridge* (New York: Paragon House, 1989). For another example, see Isabelle de Courtivron, "Of First Wives and Solitary Heroes: Clara and André Malraux," in Whitney Chadwick and Isabelle de Courtivron, eds., *Significant Others: Creativity and Intimate Partnership* (London: Thames

and Hudson, 1993), pp. 51–63. An especially moving example is presented by Fumiko Enchi in her novel *The Waiting Years,* trans. John Bester (New York: Kodansha International, 1980).

11. Card, "Gratitude and Obligation," pp. 124–125.

12. See McConnell, *Gratitude,* pp. 81–113.

13. Fred R. Berger, "Gratitude," *Ethics* 85 (1974–1975), p. 302.

14. Paul F. Camenisch, "Gift and Gratitude in Ethics," *The Journal of Religious Ethics* 9 (1981): 15.

15. Ibid.

16. Ibid., p. 14.

17. Robert C. Solomon, *The Passions* (Garden City, NY: Anchor Press, 1977), pp. 335–337.

18. Chris M. Meadows, "The Phenomenology of Joy, An Empirical Investigation," *Psychological Reports* 37 (1975): 39–54.

19. Nel Noddings, *Caring: A Feminine Approach to Ethics and Moral Education* (Berkeley: University of California Press, 1984), p. 132.

20. Carroll E. Izard, *Human Emotions* (New York: Plenum Press, 1977), pp. 244–246.

21. Robb Forman Dew, *Dale Loves Sophie to Death* (New York: Penguin Books, 1982), p. 86; also see the sequel, *Fortunate Lives* (New York: William Morrow, 1992).

22. Forman Dew, *Dale Loves Sophie to Death,* p. 217.

23. Verena Kast, *Joy, Inspiration, and Hope,* trans. Douglas Whitcher (College Station: Texas A&M University Press, 1991), pp. 67–74.

24. Camenisch, "Gift and Gratitude in Ethics," p. 23.

25. In the novel the word "gratitude" is not often used, although "appreciate" is, and hence what I am offering is an interpretation of appreciation as grateful cherishing.

26. Parenthetical page references are to Alice Walker, *The Color Purple* (New York: Pocket Books, 1985).

27. Cf. my essay *"Invisible Man* and the Indictment of Innocence," *CLA Journal* 25 (1982): 288–302.

28. Cf. Linda Abbandonato, "Rewriting the Heroine's Story in *The Color Purple,"* in Henry Louis Gates, Jr., and K. A. Appiah, eds., *Alice Walker: Critical Perspectives Past and Present* (New York: Amistad Press, 1993), p. 306. In exploring the novel's rich symbolism, see the other essays in this volume and also the essays in Harold Bloom, ed., *Alice Walker: Modern Critical Views* (New York: Chelsea House, 1989).

EPILOGUE

1. Bharati Mukherjee, *Jasmine* (New York: Fawcett Crest, 1989), p. 69.
2. Ibid., p. 25.
3. Ibid., pp. 213-214.

BIBLIOGRAPHY

Abbandonato, Linda. "Rewriting the Heroine's Story in *The Color Purple*." In *Alice Walker: Critical Perspectives Past and Present,* edited by Henry Louis Gates, Jr., and K. A. Appiah, pp. 296-308. New York: Amistad Press, 1993.

Abraham, Laurie, ed. *Reinventing Love.* New York: Plume, 1993.

Ackerman, Diane. *A Natural History of Love.* New York: Random House, 1994.

Adams, Margaret. "The Compassion Trap." In *Woman in Sexist Society,* edited by Vivian Gornick and Barbara K. Moran, pp. 555-575. New York: New American Library, 1972.

Adams, Robert. "Pure Love." In Adams, *The Virtue of Faith,* pp. 174-192. New York: Oxford University Press, 1987.

Atwater, Lynn. *The Extramarital Connection.* New York: Irvington Publishers, 1982.

Austen, Jane. *Pride and Prejudice.* New York: Penguin Books, 1972.

Awkward, Michael. *New Essays on Their Eyes Were Watching God.* New York: Cambridge University Press, 1990.

Badhwar, Neera Kapur. "Friends as Ends in Themselves." In *Eros, Agape and Philia,* edited by Alan Soble, pp. 165-186. New York: Paragon House, 1989.

Badhwar, Neera Kapur, ed. *Friendship: A Philosophical Reader.* Ithaca, NY: Cornell University Press, 1993.

Baier, Annette. *Moral Prejudices: Essays on Ethics.* Cambridge: Harvard University Press, 1994.

———. "Trust and Antitrust." *Ethics* 96 (1986): 231-260.

———. "Unsafe Loves." In *The Philosophy of (Erotic) Love,* edited by Robert C. Solomon and Kathleen M. Higgins, pp. 433-450. Lawrence: University Press of Kansas, 1991.

————. "Why Honesty Is a Hard Virtue." In *Identity, Character, and Morality,* edited by Owen Flanagan and Amélie Oksenberg Rorty, pp. 259–282. Cambridge, MA: MIT Press, 1990.

Bair, Deirdre. *Simone de Beauvoir: A Biography.* New York: Simon and Schuster, 1990.

Baker, Robert, and Frederick Elliston, eds. *Philosophy and Sex.,* 2d ed. Buffalo, NY: Prometheus Books, 1984.

Barnhart, J. E., and Mary Ann Barnhart. "Marital Faithfulness and Unfaithfulness." *Journal of Social Philosophy* 4 (1973): 10–15.

Barthes, Roland. *A Lover's Discourse: Fragments.* Translated by Richard Howard. New York: Hill and Wang, 1978.

Bartky, Sandra Lee. *Femininity and Domination.* New York: Routledge, 1990.

Bayles, Michael D. "Marriage, Love, and Procreation." In *Philosophy and Sex,* 2d ed., edited by Robert Baker and Frederick Elliston, pp. 130–145. Buffalo, NY: Prometheus Books, 1984.

Bayley, John. *The Characters of Love: A Study in the Literature of Personality.* New York: Basic Books, 1960.

————. *Tolstoy and the Novel.* New York: Viking Press, 1967.

Becker, Lawrence C. *Reciprocity.* New York: Routledge and Kegan Paul, 1986.

Bellah, Robert N., Richard Madsen, William M. Sullivan, Ann Swidler, and Steven M. Tipton. *Habits of the Heart: Individualism and Commitment in American Life.* Berkeley: University of California Press, 1985.

Belliotti, Raymond A. *Good Sex: Perspectives on Sexual Ethics.* Lawrence: University Press of Kansas, 1993.

Benjamin, Jessica. *The Bonds of Love: Psychoanalysis, Feminism, and the Problem of Domination.* New York: Pantheon Books, 1988.

Berenson, Frances. "What Is this Thing Called 'Love'?" *Philosophy* 66 (1991): 65–79.

Berger, Fred R. "Gratitude." *Ethics* 85 (1974–1975): 298–309.

Bergman, Ingmar. *Scenes from a Marriage.* In *The Marriage Scenarios,* translated by Alan Blair, pp. 1–202. New York: Pantheon Books, 1983.

Bergmann, Martin S. *The Anatomy of Loving.* New York: Columbia University Press, 1987.

Berlin, Isaiah. "The Pursuit of the Ideal." In *The Crooked Timber of Humanity,* edited by Henry Hardy, pp. 1–19. New York: Vintage Books, 1992.

Bishop, Sharon. "Love and Dependency." In *Philosophy and Women,* edited by Sharon Bishop and Marjorie Weinzweig, pp. 147–154. Belmont, CA: Wadsworth, 1979.

Bloom, Allan. *Love and Friendship.* New York: Simon and Schuster, 1993.

Bloom, Harold, ed. *Alice Walker: Modern Critical Views.* New York: Chelsea House, 1989.

————. *Zora Neale Hurston's Their Eyes Were Watching God.* New York: Chelsea House, 1987.

Blum, Lawrence A. *Friendship, Altruism and Morality.* London: Routledge and Kegan Paul, 1980.

————. *Moral Perception and Particularity.* Cambridge: Cambridge University Press, 1994.

Blum, Lawrence A., Marcia Homiak, Judy Housman, and Naomi Scheman. "Altruism and Women's Oppression." *Philosophical Forum* 5 (1975): 222–247.

Blumstein, Philip, and Pepper Schwartz. *American Couples.* New York: William Morrow, 1983.

Blustein, Jeffrey. *Care and Commitment.* New York: Oxford University Press, 1991.

Bok, Sissela. *Alva Myrdal: A Daughter's Memoir.* New York: Addison-Wesley, 1991.

Boone, Joseph Allen. *Tradition Counter Tradition: Love and the Form of Fiction.* Chicago: University of Chicago Press, 1987.

Branden, Nathaniel. *The Psychology of Romantic Love.* New York: Bantam Books, 1981.

Broudy, Harry S. *Enlightened Cherishing.* Urbana: University of Illinois Press, 1972.

Brown, Robert. *Analyzing Love.* Cambridge: Cambridge University Press, 1987.

Browning, Elizabeth Barrett. *Sonnets from the Portuguese,* Sonnet 43. In *A Book of Love Poetry,* edited by Jon Stallworthy, p. 51. New York: Oxford University Press, 1974.

Brummer, Vincent. *The Model of Love: A Study in Philosophical Theology.* Cambridge: Cambridge University Press, 1993.

Byron, George Gordon. *Don Juan.* In *English Romantic Poetry and Prose,* edited by Russell Noyes, pp. 856–913. New York: Oxford University Press, 1956.

Camenisch, Paul F. "Gift and Gratitude in Ethics." *The Journal of Religious Ethics* 9 (1981): 1–34.

Campbell, Anne. *Men, Women, and Aggression.* New York: Basic Books, 1993.

Cancian, Francesca M. *Love in America: Gender and Self-Development.* New York: Cambridge University Press, 1987.

Card, Claudia. "Gratitude and Obligation." *American Philosophical Quarterly* 25 (1988): 115-127.

Card, Claudia, ed. *Feminist Ethics.* Lawrence: University Press of Kansas, 1991.

Carson, Anne. *Eros the Bittersweet.* Princeton: Princeton University Press, 1986.

Cartledge, Sue, and Joanna Ryan, eds. *Sex and Love: New Thoughts on Old Contradictions.* London: Women's Press, 1983.

Cavell, Stanley. "Othello and the Stake of the Other." In Cavell, *Disowning Knowledge, in Six Plays of Shakespeare,* pp. 125-142. New York: Cambridge University Press, 1987.

Centilivre, Susanna. *Love at a Venture,* in *The Plays of Susanna Centilivre,* 1706. Reprint edited by Richard C. Frushell. New York: Garland, 1982.

Chadwick, Whitney, and Isabelle De Courtivron. eds. *Significant Others: Creativity and Intimate Partnership.* New York: Thames and Hudson, 1993.

Chipps, Genie D., and Bill Henderson, eds. *Love Stories for the Time Being.* Wainscott, NY: Pushcart Press, 1989.

Clanton, G., and L. G. Smith, eds. *Jealousy.* Lanham, MD: University Press of America, 1986.

Cole, Eve Browning, and Susan Coultrap-McQuin, eds. *Explorations in Feminist Ethics: Theory and Practice.* Bloomington: Indiana University Press, 1992.

Cooey, Paula M., Sharon A. Farmer, and Mary Ellen Ross, eds. *Embodied Love: Sensuality and Relationship as Feminist Values.* San Francisco: Harper and Row, 1987.

Connelly, R. J. "Philosophy and Adultery." In *Adultery in the United States,* edited by Philip E. Lampe, pp. 131-164. Buffalo, NY: Prometheus Books, 1987.

Council, Norman. *When Honour's at the Stake: Ideas of Honour in Shakespeare's Plays.* London: George Allen and Unwin, 1973.

Courtivron, Isabelle de. "Of First Wives and Solitary Heroes: Clara and André Malraux." In *Significant Others: Creativity and Intimate Partnership,* edited by Whitney Chadwick and Isabelle de Courtivron, pp. 51-63. London: Thames and Hudson, 1993.

Cua, A. S. *Dimensions of Moral Creativity: Paradigms, Principles, and Ideals.* University Park: Pennsylvania State University Press, 1978.

Daniels, Arlene Kaplan. *Invisible Careers: Women Civic Leaders from the Volunteer World.* Chicago: University of Chicago Press, 1988.

Dark, Larry, ed. *The Literary Lover.* New York: Viking, 1993.

Darwall, Stephen L. "Two Kinds of Respect. *Ethics* 88 (1977): 36-49.

Day, Dorothy. *The Long Loneliness.* New York: Harper and Row, 1952.

De Beauvoir, Simone. *The Ethics of Ambiguity.* Translated by Bernard Frechtman. Secaucus, NJ: Citadel Press, 1980.

_____. *The Second Sex.* Translated by H. M. Parshley. New York: Vintage Books, 1974.

D'Emilio, John, and Estelle B. Freedman. *Intimate Matters: A History of Sexuality in America.* New York: Harper and Row, 1988.

Derlega, Valerian J., Sandra Metts, Sandra Petronia, and Stephen T. Margulis. *Self-Disclosure.* Newbury Park, CA: Sage Publications, 1993.

De Rougement, Denis. *Love in the Western World.* Rev. ed. Translated by Montgomery Belgion. New York: Harper and Row, 1974.

De Sousa, Ronald. *The Rationality of Emotion.* Cambridge, MA: MIT Press, 1987.

Deutsch, Eliot. *Personhood, Creativity and Freedom.* Honolulu: University of Hawaii Press, 1982.

Dew, Robb Forman. *Dale Loves Sophie to Death.* New York: Penguin Books, 1982.

_____. *Fortunate Lives.* New York: William Morrow,, 1992.

Dewey, John. *Human Nature and Conduct.* New York: Modern Library, 1930.

Diamond, Irene, ed. *Families, Politics, and Public Policy.* New York: Longman, 1983.

Dillon, Robin S. "Care and Respect." In *Explorations in Feminist Ethics,* edited by E. B. Cole and S. Coultrap-McQuin, pp. 69–81. Bloomington: Indiana University Press, 1992.

_____. "How to Lose Your Self-Respect." *American Philosophical Quarterly* 29 (1992): 125–139.

_____. "Toward a Feminist Conception of Self-Respect." *Hypatia* 7 (1992): 52–69.

Dilman, İlham. *Love and Human Separateness.* New York: Basil Blackwell, 1987.

Dinesen, Isak. *On Marriage and Other Observations.* Translated by Anne Born. New York: St. Martin's Press, 1986.

Dion, K. L., and K. K. Dion. "Romantic Love: Individual and Cultural Perspectives." In *The Psychology of Love,* edited by Robert J. Sternberg and Michael L. Barnes, pp. 264–289. New Haven: Yale University Press, 1988.

Dostoyevsky, Fyodor. *The Brothers Karamazov.* Translated by Constance Garnett. New York: New American Library, 1957.

_____. *Notes from the Underground.* Translated by Ralph E. Matlaw. New York: E. P. Dutton, 1960.

Douglas, Jack D., and Freda Cruse Atwell. *Love, Intimacy and Sex*. Newbury Park, CA: Sage Publications, 1988.

Draft, Scott. "Murderous Affair Shocks Kansas Town." *Los Angeles Times* (March 17, 1986): 1, 14–15.

Dworkin, Ronald. *Taking Rights Seriously*. Cambridge: Harvard University Press, 1977.

Ehman, Robert R. "Personal Love." *The Personalist* 49 (1968): 116–141; reprinted, in *Eros, Agape and Philia: Readings in the Philosophy of Love*, edited by Alan Soble, pp. 254–271. New York: Paragon House, 1989.

Eliot, George. *Daniel Deronda*. 1876. Reprint. New York: Penguin Books, 1967.

———. *The Mill on the Floss*. New York: New American Library, 1965.

Elliott, Martin. *Shakespeare's Invention of Othello: A Study in Early Modern English*. New York: Macmillan, 1988.

Enchi, Fumiko. *The Waiting Years*. Translated by John Bester. New York: Kodansha International, 1980.

Feinberg, Joel. "Absurd Self-Fulfillment." In Feinberg, *Freedom and Fulfillment*, pp. 297–330. Princeton: Princeton University Press, 1992.

———. "The Child's Right to an Open Future." In *Whose Child?* edited by William Aiken and Hugh LaFollette, pp. 124–153. Totowa, NJ: Littlefield, Adams, 1980.

Fiedler, Leslie A. *Love and Death in the American Novel*. Rev. ed. New York: Stein and Day, 1966.

Firestone, Shulamith. *The Dialectic of Sex*. New York: William Morrow, 1970.

Fisher, Helen E. *Anatomy of Love: The Natural History of Monogamy, Adultery, and Divorce*. New York: W. W. Norton, 1992.

Flanagan, Owen. *Varieties of Moral Personality*. Cambridge: Harvard University Press, 1991.

Flanagan, Owen, and Amélie Oksenberg Rorty, eds. *Identity, Character, and Morality*. Cambridge: MIT Press, 1990.

Fletcher, George P. *Loyalty: An Essay on The Morality of Relationships*. New York: Oxford University Press, 1993.

Foucault, Michel. *The History of Sexuality*. 3 vols. New York: Vintage Books, 1980–1988.

Frankena, William K. "The Ethics of Love Conceived as an Ethics of Virtue." *Journal of Religious Ethics* 1 (1973): 21–36.

Frankfurt, Harry G. *The Importance of What We Care About*. New York: Cambridge University Press, 1988.

French, Marilyn. *The Women's Room*. New York: Jove, 1977.

French, Peter. "The Corporation as a Moral Person." In French, *Collective and Corporate Responsibility,* pp. 31–47. New York: Columbia University Press, 1984.

Friday, Nancy. *Jealousy.* New York: William Morrow, 1985.

Friedman, Marilyn. "Beyond Caring: The De-Moralization of Gender." *Canadian Journal of Philosophy,* supplementary vol. 13, *Science, Morality and Feminist Theory* (1987): 87–110.

———. "The Social Self and the Partiality Debates." In *Feminist Ethics,* edited by Claudia Card, pp. 161–179. Lawrence: University Press of Kansas, 1991.

———. *What Are Friends For? Feminist Perspectives on Personal Relationships and Moral Theory.* Ithaca, NY: Cornell University Press, 1993.

Fromm, Erich. *The Art of Loving.* New York: Harper and Row, 1956.

———. *Man For Himself.* New York: Holt, Rinehart, and Winston, 1947.

———. "Selfishness and Self-Love." *Psychiatry* 2 (1939): 507–524.

Fullbrook, Kate, and Edward Fullbrook. *Simone de Beauvoir and Jean-Paul Sartre: The Remaking of a Twentieth-Century Legend.* New York: Basic Books, 1994.

Gajowski, Evelyn. *The Art of Loving: Female Subjectivity and Male Discursive Traditions in Shakespeare's Tragedies.* Newark: University of Delaware Press, 1992.

Gaylin, Willard. *Rediscovering Love.* New York: Viking, 1986.

Giddens, Anthony. *The Transformation of Intimacy: Sexuality, Love and Eroticism in Modern Societies.* Stanford: Stanford University Press, 1992.

Gilbert Paul. *Human Relationships.* Oxford: Blackwell, 1991.

Gilligan, Carol. "The Conquistador and the Dark Continent: Reflections on the Psychology of Love." *Daedalus* 11 (1984): 75–95.

———. *In a Different Voice.* Cambridge: Harvard University Press, 1982.

Glaser, Elizabeth, and Laura Palmer. *In the Absence of Angels.* New York: Berkley Books, 1991.

Glasgow, Ellen. *The Woman Within.* New York: Hill and Wang, 1980.

Glickman, Jack. "On Creating." In *Perspectives in Education, Religion, and the Arts,* edited by M. K. Munitz, pp. 262–265. Albany: State University of New York Press, 1970.

Goethe, Johann Wolfgang von. *The Sorrows of Young Werther.* Translated by Michael Hulse. New York: Penguin Books, 1989.

Goicoechea, David, ed. *The Nature and Pursuit of Love: The Philosophy of Irving Singer.* Amherst, NY: Prometheus Books, 1995.

Gooch, Paul. "A Mind to Love: Friends and Lovers in Ancient Greek Philosophy." In *The Nature and Pursuit of Love: The Philosophy of Irving*

Singer, edited by David Goicoechea, pp. 83–97. Amherst, NY: Prometheus Books, 1995.

Gottfried von Strassburg. *Tristan.* Translated by A. T. Hatto. New York: Penguin Books, 1960.

Gould, James A., and John J. Iorio, eds. *Love, Sex and Identity.* San Francisco: Boyd and Fraser, 1972.

Graham, George, and Hugh LaFollette. "Honesty and Intimacy." In *Person to Person,* edited by George Graham and Hugh LaFollette, pp. 167–181. Philadelphia: Temple University Press, 1989.

Green, Laura. "Never Confess." In *Reinventing Love,* edited by Laurie Abraham, pp. 192–197. New York: Plume, 1993.

Greenspan, Patricia S. *Emotions and Reasons.* New York: Routledge, 1988.

Greiner, Donald J. *Adultery in the American Novel: Updike, James, and Hawthorne.* Columbia: University of South Carolina Press, 1985.

Grimshaw, Jean. *Philosophy and Feminist Thinking.* Minneapolis: University of Minnesota Press, 1986.

Guggenbuhl-Craig, Adolf. *Marriage: Dead or Alive.* Translated by Murray Stein. Dallas: Spring Publications, 1977.

Hamburger, Lotte, and Joseph Hamburger. *Contemplating Adultery.* New York: Fawcett Columbine, 1991.

Hansen, Ron, ed. *You Don't Know What Love Is: Contemporary American Stories.* Princeton, NJ: Ontario Review Press, 1987.

Haskell, Molly. *Love and Other Infectious Diseases.* New York: Citadel Press, 1992.

Haworth, Lawrence. *Autonomy.* New Haven: Yale University Press, 1986.

Hazo, Robert G. *The Idea of Love.* New York: Frederick A. Praeger, 1967.

Heidegger, Martin. *Being and Time.* Translated by John Macquarrie and Edward Robinson. New York: Harper and Row, 1962.

Held, Virginia. *Feminist Morality: Transforming Culture, Society, and Politics.* Chicago: University of Chicago Press, 1993.

———. *Rights and Goods.* Chicago: University of Chicago Press, 1984.

Heyn, Dalma. *The Erotic Silence of the American Wife.* New York: Signet, 1993.

Hijuelos, Oscar. *The Mambo Kings Play Songs of Love.* New York: Harper and Row, 1989.

Hill, Thomas E., Jr. *Autonomy and Self-Respect.* New York: Cambridge University Press, 1991.

Hochschild, Arlie Russell. "Emotion Work, Feeling Rules, and Social Structure." *American Journal of Sociology* 85 (1970): 551–575.

———. *The Managed Heart.* Berkeley: University of California Press, 1983.

Hochschild, Arlie Russell, and Anne Machung. *The Second Shift.* New York: Avon Books, 1989.

Horsburgh, H. J. N. "The Ethics of Trust." *The Philosophical Quarterly* 10 (1960): 343–354.

Hunt, Morton. *The Affair.* New York: World Publishing, 1969.

_____. *The Natural History of Love.* Rev. ed. New York: Anchor Books, 1994.

Hunter, J. F. M. *Thinking About Sex and Love.* Toronto: Macmillan of Canada, 1980.

Hunter, James Davison. *Culture Wars: The Struggle to Define America.* New York: Basic Books, 1991.

Hurston, Zora Neale. *Dust Tracks on a Road.* New York: Harper Perennial, 1991.

_____. *Their Eyes Were Watching God.* New York: Harper and Row, 1990.

Hutchings, P. E. "Conjugal Faithfulness." In *Human Values,* edited by Godfrey Vesey, pp. 61–85. Atlantic Highlands, NJ: Humanities Press, 1978.

Hwang, David Henry. *M. Butterfly.* New York: Penguin Books, 1989.

Izard, Carroll E. *Human Emotions.* New York: Plenum Press, 1977.

Jaggar, Alison M. "Love and Knowledge: Emotion in Feminist Epistemology." In *Gender/Body/Knowledge,* edited by Alison M. Jaggar and Susan R. Bordo, pp. 145–187. New Brunswick, NJ: Rutgers University Press, 1989.

Jaggar, Alison M., ed. *Living with Contradictions: Controversies in Feminist Social Ethics.* Boulder, CO: Westview Press, 1994.

Johnson, Sonia. *From Housewife to Heretic.* Garden City, NY: Anchor Books, 1983.

Jong, Erica. *How To Save Your Own Life.* New York: New American Library, 1977.

Kahn, Coppelia. *Man's Estate: Masculine Identity in Shakespeare.* Berkeley: University of California Press, 1981.

Kant, Immanuel. *The Doctrine of Virtue.* Translated by M. J. Gregor. Philadelphia: University of Pennsylvania Press, 1964.

_____. *Lectures on Ethics.* Translated by Louis Infield. New York: Harper and Row, 1963.

Kast, Verena. *Joy, Inspiration, and Hope.* Translated by Douglas Whitcher. College Station: Texas A&M University Press, 1991.

Kavka, Gregory S. *Hobbesian Moral and Political Theory.* Princeton: Princeton University Press, 1986.

Kekes, John. "Good Lives and Happiness." In Kekes, *The Examined Life,* pp. 161–173. Lewisburg, PA: Bucknell University Press, 1988.

———. *The Morality of Pluralism.* Princeton: Princeton University Press, 1993.

Kermode, Frank. "Introduction to *Romeo and Juliet, Othello,* and *Anthony and Cleopatra.*" In *The Riverside Shakespeare,* edited by G. Blakemore Evans, p. 1201. Boston: Houghton Mifflin, 1974.

Kierkegaard, Søren. *Concluding Unscientific Postscript.* Translated by David F. Swenson and Walter Lowrie. Princeton: Princeton University Press, 1941.

———. *Either/Or,* vol. 2. Translated by Walter Lowrie. Princeton: Princeton University Press, 1959.

Kimball, Gayle. *The 50/50 Marriage.* Boston: Beacon Press, 1983.

Kirsch, Arthur. *Shakespeare and the Experience of Love.* Cambridge: Cambridge University Press, 1981.

Kittay, Eva Feder, and Diana T. Meyers, eds. *Women and Moral Theory.* Totowa, NJ: Rowman and Littlefield, 1987.

Kohl, Marvin. "Caring Love and Liberty: Some Questions." In *The Nature and Pursuit of Love: The Philosophy of Irving Singer,* edited by David Goicoechea, pp. 221–228. Amherst, NY: Prometheus Books, 1995.

Kristeva, Julia. *Tales of Love.* Translated by Leon S. Roudiez. New York: Columbia University Press, 1987.

Kubitschek, Missy Dehn. "Tuh de Horizon and Back: The Female Quest in *Their Eyes Were Watching God.*" In *Zora Neale Hurston's Their Eyes Were Watching God,* edited by Harold Bloom, pp. 19–33. New York: Chelsea House, 1987.

Kundera, Milan. *The Unbearable Lightness of Being.* Translated by Michael Henry Heim. New York: Harper Perennial, 1991.

Lahr, Jane, and Lena Tabori, eds. *Love: A Celebration in Art and Literature.* New York: Stewart, Tabori, and Chang, 1982.

Lampe, Philip E. "The Many Dimensions of Adultery." In *Adultery in the United States,* edited by Philip E. Lampe. Buffalo, NY: Prometheus Books, 1987.

Larrabee, Mary Jeanne, ed. *An Ethic of Care: Feminist and Interdisciplinary Perspectives.* New York: Routledge, 1993.

Lawrence, D. H. *Women in Love.* New York: Penguin Books, 1982.

Lawson, Annette. *Adultery: An Analysis of Love and Betrayal.* New York: Basic Books, 1988.

Leavis, F. R. "Diabolic Intellect and the Noble Hero." *Scrutiny* 6 (1937). Reprinted in Leavis, *The Common Pursuit,* pp. 136–159. London: Penguin Books, 1966.

Lee, John Alan. *The Colors of Love.* Englewood Cliffs, NJ: Prentice-Hall, 1976.

_____. "Love-Styles." In *The Psychology of Love,* edited by Robert J. Sternberg and Michael L. Barnes, pp. 38–67. New Haven: Yale University Press, 1988.

Lefebure, Molly. *The Bondage of Love: A Life of Mrs. Samuel Taylor Coleridge.* New York: Paragon House, 1989.

Leites, Edmund. *The Puritan Conscience and Modern Sexuality.* New Haven: Yale University Press, 1986.

Lessing, Doris. *Landlocked.* New York: Plume, 1970.

Lewis, C. S. *The Four Loves.* San Diego: Harcourt Brace Jovanovich, 1960.

Lockard, Joan S., and Delroy L. Paulhus, eds. *Self-Deception: An Adaptive Mechanism?* Englewood Cliffs, NJ: Prentice-Hall, 1988.

Lurie, Alison. *Love and Friendship.* New York: Macmillan, 1962.

McConnell, Terrance. *Gratitude.* Philadelphia: Temple University Press, 1993.

MacIntyre, Alasdair. *After Virtue.* 2d ed. Notre Dame: University of Notre Dame Press, 1984.

McMurtry, John. "Monogamy: A Critique." *The Monist* 56 (1972). Reprinted in *Philosophy and Sex,* rev. ed., edited by Robert Baker and Frederick Elliston, pp. 107–118. Buffalo, NY: Prometheus Books, 1984.

Manning, Rita C. *Speaking from the Heart: A Feminist Perspective on Ethics.* Lanham, MD: Rowman and Littlefield, 1992.

Markus, Julia. *Dared and Done: The Marriage of Elizabeth Barrett and Robert Browning.* New York: Alfred A. Knopf, 1995.

Marquez, Gabriel Garcia. *Love in the Time of Cholera.* Translated by Edith Grossman. New York: Penguin Books, 1989.

Martin, Del. *Battered Wives.* New York: Pocket Books, 1983.

Martin, Mike W. "Adultery and Fidelity." *Journal of Social Philosophy* 25 (1994): 76–91.

_____. *Everyday Morality: An Introduction to Applied Ethics.* 2d ed. Belmont, CA: Wadsworth, 1995.

_____. "Honesty in Love." *The Journal of Value Inquiry* 27 (1993): 497–507.

_____. "Honesty with Oneself." In *Rules, Rituals, and Responsibility: Essays Dedicated to Herbert Fingarette,* edited by Mary I. Bockover, pp. 115–136. La Salle, IL: Open Court, 1991.

_____. "*Invisible Man* and the Indictment of Innocence." *CLA Journal* 25 (1982): 288–302.

_____. "Love's Constancy." *Philosophy* 68 (1993): 63–77. Also published in German as "Die Bestandigkeit der Liebe," trans. Otto Neumaier. *Conceptus* (Austria) 27 (1994): 21–40.

————. *Self-Deception and Morality.* Lawrence: University Press of Kansas, 1986.

————. *Virtuous Giving: Philanthropy, Voluntary Service, and Caring.* Bloomington: Indiana University Press, 1994.

————. "What's Fair in Love?" *The Southern Journal of Philosophy* 31 (1993): 393–407.

Martin, Mike W., ed. *Self-Deception and Self-Understanding: New Essays in Philosophy and Psychology.* Lawrence: University Press of Kansas, 1985.

Maslow, Abraham H. *Toward a Psychology of Being.* New York: Van Nostrand Reinhold, 1968.

Mason, H. A. *Shakespeare's Tragedies of Love.* London: Chatto and Windus, 1970.

Massey, Stephen J. "Is Self-Respect a Moral or a Psychological Concept?" *Ethics* 93 (1983): 246–261.

May, Rollo. *Love and Will.* New York: Dell, 1974.

Mayeroff, Milton. *On Caring.* New York: Harper and Row, 1971.

Meadows, Chris M. "The Phenomenology of Joy, An Empirical Investigation." *Psychological Reports* 37 (1975): 39–54.

Melden, A. I. *Rights and Persons.* Berkeley: University of California Press, 1979.

Mendus, Susan. "Marital Faithfulness." *Philosophy* 59 (1984): 243–252.

Meyers, Diana T. *Self, Society, and Personal Choice.* New York: Columbia University Press, 1989.

Michael, Robert T., John H. Gagnon, Edward O. Laumann, and Gina Kolata. *Sex in America: A Definitive Survey.* Boston: Little, Brown, 1994.

Midgley, Mary. *Beast and Man.* New York: New American Library, 1980.

————. "Creation and Originality." In Midgley, *Heart and Mind: The Varieties of Moral Experience,* pp. 43–58. New York: St. Martin's Press, 1981.

————. *Wisdom, Information and Wonder.* New York: Routledge, 1989.

Midgley, Mary, and Judith Hughes. *Women's Choices: Philosophical Problems Facing Feminism.* New York: St. Martin's Press, 1983.

Miles, Sian, ed. *Simone Weil: An Anthology.* London: Virago, 1986.

Mill, John Stuart. *Autobiography.* Garden City, NY: Doubleday, 1873.

————. *On Liberty.* Indianapolis: Hackett, 1978.

Misurella, Fred. *Understanding Milan Kundera.* Columbia: University of South Carolina Press, 1992.

Molière (Jean Baptiste Paquelin). *The Misanthrope.* Translated by Richard Wilbur. New York: Harcourt, Brace and World, 1954.

Morgan, Kathryn Pauly. "Romantic Love, Altruism, and Self-Respect: An Analysis of Simone De Beauvoir." *Hypatia* 1 (1986): 117–148.

Morrison, Toni. *Song of Solomon.* New York: New American Library, 1977.

Mukherjee, Bharati. *Jasmine.* New York: Fawcett Crest, 1989.

Murdoch, Iris. *The Sovereignty of Good.* 1970. Reprint. Boston: Routledge and Kegan Paul, 1985.

Muyskens, James L. *The Sufficiency of Hope.* Philadelphia: Temple University Press, 1979.

Nagler, Michael, and William Swanson, eds. *Wives and Husbands: 20 Short Stories About Marriage.* New York: New American Library, 1989.

Nakhnikian, George. "Love in Human Reason." *Midwest Studies in Philosophy* 3 (1978): 286–317.

Neely, Carol Thomas. "Women and Men in *Othello.*" In *The Woman's Part: Feminist Criticism of Shakespeare,* edited by Carolyn Ruth Swift Lenz, Gayle Greene, and Carol Thomas Neely, pp. 211–238. Urbana: University of Illinois Press, 1983.

Neu, Jerome. "Jealous Thoughts." In *Explaining Emotions,* edited by Amélie O. Rorty, pp. 425–463. Berkeley: University of California Press, 1980.

Newton-Smith, W. "A Conceptual Investigation of Love." In *Philosophy and Personal Relations,* edited by Alan Montefiore, pp. 113–136. London: Routledge and Kegan Paul, 1973.

Nicolson, Nigel. *Portrait of a Marriage.* New York: Atheneum, 1973.

Nietzsche, Friedrich. *Beyond Good and Evil.* Translated by Walter Kaufmann. New York: Vintage Books, 1966.

———. *The Gay Science.* Translated by Walter Kaufmann. New York: Vintage Books, 1974.

———. "On the Thousand and One Goals." In *Thus Spoke Zarathustra,* pp. 58–60. Translated by Walter Kaufmann. New York: Penguin Books, 1978.

Nin, Anaïs. *The Diary of Anaïs Nin.* Edited by Gunther Stuhlmann. New York: Harcourt Brace Jovanovich, 1969.

———. *Henry and June.* New York: Harcourt Brace Jovanovich, 1986.

Noddings, Nel. *Caring: A Feminine Approach to Ethics and Moral Education.* Berkeley: University of California Press, 1984.

Norton, David L., and Mary F. Kille, eds. *Philosophies of Love.* Totowa, NJ: Rowman and Allanheld, 1983.

Norwood, Robin. *Women Who Love Too Much.* New York: Pocket Books, 1986.

Novy, Marianne. *Love's Argument: Gender Relations in Shakespeare.* Chapel Hill: University of North Carolina Press, 1984.

Nozick, Robert. *Anarchy, State and Utopia.* New York: Basic Books, 1974.

———. "Love's Bond." In Nozick, *The Examined Life,* pp. 68-86. New York: Simon and Schuster, 1989.

Nussbaum, Martha C. *The Fragility of Goodness.* New York: Cambridge University Press, 1986.

———. *Love's Knowledge: Essays on Philosophy and Literature.* New York: Oxford University Press, 1990.

———. "The Speech of Alcibiades: A Reading of Plato's *Symposium.*" *Philosophy and Literature* 3 (1979): 131-169; reprinted in *The Philosophy of (Erotic) Love,* edited by Robert C. Solomon and Kathleen M. Higgins, pp. 279-316. Lawrence: University Press of Kansas, 1991.

Nygren, Anders. *Agape and Eros: The Christian Idea of Love.* Translated by Philip S. Watson. Chicago: University of Chicago Press, 1982.

Okin, Susan Moller. *Justice, Gender, and the Family.* New York: Basic Books, 1989.

O'Neill, Eugene. *The Iceman Cometh.* New York: Vintage Books, 1957.

Ortega y Gasset, José. *On Love.* Translated by Toby Talbot. New York: New American Library, 1957.

Outka, Gene. *Agape: An Ethical Analysis.* New Haven: Yale University Press, 1972.

Palmer, David. "The Consolation of the Wedded." In *Philosophy and Sex,* rev. ed. edited by Robert Baker and Frederick Elliston, pp. 119-129. Buffalo, NY: Prometheus Books, 1984.

Parfit, Derek. "Later Selves and Moral Principles." In *Philosophy and Personal Relations,* edited by A. Montefiore, pp. 137-169. London: Routledge and Kegan Paul, 1973.

Parker, Barbara L. *Precious Seeing: Love and Reason in Shakespeare's Plays.* New York: New York University Press, 1987.

Paul, Ellen Frankel, Fred D. Miller, Jr., and Jeffrey Paul, eds. *Cultural Pluralism and Moral Knowledge.* Cambridge: Cambridge University Press, 1994.

Peck, M. Scott. *The Road Less Traveled.* New York: Simon and Schuster, 1978.

Peele, Stanton. *Love and Addiction.* New York: New American Library, 1975.

Perkins, D. N. *The Mind's Best Work.* Cambridge: Harvard University Press, 1981.

Person, Ethel Spector. *Dreams of Love and Fateful Encounters: The Power of Romantic Passion.* New York: W. W. Norton, 1988.

Pincoffs, Edmund L. *Quandaries and Virtues.* Lawrence: University Press of Kansas, 1986.

Pittman, Frank. *Private Lies: Infidelity and the Betrayal of Intimacy.* New York: W. W. Norton, 1989.

Plato. *Euthyphro.* Translated by Lane Cooper. In *The Collected Dialogues of Plato,* edited by Edith Hamilton and Huntington Cairns, pp. 169–185. Princeton: Princeton University Press, 1961.

————. *Symposium.* Translated by Alexander Nehamas and Paul Woodruff. Indianapolis: Hackett, 1989.

Polhemus, Robert M. *Erotic Faith: Being in Love from Jane Austen to D. H. Lawrence.* Chicago: University of Chicago Press, 1990.

Pope, Kenneth S., ed. *On Love and Loving.* San Francisco: Jossey-Bass, 1980.

Posner, Richard A. *Sex and Reason.* Cambridge: Harvard University Press, 1992.

Rawls, John. *A Theory of Justice.* Cambridge: Harvard University Press, 1971.

Rescher, Nicholas. *Ethical Idealism: An Inquiry into the Nature and Function of Ideals.* Berkeley: University of California Press, 1987.

Rhode, Deborah L. *Justice and Gender.* Cambridge: Harvard University Press, 1989.

Roberts, Robert C. "What an Emotion Is: A Sketch." *Philosophical Review* 97 (April 1988): 183–209.

Rogers, Carl R. *Becoming Partners: Marriage and Its Alternatives.* New York: Dell, 1972.

Rorty, Amélie Oksenberg. "Explaining Emotions." In Amélie Oksenberg Rorty, ed., *Explaining Emotions,* pp. 103–126. Berkeley: University of California Press, 1980.

Rose, Phyllis. *Parallel Lives: Five Victorian Marriages.* New York: Vintage Books, 1984.

Rosenberg, Janice. "Fidelity." In *Reinventing Love,* edited by Laurie Abraham, pp. 101–106. New York: Plume, 1993.

Rosenthal, Lucy, ed. *Great American Love Stories.* Boston: Little, Brown, 1988.

Rostand, Edmond. *Cyrano de Bergerac.* Translated by Brian Hooker. New York: Bantam Books, 1950.

Rubinstein, Helge, ed. *The Oxford Book of Marriage.* New York: Oxford University Press, 1990.

Russell, Bertrand. *The Autobiography of Bertrand Russell.* Vol. 1. New York: Bantam Books, 1968.

————. *Marriage and Morals.* 1929. Reprint. New York: Liveright, 1970.

Sachs, David. "How to Distinguish Self-Respect from Self-Esteem." *Philosophy and Public Affairs* 10 (1981): 346–360.

Sanford, L. T., and M. E. Donovan. *Women and Self-Esteem*. New York: Penguin Books, 1984.

Sankowski, Edward. "Responsibility of Persons for Their Emotions." *Canadian Journal of Philosophy* 12 (1977): 829–840.

Santas, Gerasimos. *Plato and Freud: Two Theories of Love*. New York: Basil Blackwell, 1988.

Sartre, Jean-Paul. *Being and Nothingness*. Translated by Hazel E. Barnes. New York: Washington Square Press, 1966.

―――. "Existentialism Is a Humanism." Translated by Philip Maivet. In *Existentialism from Dostoevsky to Sartre*, rev. ed., edited by Walter Kaufmann, pp. 345–369. New York: Meridian Books, 1975.

―――. "Interview with Jean-Paul Sartre." In *The Philosophy of Jean-Paul Sartre*, edited by Paul Arthur Schilpp, pp. 5–51. La Salle, IL: Open Court, 1981.

―――. *No Exit and Three Other Plays*. New York: Vintage Books, 1955.

Scharfman, Ronnie. "Significantly Other: Simone and Andre Schwarz-Bart." In *Significant Others: Creativity and Intimate Partnership*, edited by Whitney Chadwick and Isabelle De Courtivron, pp. 209–221. New York: Thames and Hudson, 1993.

Scheff, Thomas J., and Suzanne M. Retzinger. *Emotions and Violence: Shame and Rage in Destructive Conflicts*. Lexington, MA: Lexington Books, 1991.

Scheler, Max. "Love and Knowledge." In *On Feeling, Knowing, and Valuing*, edited by Harold J. Bershady, pp. 147–165. Chicago: University of Chicago Press, 1992.

Schneir, Miriam, ed. *Feminism in Our Time*. New York: Vintage Books, 1994.

Schoeman, Ferdinand D. "Privacy and Intimate Information." In *Philosophical Dimensions of Privacy*, edited by Ferdinand D. Schoeman, pp. 403–418. Cambridge: Cambridge University Press, 1984.

Scruton, Roger. *Sexual Desire*. New York: Free Press, 1986.

Seidman, Steven. *Embattled Eros: Sexual Politics and Ethics in Contemporary America*. New York: Routledge, 1992.

Seligman, Martin E. P. *Learned Optimism*. New York: Alfred A. Knopf, 1991.

Sessions, William Lad. *The Concept of Faith: A Philosophical Investigation*. Ithaca, NY: Cornell University Press, 1994.

Shakespeare, William. *Othello*. Edited by David Bevington. New York: Bantam Books, 1988.

―――. *The Sonnets*. New York: New American Library, 1964.

Shelley, Percy Bysshe. "Love's Philosophy." Reprinted in *A Book of Love Po-

etry, edited by Jon Stallworthy, p. 80. New York: Oxford University Press, 1974.

Simmons, John A. *Moral Principles and Political Obligations.* Princeton: Princeton University Press, 1979.

Singer, Irving. *The Nature of Love.* Vol. 1, *Plato to Luther,* 2d ed.; vol. 2, *Courtly and Romantic;* vol. 3, *The Modern World.* Chicago: University of Chicago Press, 1984–1987.

————. *The Pursuit of Love.* Baltimore: Johns Hopkins University Press, 1994.

Sircello, Guy. *Love and Beauty.* Princeton: Princeton University Press, 1989.

Slote, Michael. *Goods and Virtues.* Oxford: Clarendon Press, 1983.

Smedley, Francis Edward. *Frank Fairlegh.* London: George Routledge and Sons, 1850.

Smelser, Neil J., and Erik H. Erikson, eds. *Themes of Work and Love in Adulthood.* Cambridge: Harvard University Press, 1980.

Smith, Danny L. *"To Be Once in Doubt": Certainty and Marriage of Minds in Othello.* New York: Peter Lang, 1989.

Soble, Alan. *The Structure of Love.* New Haven: Yale University Press, 1990.

Soble, Alan, ed. *Eros, Agape, and Philia: Readings in the Philosophy of Love.* New York: Paragon House, 1989.

————. *The Philosophy of Sex.* 2d ed. Savage, MD: Rowman and Littlefield, 1991.

Solomon, Robert C. *About Love.* New York: Simon and Schuster, 1988.

————. *Love: Emotion, Myth, and Metaphor.* Garden City, NY: Anchor Press, 1981.

————. *The Passions.* Garden City, NY: Anchor Press, 1977.

————. "The Virtue of (Erotic) Love." In *The Philosophy of (Erotic) Love,* edited by Robert C. Solomon and Kathleen M. Higgins, pp. 492–518. Lawrence: University Press of Kansas, 1991.

Solomon, Robert C., and Kathleen M. Higgins, eds. *The Philosophy of (Erotic) Love.* Lawrence: University Press of Kansas, 1991.

Solovyov, Vladimir. *The Meaning of Love.* Translated by Thomas R. Beyer, Jr. West Stockbridge, MA: Lindisfarne Press, 1985.

Souhami, Diana. *Gertrude and Alice.* San Francisco: Pandora, 1991.

Stallworthy, Jon, ed. *A Book of Love Poetry.* New York: Oxford University Press, 1974.

Stearns, Peter N. *Jealousy.* New York: New York University Press, 1989.

Steinbock, Bonnie. "Adultery." In *The Philosophy of Sex,* 2d ed., edited by Alan Soble, pp. 187–192. Savage, MD: Rowman and Littlefield, 1991.

Stendhal. *Love*. Translated by Gilbert Sale and Suzanne Sale. New York: Penguin Books, 1975.

———. *On Love*. Translated by H. B. V. Scott-Moncrieff and C. K. Scott-Moncrieff. New York: Liveright, 1983.

Stepto, Robert B. "Ascent, Immersion, Narration." In *Zora Neale Hurston's Their Eyes Were Watching God*, edited by Harold Bloom, pp. 5–8. New York: Chelsea House, 1987.

Sternberg, Robert J. "Triangulating Love." In *The Psychology of Love*, edited by Robert J. Sternberg and Michael L. Barnes, pp. 119–138. New Haven: Yale University Press, 1988.

Sternberg, Robert J., ed. *Wisdom: Its Nature, Origins, and Development*. New York: Cambridge University Press, 1990.

Stewart, Robert M. *Philosophical Perspectives on Sex and Love*. Oxford: Oxford University Press, 1995.

Stout, Jeffrey. *Ethics After Babel: The Languages of Morals and Their Discontents*. Boston: Beacon Press, 1988.

Strachey, Barbara. *Remarkable Relations*. London: Victor Gollancz, 1980.

Strassburg, Gottfried von. *Tristan*. Translated by A. T. Hatto. New York: Penguin Books, 1975.

Strean, Herbert S. *The Extramarital Affair*. New York: Free Press, 1980.

Sunstein, Cass R. *Feminism and Political Theory*. Chicago: University of Chicago Press, 1990.

Tannen, Deborah. *That's Not What I Meant!* New York: Ballantine Books, 1986.

———. *You Just Don't Understand*. New York: Ballantine Books, 1990.

Tanner, Tony. *Adultery in the Novel: Contract and Transgression*. Baltimore: Johns Hopkins University Press, 1979.

Taylor, Gabriele. "Love." *Proceedings of the Aristotelian Society* 76 (1975–1976): 147–164.

Taylor, Richard. *Ethics, Faith and Reason*. Englewood Cliffs, NJ: Prentice-Hall, 1985.

———. *Having Love Affairs*. Buffalo, NY: Prometheus Books, 1982.

Taylor, Shelley E. *Positive Illusions*. New York: Basic Books, 1989.

Telfer, Elizabeth. *Happiness*. New York: St. Martin's Press, 1980.

Tennov, Dorothy. *Love and Limerence*. Chelsea, MI: Scarborough House, 1979.

Theweleit, Klaus. *Object-Choice: (All You Need Is Love. . .)*. Translated by Malcolm Green. New York: Verso, 1994.

Thomas, Laurence. *Living Morally: A Psychology of Moral Character*. Philadelphia: Temple University Press, 1989.

———. "Trust, Affirmation, and Moral Character: A Critique of Kantian

Morality." In Owen Flanagan and Amélie Oksenberg Rorty, eds., *Identity, Character and Morality: Essays in Moral Psychology*, pp. 235–257. Cambridge, MA: MIT Press, 1990.

Thorne, Barrie, and Marilyn Yalom, eds. *Rethinking the Family: Some Feminist Questions*. New York: Longman, 1982.

Tolstoy, Leo. *Anna Karenina*. Translated by David Magarshack. New York: New American Library, 1961.

————. *Kreutzer Sonata*. In *Great Short Works of Leo Tolstoy*, pp. 353–449. Translated by Louise and Aylmer Maude. New York: Harper and Row, 1967.

Tong, Rosemarie. *Feminine and Feminist Ethics*. Belmont, CA: Wadsworth, 1993.

Tormey, Judith Farr. "Exploitation, Oppression and Self-Sacrifice." *Philosophical Forum* 5 (1975): 206–221.

Tronto, Joan C. *Moral Boundaries: A Political Argument for an Ethic of Care*. New York: Routledge, 1993.

Tusquets, Esther. *Love Is a Solitary Game*. Translated by Bruce Penman. New York: Riverrun Press, 1985.

Van de Vate, Dwight. *Romantic Love: A Philosophical Inquiry*. University Park: Pennsylvania State University Press, 1981.

Vannoy, Russell. *Sex Without Love*. Buffalo, NY: Prometheus Books, 1980.

Verene, D. P., ed. *Sexual Love and Western Morality: A Philosophical Anthology*. New York: Harper and Row, 1972.

Vlastos, Gregory. "The Individual as an Object of Love in Plato." In Vlastos, *Platonic Studies*, 2d ed., pp. 3–34. Princeton: Princeton University Press, 1973.

Von Strassburg, Gottfried. *Tristan*. Translated by A. T. Hatto. New York: Penguin Books, 1960.

Walker, A. D. M. "Gratefulness and Gratitude." *Proceedings of the Aristotelian Society* 81 (1980–1981): 39–55.

Walker, Alice. *The Color Purple*. New York: Pocket Books, 1985.

————. *In Search of Our Mothers' Gardens*. New York: Harcourt Brace Jovanovich, 1983.

Wallace, James D. *Moral Relevance and Moral Conflict*. Ithaca, NY: Cornell University Press, 1988.

Waller, Robert James. *The Bridges of Madison County*. New York: Warner Books, 1992.

Walton, Douglas N. *Courage: A Philosophical Investigation*. Berkeley: University of California Press, 1986.

Walzer, Michael. *Spheres of Justice: A Defense of Pluralism and Equality*. New York: Basic Books, 1983.

Washington, Mary Helen. "'I Love the Way Janie Crawford Left Her Husbands': Emergent Female Hero." In *Zora Neale Hurston: Critical Perspectives Past and Present,* edited by Henry Louis Gates, Jr., and K. A. Appiah, pp. 98–109. New York: Amistad Press, 1993.

Wasserstrom, Richard. "Is Adultery Immoral?" *Philosophical Forum* 5 (1974): 513–528.

Weeks, Jeffrey. *Sexuality.* New York: Routledge, 1986.

Weiss, Roslyn. "The Moral and Social Dimensions of Gratitude." *The Southern Journal of Philosophy* 23 (1985): 491–501.

Weitzman, Lenore J. *The Marriage Contract.* New York: Free Press, 1981.

West, Uta. *If Love Is the Answer, What Is the Question?* New York: McGraw-Hill, 1977.

Whitbeck, Caroline. "The Trouble with Dilemmas: Rethinking Applied Ethics." *Professional Ethics* 1 (1992): 119–142.

Williams, Bernard. *Moral Luck.* New York: Cambridge University Press, 1981.

Williams, Clifford, ed. *On Love and Friendship: Philosophical Readings.* Boston: Jones and Bartlett, 1995.

Wilson, A. N. *Tolstoy.* London: Hamish Hamilton, 1988.

Wilson, James Q. *The Moral Sense.* New York: Free Press, 1993.

Wilson, John. "Can One Promise to Love Another?" *Philosophy* 64 (1989): 557–563.

————. *Love, Sex, and Feminism.* New York: Praeger, 1980.

Winch, Peter. *Simone Weil: "The Just Balance."* New York: Cambridge University Press, 1989.

Wittgenstein, Ludwig. *Philosophical Investigations.* Translated by G. E. M. Anscombe. New York: Macmillan, 1958.

Wood, David. "Honesty." In *Philosophy and Personal Relationships,* edited by Alan Montefiore, pp. 191–223. London: Routledge and Kegan Paul, 1973.

Woolf, Virginia. *To the Lighthouse.* San Diego: Harcourt Brace Jovanovich, 1927.

Wreen, Michael J. "What's Really Wrong with Adultery?" *Journal of Applied Philosophy* 3 (1986): 45–49.

Yalom, Irvin D. *Love's Executioner.* New York: Harper Collins, 1989.

Young-Bruehl, Elisabeth. *Creative Characters.* New York: Routledge, 1991.

Zola, Émile. *Thérèse Raquin.* Translated by Leonard Tancock. New York: Penguin Books, 1984.

INDEX

231